Silvia Ballarè and Guglielmo Inglese (Eds.)
Sociolinguistic and Typological Perspectives on Language Variation

Trends in Linguistics
Studies and Monographs

Editors
Chiara Gianollo
Daniël Van Olmen

Editorial Board
Walter Bisang
Tine Breban
Volker Gast
Hans Henrich Hock
Karen Lahousse
Natalia Levshina
Caterina Mauri
Heiko Narrog
Salvador Pons
Niina Ning Zhang
Amir Zeldes

Editor responsible for this volume
Daniël Van Olmen

Volume 374

Sociolinguistic and Typological Perspectives on Language Variation

Edited by
Silvia Ballarè and Guglielmo Inglese

DE GRUYTER
MOUTON

ISBN 978-3-11-221410-7
e-ISBN (PDF) 978-3-11-078116-8
e-ISBN (EPUB) 978-3-11-078123-6
ISSN 1861-4302

Library of Congress Control Number: 2023940160

Bibliographic information published by the Deutsche Nationalbibliothek
The Deutsche Nationalbibliothek lists this publication in the Deutsche Nationalbibliografie;
detailed bibliographic data are available on the internet at http://dnb.dnb.de.

© 2025 Walter de Gruyter GmbH, Berlin/Boston
This volume is text- and page-identical with the hardback published in 2023.
Typesetting: Integra Software Services Pvt. Ltd.
Printing and binding: CPI books GmbH, Leck

www.degruyter.com

Contents

Guglielmo Inglese and Silvia Ballarè
1 Analyzing language variation: Where sociolinguistics and linguistic typology meet —— 1

Lorenzo Ferrarotti
2 Isolation, complexification, and development of unusual features: A case study from some Gallo-Italian dialects of Northern Italy —— 29

Konstantinos Sampanis
3 On typological shift in Inner Anatolian Greek —— 53

Anja Hasse and Guido Seiler
4 Social factors in mixed language emergence: Solving the puzzle of Amish Shwitzer —— 85

Laura Becker, Matías Guzmán Naranjo and Samira Ochs
5 Socio-linguistic effects on conditional constructions: A quantitative typological study —— 121

Caterina Mauri, Alessandra Barotto and Simone Mattiola
6 Counterfactual conditionals: Linguistic variation in Italian and beyond —— 155

Bert Cornillie and Malte Rosemeyer
7 Syntactic elaboration in the domain of periphrasticity: Evidence from Spanish —— 197

Index —— 219

Guglielmo Inglese and Silvia Ballarè
1 Analyzing language variation: Where sociolinguistics and linguistic typology meet

1 Introduction

This book offers a collection of chapters that explore the interplay between cross-linguistic and intra-linguistic perspectives to the study of language variation.[1]

Variation is an inherent property of natural languages and is pervasive across several layers: in the performance of individual speakers, within speech communities, across languages distant in time and space. As a general definition, variation can be understood as the co-existence of formally distinct linguistic forms to express the same content. Nevertheless, the nature of variation itself remains constant irrespective of its locus of manifestation. As Croft (2022: 27) observes "the patterns of variation and change found in [. . .] a particular language are in many cases simply instances of patterns of variation and change found across languages".

Language variation has constituted the core of the research agenda of at least two disciplines of linguistics, that is, variationist sociolinguistics and linguistic typology.[2] At a superficial glance, the two appear to deal with quite distinct domains. Typology "concerns itself with the study of structural differences and similarities between languages" (Velupillai 2012: 15), and is based on the study of linguistic phenomena in more or less large samples of languages representing the genetic and geographic diversity of the languages of the world.[3] By contrast, sociolinguistics focuses on "the correlation of dependent linguistic variables with independent

---

[1] The ideas that inform this chapter have partly been published in an earlier chapter in Italian, which served as an introduction to the edited volume *Tipologia e sociolinguistica: verso un approccio integrato allo studio della variazione. Atti del Workshop SLI 2020*, published in 2021 by Officinaventuno (Milano).
[2] To these, one should also add historical (comparative) linguistics, whose main focus is however variation across the diachronic dimension, as we discuss in Section 4.
[3] Interestingly, typology has also been subsumed under the more general heading of *diversity linguistics* (see Haspelmath 2014-).

Guglielmo Inglese, University of Turin, e-mail: guglielmo.inglese@unito.it
Silvia Ballarè, University of Bologna, e-mail: silvia.ballare@unibo.it

https://doi.org/10.1515/9783110781168-001

social variables" (Chambers 2003: ix), and does so by typically focusing on speakers of a single language.[4]

As a matter of fact, typology and sociolinguistics approach variation with distinct premises and goals. Broadly speaking, typology is interested in crosslinguistic variation because it seeks to explore what the limits of such variation are, and, based on the empirical large-scale study of which linguistic structures are attested and which are not in the languages of the world, it aims at understanding the universal properties of human language.[5] Conversely, sociolinguistics takes a keen interest in those linguistic phenomena that have a social meaning, so as to unveil "the mechanisms which link extra linguistic phenomena (the social and cultural) with patterned linguistic heterogeneity (the internal, variable, system of language)" (Tagliamonte 2012: XIV).

What the two fields have in common is the effort to show that language variation, in all its shapes, is not random, but systematically takes place within well-defined boundaries. As a result, sociolinguistics and typology have developed over time a number of theoretical models and tools that share remarkable similarities. Nevertheless, while a number of studies attempting to address at least aspects of this relationship have appeared in recent years (see e.g. Kortmann 2004a, Trudgill 2011a), a principled discussion on how the two disciplines may interact has not yet been carried out in a programmatic way. This volume aims to fill this gap and to provide a venue for chapters discussing the bridging between sociolinguistic and typological research from various angles, with the ultimate goal of laying out the methodological and conceptual foundations of an integrated research agenda for the study of linguistic variation.

In this introductory chapter we take a closer look at the main intersections that exist between sociolinguistics and typology, with a particular focus on their theoretical and methodological apparatus. The chapter is structured as follows. Section 2 focuses on similarities among the conceptual tools developed by sociolinguistics and typology, while Section 3 deals with shared methodologies and practices. Section 4 addresses the role that diachrony plays in the study of cross- and intra-linguistic variation. Section 5 discusses a number of recent studies that showcase the mutual benefits between sociolinguistic and typological approaches, and introduces the chapters featured in this volume. Section 6 features some conclusive remarks.

---

[4] We do not address here the thorny issue of how to distinguish languages from dialects, that is, whether two linguistic entities shall be seen as independent languages (and therefor attest to cross-linguistic variation) or instantiate varieties of the same languages (thus attesting to intra-linguistic variation). We refer to Gil (2016) for an insightful discussion.

[5] The inquiry on universals carried out by typology remains fundamentally alternative to the one pursued by generative linguistics (see Daniel 2010 for discussion).

2 Analyzing variation: Theoretical models

In addressing the study of variation, sociolinguistics and typology have been confronted with a number of strikingly similar methodological issues, to address which the two fields have, quite independently, come up with comparable theoretical toolkits. In this section, we focus on three key issues, that is (i) the individuation of the linguistic trait to be taken into account when analyzing variation, that is, the notions of variables and comparative concepts (ii) the study of the aggregation of linguistic traits, be it either sociolinguistic varieties or linguistic types (iii) the relationship among linguistic traits and their systematization in terms of implicational hierarchies and universals.

2.1 How to describe variation: Sociolinguistic variables and comparative concepts

The first step in describing variation concerns the need to set the boundaries of the linguistic phenomenon under investigation, that is, the boundaries of the domain of variation. To this end, variationist sociolinguistics relies on the notion of *sociolinguistic variable*, whose definition is "is the first and also the last step in the analysis of variation" (Labov 2004: 7). A sociolinguistic variable can be defined as the set of "alternative ways of saying "the same" thing" (Labov 1972: 188). In addition to "semantic equivalence", variants as understood by variationist sociolinguistics also correlate with social factors (such as the formality of the context, the geographic origin of the speaker, etc.).

The debate around "semantic equivalence" among variants started in the '70s (see Berruto 2007 [1995]: 139–145 and Tagliamonte 2006: 70–76). Specifically, it soon became clear that while this methodology is particularly apt to describe phonetic variation, its application to other domains of linguistic analysis is far from straightforward. This is a consequence of the fact that more complex linguistic structures necessarily carry a meaning component, which poses a challenge to the individuation of semantic equivalence. This is why Sankoff (1972: 58) broadens his definition of variable and argues that "whenever there are options open to a speaker, we can infer from his or her behaviour an underlying set of probabilities". Similarly, to account for variation outside of the phonetic domain, Lavandera (1978: 181) invokes the principle of *functional comparability* of linguistic forms in individual contexts. Labov, turning to morphosyntactic variation, offers a narrower interpretation of "semantic equivalence" as pertaining to the referential level only (Labov 1972: 271; 1978; Weiner and Labov 1983).

Over the decades, the boundaries of the notion of variable have been extended so as to include variation at other levels, including morphology, syntax and the lexicon. The most problematic level undoubtedly remains that of pragmatics, and for obvious reasons, if one considers the level of abstractness of the categories used to describe pragmatic phenomena (see Pichler 2013: 6–9; on the variationist approach to pragmatic phenomena see also Tagliamonte 2005, Schneider and Barron 2008, Cameron and Schwenter 2013, and Sansò 2020: 81–104).

Linguistic typology is essentially a comparative branch of linguistics, which deals with the categorization of linguistic traits across languages (Moravcsik 2016). This means that delimiting the domain of variation is a necessary prequisite of the typological inquiry, so as to ensure the comparability and the correct categorization of linguistic traits. As Koptjevskaja-Tamm et al. (2015: 436) put it "cross-linguistic identification of studied phenomena presupposes a procedure which ensures that we compare like with like". This is a relatively straightforward task in the case of the most basic domains of lexical typology (Koptjevskaja-Tamm 2012). Things become more difficult when one tries to compare morphosyntactic entities across languages – which constitutes the core of the typological enterprise (Evans 2020; on the comparability issue see in particular two special issues of *Linguistic Typology* 20(2) [2016] and 24(3) [2020] and Alfieri et al. 2021) – since most of the notions developed in the Western grammatical thought (and on the basis of Classical languages) cannot be straightforwardly applied across languages: this concerns basic notions such as subject and object (cf. Bickel 2010; Witzlack-Makarevich 2019), subordinate clause (Cristofaro 2003) and even the notion of 'word' itself (Haspelmath 2011).

To overcome these difficulties, and achieve a meaningful comparison disregarding the structural and formal peculiarities of individual languages, scholars have argued that cross-linguistic comparison must be based on universally applicable semantic notions (cfr. Stassen 1985: 14; Croft 2003: 13–19). These have more explicitly been defined by Haspelmath (2010, 2018) as *comparative concepts* (as opposed to language-specific *descriptive categories*). Comparative concepts constitute the key tool for typologists to compare linguistic phenomena across languages and draw generalizations on the distribution of linguistic patterns, from the domain of phonetics to that of pragmatics.

In this respect, typology echoes the notion of "semantic equivalence" discussed above for sociolinguistics, in the sense that both in the case of comparative concepts and in that of sociolinguistic variables, the comparability issue has been resolved by according primacy to semantic-functional parameters in delimiting the object of investigation. Nevertheless, it must be remarked that more recent studies have also argued that typology needs *hybrid* comparative concepts, in which formal and structural parameters are taken into account (e.g., Miestamo 2005: 39–45; Stassen

2010; Croft 2016), as long as these are not based on language-specific criteria and are in their turn based on comparative concepts (e.g., the concept of root or affix).

2.2 Systematizing variation: Sociolinguistic varieties and linguistic types

Another common trait between sociolinguistics and typology is that, once the domain of variation has been identified as discussed in Section 2.1, individual traits can be organized in more general aggregates that better capture the systematicity of variation (see Grandi 2018, 2020 *inter al.*). The two disciplines achieve this by resorting to the notions of *sociolinguistic variety* and *linguistic type*, respectively.

The notion of sociolinguistic variety has been formulated in order to account for the fact that variation in languages is not random, but that instead language should be thought of as "as an object possessing orderly heterogeneity" (Weinreich et al. 1968: 100). A linguistic variety is "the realization of the linguistic system, in, or better among, classes of speakers and usages" (Berruto 2007 [1995]: 63; see further Hudson 1980, *inter al.*). In other words, varieties are constituted by a bundle of linguistic traits – at various levels – that tend to co-occur systematically, for example, in the productions of speakers that share some social features or in a certain situational context. It must also be added at this point that varieties are not discrete entities, but rather can be placed along a continuum, giving rise to an "ordered set of elements arranged in such a way that between two adjacent entities of the set (in this case, language varieties) there are no sharp boundaries, but rather a gradual, fuzzy differentiation, each variety sharing some sociolinguistically marked features with adjacent varieties" (Berruto 2010: 235).

This view on language as an entity organized in a set of varieties, which shows an evident structuralist footprint, has been variously criticized over the years by scholars who have questioned the very existence of varieties; this debate has recently been revived by studies based on large-scale annotated corpora, which have shown, by means of quantitative methods, the reality of linguistic varieties (see Hinskens and Guy 2016 and Ghyselen and De Vogelaer 2018 for an overview).

The notion of linguistic type lies at the very historical roots of typology, and is based on the assumption that the diversity of the languages of the world is amenable to a few general types (see Ramat 2010; on the notion of type see further Round and Corbett 2020). In fact, typology itself can be understood as "the study and interpretation of linguistic or language types" (Velupillai 2012: 15). A relevant feature of linguistic types, as also argued by Grandi (2014: 11–15), is that they constitute a structured and not random set of traits. This means that the usefulness of linguistic types is that they allow predictions on the co-occurrence of specific traits. For example, as already discussed by Greenberg (1963), knowing that in one language the object is typically placed before the verb allows one to predict that, with a frequency higher than chance, the same language will also have genitives preceding their head nouns (see Song 2010). Still, the idea that types effectively provide a holistic and discrete categorization of languages, whereby a given language fully instantiate a given type, with types neatly distinct from one another, has been largely abandoned by typologists (Croft 2003: 42–45). Types are better conceived of as ideal constructs, to which languages may adhere to various extents (Coseriu 1973: 253). For example, already Sapir (1921) casted doubt on the validity of a binary distinction between isolating vs. flexional languages, arguing that morphological complexity can be computed based on the range of synthetic/analytic strategies attested within individual languages (see Greenberg 1960; Siegel et al. 2014).

Overall, it is clear that cross-linguistic diversity in most cases cannot be reduced to a few discrete types, but should be intended as a multidimensional space, featuring a number of parameters, in which languages may be variously placed (see, e.g., Arkadiev and Klamer 2018: 444 on morphological typology). A key contribution in this respect has come from the ever-increasing inclusion in typology of large-scale quantitative data from corpora (see Section 3.2.3). For example, studies carried out on treebanks have revealed how languages do not follow a single word order pattern, but various patterns coexist (with different degrees) within individual languages (Levshina 2019; Gerdes et al. 2021). This is yet another similarity between linguistic varieties and linguistic types, as they can both be ordered in continua.

2.3 Implicational relations: Universals, hierarchies and scales

Besides the notion of variety and type, sociolinguistics and typology have also come up with powerful tools to capture the relationship between traits, within and across languages.

Implicational relations, which can be expressed as either implicational universals or hierarchies, have been introduced in modern linguistics by Joseph Greenberg (1963). Typological universals constitute perhaps the major achievement of the study of cross-linguistic variation, as it is thanks to language universal that one can assess the limit of linguistic diversity and predict which languages are possible and which not (Croft 2003: Cap. 3; Moravcsik 2010). Universals can be distinguished into absolute and implicational ones, as in (1a-b) (Croft 2003: 52–53):

(1) a. All languages have oral vowels.
    b. If a language has nasal vowels, it will also have oral vowels, but not viceversa.

The universal in (1a) is absolute because it describes a property equally shared by all (spoken) languages of the world. Universals of this type are rather the exception. Most universals are implicational, as (1b), as it establishes an implicational relationship between the occurrence of distinct linguistic traits. Implicational universals are theoretically more interesting than absolute ones, as only the former allow typologists to delimit the domain of cross-linguistic variation, so as to exclude impossible language types. Coming back to (1b), this universal also rules out the possibility that languages exist in which only nasal vowels, but not oral ones, are found.

Implicational hierarchies merely constitute a mono-dimensional chain of implicational universals, whereby the implicans of one universal is the implicatum of the following one (Croft 2003: 122). Hierarchies are particularly suitable to capture the systematic relation between a high number of traits, and have been used in various domain from the lexicon to morphosyntax (Croft 2003: Cap. 5; Corbett 2010). Famous hierarchies are the hierarchy of accessibility relativization (Keenan and Comrie 1977, 1979) and the animacy or referential hierarchy (e.g., Corbett 2000; Cristofaro 2013). In the lexical domain, mostly pertaining to the verbal lexicon, important hierarchies are the hierarchy of perception modalities (Viberg 1984), as well as transitivity (Tsunoda 1985; Malchukov 2005) and spontaneity scales (Haspelmath 2016).

Within the functional-typological approach, regular correlations among linguistic traits are not treated as random, but have traditionally been explained by resorting to specific underling functional and cognitive principles, including economy, iconicity, markedness, memory, ease of processing etc. (Moravcsik 2010; Sansò 2018). As a matter of fact, more recent research has questioned the validity of such explanations, which are strictly functional and synchronic. First – and this is an input coming from usage-based approaches to the study of language – it has been argued that frequency of occurrence, correlating with predictability and with coding efficiency, plays a key role in explaining some of the universals that have been proposed, in particular those that have to do with marking asymmetries, i.e. those cases in which a value of a given grammatical category (e.g., plural) receives extra marking as compared to another, more frequent one (e.g., singular) (see Haspelmath 2006, 2021). The second kind of criticism instead comes from adopting a diachronic perspective to cross-linguistic regularities (Section 4.1).

Comparable tools have been devised in sociolinguistics. For example, implicational scales have been traditionally regarded as an alternative model to variable rules, understood as the expression of the behavior of a variable (see Rickford 2002 inter al.). In fact, implicational scales and variable rules might be (and as a matter of fact have been) used in combination, partly because they represent distinct objects. Scales account for the relationships that may exist among variables

(Berruto 2007 [1995]: 156), by establishing implicational co-occurrence patterns among traits in a given sociolinguistic variety or in the speech of speakers with specific social connotations. In practice, a scale is made up as a cross-table in which linguistic traits are ordered on one side and (groups of) speakers or varieties on the other side. Cells of this matrix can be filled by either binary values (e.g., +/-) which account for the (non-)occurrence of a given trait in a given production, or by intervals of frequencies relative to the occurrence of a specific trait (as an example, see Cerruti 2009: 235–254).

3 Exploring variation: Empirical tools

A shared feature between typology and sociolinguistics is that these are two heavily empirically based branches of linguistics. In fact, they both proceed from the assumption that variation can only be captured by analyzing the distribution of linguistic patterns in real data. It should come as no surprise, at this point, that, besides having developed similar theoretical models for the study of variation (Section 2), the two disciplines have also come up with a number of remarkably similar research tools. In this section, we highlight commonalities that can be detected among these, so as to highlight how they have been independently created as a response to similar theoretical and methodological pressures. Even though the tools are essentially the same, it is interesting to observe how they have become part of the toolkit of sociolinguists and typologists at different times, reflecting the different priorities of the two fields along their history.

3.1 The empirical turn: Corpora and questionnaires

In order to obtain comparable data on specific linguistic features from speakers of a given language, while at the same time collecting the relevant extralinguistic metadata on informants, sociolinguistics has long relied on questionnaires. Questionnaires are usually made up of two components, one concerning the linguistic data, which is typically elicited by administering specific stimuli to informants, the other one adding various type of metadata.

Questionnaires are widely used in sociolinguistics and dialectology to gather various types of data, including acceptability judgements, information on repertories, etc. (see Meyerhoff et al. 2015: 71–73). This linguistic information comes with metadata on informants (age, geographic origin, degree of education, etc.), so as to allow the researcher to evaluate possible correlations between the distribution of linguistic features and extra-linguistic factors. Questionnaires are particularly suitable when one wishes to explore the sociolinguistic characterization of a given trait, as they can be administered to a sample of informants that has been selected specifically for the purpose of the investigation. Nevertheless, questionnaires are not free of shortcomings, first and foremost the fact that their responses generally also represent the informants' evaluation on the stimulus, which might be distinct from their actual usage of the language (see Iannàccaro 2000 and more generally the methodological remarks in Sanga 1991).

Typological inquiries, in the most traditional sense, usually proceed with gathering a representative sample of the languages of the world and then sifting through grammatical descriptions of these languages in order to obtain data on the phenomenon under analysis. This methodology has been defined *type-based* by Levshina (2019), in the sense that languages are typically classified as having (a specific value of) vs. lacking a certain feature. However, as grammatical descriptions greatly differ in their granularity and thoroughness, in some cases, especially when one wishes to investigate less documented phenomena with a high degree of detail, questionnaires might supply a crucial additional source of data. One of the most renowned typological questionnaires has been devised by Östen Dahl to investigate the cross-linguistic realization of TAM systems (Dahl 1985).

In general, the main advantage of questionnaires is that they allow the researcher to gather highly detailed and comparable data for the linguistic trait under investigation. By directly eliciting data through standardized stimuli, one minimizes the risk of overlooking traits that exist in a language but are not described in reference grammars and/or are less documented in corpora. To further minimize the limits of linguistic stimuli, including translation biases and speakers' attitudes, a number of questionnaires featuring a set of non-linguistic (typically visual) stimuli has been elaborated. These cover both morphosyntactic and lexical domains (Koptjevskaja-Tamm et al. 2015: 441–442 for an overview).[6] Non-linguistic visual stimuli have also long been used in sociolinguistic research and still constitute a valuable tool (see for example de Benito Moreno 2022 for a recent application).

Some of the limits inherent to questionnaires can be overcome by looking for linguistic data in corpora. Corpora constitute a long-standing resource in sociolinguistics, as they enable access to a considerable amount of linguistic data naturally produced by speakers, thereby avoiding possible biases introduced by the controlled setting in which data from questionnaires is elicited. Clearly, in order to be useful for sociolinguists, corpora must also be supplied with extra-linguistic

---

6 A useful collection of typological questionnaires can be found at https://www.eva.mpg.de/lingua/tools-at-lingboard/questionnaires.php.

metadata. Such resources are extremely valuable in that they allow fine-grained quantitative analyses, which have been a hallmark of sociolinguistics since its earliest phase. Over the years, several sociolinguists have devoted time and effort to the creation of corpora, as well as to the discussion of the more suitable methodologies for corpus building (e.g., Tagliamonte 2006) and of the relevance of corpora for sociolinguistic research (Poplack 2021).

By contrast, even though quantitative approaches are not new to typology (see already Greenberg 1960), it is only recently that the use of corpora has opened the way for a new quantitative oriented typology based on a rich empirical basis. Levshina (2021) offers an excellent overview of the type of corpora used in typology, the typological research questions that can be approached with quantitative methods, and the advantages and limits of corpus-based, or better *token-based*, typology.

It must be remarked that the use of corpora for typology is practically and methodologically more challenging than for sociolinguistics. The main issue is that cross-linguistic corpus-based studies need a reasonable number of corpora of different languages, which additionally must be sufficiently similar to allow a meaningful comparison. Two main solutions to this issue have been proposed, that is, either parallel corpora consisting of the translation of the same text in several languages (Cysouw and Wälchi 2007), or, more recently, corpora that share a common annotation schema, such as the treebanks featured in the Universal Dependency project (Zeman et al. 2020). Another relevant ongoing project is the DoReCo, which aims at publishing annotated spoken corpora of 150 languages, with a focus on endangered and/or underdescribed languages (Paschen et al. 2020). The latter project in particular has constituted a major step forward in advocating for the need of typological studies not based on grammatical description, but rather grounded on corpora of spoken language (Haig et al. 2021).

Notably, corpora in typology do not merely constitute a source of cross-linguistic data, but the shift from type- to token-based typology also bears remarkable theoretical consequence. Specifically, while in traditional type-based typology languages are typically treated as either featuring/lacking a certain trait, token-based typology is more suitable to describe much more accurately the gradual nature of specific linguistic phenomena. This entails, among other thing, replacing the categorial approach to types with a description of variation into continua (see Section 2.1). Token-based typology has given important results in the study of word order (Levshina 2019, Gerdes et al. 2012, Choi et al. 2021), in phonetic studies (e.g., Paschen et al. 2022), and in the study of morphological complexity (e.g., Brigada Villa and Inglese 2021; Stave et al. 2021). On a more general level, as Levshina (2020: 8) remarks, once typology turns to usage- (and corpus-)based models, which entail a keen interest in the gradual nature of language and the interaction between the realization of individual traits and their context of use, typologists effectively conduct variationist studies, which can then benefit from the methods and tools developed within the sociolinguistics tradition.

3.2 Visualizing data: Atlases

Geography constitutes a key aspect of linguistic variation. Linguistic atlases have been devised as means to observe diversity of languages in space. In dialectology, atlases have been devoted mostly to the description of phonetic, morphological and lexical variation. In particular, they have been thriving in European countries with a marked multilingual landscape, such as Germany, Switzerland, Italy, and Russia (Lameli 2010: 569). Modern linguistic atlases are made up by individual charts on which a specific phenomenon is mapped according to its realization in specific points within the area under consideration. Building on the tradition of dialectal atlases, the last decades have also witnessed a surge in typological and sociolinguistically informed atlases. Sociolinguistic atlases account for intralinguistic variation and typically display how the variants of a given variable are realized in space. As an example, consider the SAND – *Syntactische Atlas van de Nederlandse Dialecten* (Barbiers et al. 2005) or the ANAE – *Atlas of North American English* (Labov et al. 2006). The interest in the geographic and areal dimension constitutes in some respects a more recent acquisition in typology. The main typological atlas is the WALS – *Word Atlas of Language Structure* (Haspelmath et al. 2005, online version Dryer and Haspelmath 2013). WALS has served as the model for the creation of a number of analogous resources. Notable examples are the APiCS – *Atlas of Pidgin and Creole Language Structures* (Michaelis et al. 2013) and PHOIBLE, which gathers data on the phonological inventory of almost 2100 languages (Moran and McCloy 2019). Recently, a new typological atlas, *Grambank*, has been launched, which features information concerning 195 morphosyntactic parameters for almost 2500 languages (Skirgård et al. 2023). There exist also atlases restricted to particular linguistic areas, as is the case of SAILS – *South American Indigenous Language Structures* (Muysken et al. 2016), an atlas featuring several grammatical traits of South American languages.

As we have discussed in this section, both typology and sociolinguistics have developed practical tools to display and analyze variation in space. A peculiar resource in this respect, which shows how tools developed by one discipline can easily and fruitfully be transferred to the other, is the eWAVE – *electronic World Atlas of Varieties of Varieties of English* (Kortmann and Lunkenheimer 2013, digital version Kortmann et al. 2020). eWAVE shows a structure entirely analogous to that of WALS, but instead collects data on morphosyntactic structures in 77 geographical varieties of English. There is however one key difference with respect WALS: while WALS largely disregards intralinguistic variation, as each language is represented by only one variety, in the case of eWAVE each chart represent a given trait and for each variety the relative frequency of the trait is given (with values ranging from pervasive to absence of feature).

4 Variation and change: The role of diachrony

In the structuralist tradition initiated by de Saussure (2016 [1916]: 174), synchrony and diachrony are two complementary perspectives to the study of language. According to this view, variation pertains to the synchronic level only, while diachrony is rather concerned with change. Such a dichotomic approach has been largely superseded, and scholars nowadays agree that the two dimensions are rather "two sides of the same coin" (Seiler 2018: 82; see also Giacalone Ramat et al. 2012). The interplay between the two dimensions is twofold (e.g. Croft 2000; Luraghi 2010; Seiler 2018). On the one hand, variation is the result of change, in that change may result in the creation of new forms for a given function, thereby bringing about a new variant within a system; on the other hand, synchronic variation is also the pool from which language change, understood as a process of selection and conventionalization of a new variant against an older one, takes places. A key contribution in offering a more dynamic understanding of the interface between synchrony and diachrony comes from grammaticalization studies (see Hopper and Traugott 2003; Lehmann 2015 [1995]). Grammaticalization processes, at least in their more traditional formulation, typically involved lexical elements that progressively acquire grammatical meaning, losing their morphosyntactic autonomy in the process. Crucially, these processes take place on-line in the concrete production of speakers, thanks to the reinterpretation of specific source constructions into new target constructions (see below).

In the reminder of this section, we briefly sketch the ways in which sociolinguistics and typology have integrated the diachronic dimension within their synchronic account of intra- and cross-linguistic variation.

4.1 Diachronic typology

In spite of its apparently predominant synchronic orientation, typology has taken the diachronic dimension into account since its earliest days. Let us consider the case of morphological typology: already Humboldt, in formulating his classification of languages into isolating, agglutinative, inflected and incorporating, not only proposed that these constitute four distinct synchronic language types, but also established a diachronic relation among these, in the sense that each stage follows the other one along an ideal evolutionary process. The need for a diachronic dimension has been more recently advocated by Greenberg himself (e.g., Greenberg 1995). Nevertheless, it is only over the last couple of decades that the diachronic dimension has been more systematically integrated in the typological framework, thanks to a fruitful interaction with historical linguistics and grammaticalization studies (e.g. Narrog 2017; Heine and Narrog 2018; Bisang et al. 2020). In particular, grammaticalization studies have shown how grammatical structures recurrently arise from a well-defined set of historical sources and following a restricted number of processes across languages (es. Narrog 2017, Kuteva et al. 2019).). In this respect, diachrony offers a key to understand variation, by answering to the question "why languages have come to be the way they are" (Croft 2022: 27).

The diachronic perspective is also crucial to semasiological approaches, in the sense that grammaticalization studies offer an important tool to explain the co-existence of different functions performed by the same grammatical form, by establishing a diachronic connection among these and by providing a straightforward explanation for why certain polyfunctionality patterns recur across languages and others do not.

Studies in diachronic typology have led to an overall reassessment of the role of the synchronic functional principles that underlie language universals and implicational hierarchies. This approach to typology, which can be defined as *source-oriented*, is grounded in the assumption that cross-linguistic regularities in the distribution of linguistic forms cannot be solely based on synchronic functional motivations but can be better understood by taking into account constraints on the types of sources and diachronic processes that lead to the emergence of such forms in the first place (cf. Blevins 2004; Moravcsik 2010; Cristofaro 2019, 2021; Mithun 2018; see Haspelmath 2019 for a critical overview). As a result of this line of research, diachronic explanations have become an increasingly essential component in explaining the nature and constraints of language diversity.

4.2 Sociolinguistic varieties and patterns of change

Similarly to typology, also within sociolinguistics the study of variation has been increasingly related to historical processes. Specifically, it has been observed how variants of individual variables analyzed across different varieties of the same language might instantiate distinct diachronic stages within a single grammaticalization process (see Nevalainen and Palander-Collin 2011; Poplack 2011; Cerruti 2021). Since synchronic variation is the place where every process of change begins, one could say that the different patterns of variation may be put in relation with mutation patterns (see Lehmann 1985). In particular, sub-standard varieties show linguistic features that can be considered to be more grammaticalized when compared to the ones attested in standard (or *supra*-standard) varieties (see Cerruti 2021 for a discussion).

From our perspective, it is interesting to link the notion of *(socio)linguistic variable* to the one of *layering*, which Hopper (1991: 22) describes as follows: "withing a broad functional domain, new layers are continually emerging. As this happens, the older layers are not necessarily discarded, but may remain to coexist with and interact with the newer layers". Clearly, from a sociolinguistic point of view, these so-called "layers" can be considered variants of the same variable, and the *layering* portrays the co-existence in a certain moment in time of different ways of conveying the same functional meaning. Several variationist studies have been carried out in this perspective; it is worth mentioning, among others, Tagliamonte (2000), Poplack (2011), and Torres Cacoullos (2011).

Furthermore, to a diachronic dimension is linked the "inverse" semasiological approach to sociolinguistic variables, whereby the focus is not on how a given meaning is realized by different forms (and what governs such variation) but rather on how different functions of the same form may correlate with extra-linguistic parameters (see Cerruti 2011). In this case, the main issue is how to securely establish which and how many distinct functions should be associated to a given form, which is usually left to the individual researcher's intuition. This difficulty was already clear to Weiner and Labov (1983: 31), who argued that "theoretically, it should be possible to draw equal profit from cases where a single form is used with several meanings. But the possibility of accurate measurement is less immediate with semantic variation". Nevertheless, such an approach offers the significant advantage that it does not require the researcher to follow the principle of "semantic equivalence" and to individuate in a straightforward way all contexts to be considered as instantiating variation (that is, all contexts of occurrence of a given form). This perspective, which stems from studies in historical linguistics in which the diachronic connections among various meanings/functions of a given form are studied, has also been successfully applied to sociolinguistic studies.

5 Towards a unitary framework for the study of variation

In spite of the fact that structural variation has been the main object of interest of both typology and sociolinguistics, the kinds of explanations for variation that the two disciplines have formulated are rather different. Patterns of cross-linguistic distributions are usually explained in terms of functional properties (economy, iconicity, processing, etc.). Conversely, language internal variation is often explained by variationist sociolinguistics by also appealing to extra-linguistic socio-demographic factors (speakers' age and education, register, etc.). Likewise, in a historical perspective, typology has been concerned with the general mechanisms of language change that bring about specific cross-linguistic patterns of distribution (Cristofaro 2019), while sociolinguistics has put emphasis on the extra-linguistic factors behind the progressive diffusion of linguistic innovations within communities (Labov 2001).

Nevertheless, typological and sociolinguistic explanations of variation are in principle not mutually exclusive and should be integrated into a general explanatory framework of linguistic variation. As a matter of fact, building on the theoretical and methodological similarities between the two disciplines, as outlined in Sections 2 to 4, scholars have started to highlight the possible mutual benefits of a more systematic and programmatic interaction between the two (e.g., Trudgill 2011a; see also the papers in Kortmann 2004a and Ballarè and Inglese 2021). In what follows, we highlight aspects of this relationship, focusing on the way in which typology has influenced sociolinguistics and vice versa. In addition, we also discuss how the chapters included in this volume variously address these lines of research from different angles, bringing their own contribution to the overall quest of integrating language-specific and cross-linguistic research on linguistic variation on both a methodological and a conceptual level.

Sociolinguistics (and, more generally, the study of intralinguistic variation) has benefited from the influence of typology first and foremost in that the latter has offered useful *tertia comparationis* which, by virtue of their comparative crosslingusitic nature, are independent from individual languages (or families). As already remarked by Bossong (1991: 143) "broad typological comparison of data from many genetically and structurally different languages is necessary in order to be able to describe phenomena of single languages as what they really are".

One must mention in this respect the volume edited by Kortmann (2004a), whose programmatic objective was to foster the dialogue among scholars working on inter- and intra-linguistic variation, as explicitly stated in the introduction: "The purpose of this invitation is to bring together for the first time two research traditions in the study of language variation (and change) which so far have largely worked independently of each other, to make them enrich and provide new vistas for each other" (Kortmann 2004b: 1).

The benefit of a typological angle to sociolinguistic research is well exemplified in the chapters by Lorenzo Ferrarotti and Konstantinos Sampanis. In his chapter, *Isolation, complexification, and development of unusual features: a case study from some Gallo-Italian dialects of Northern Italy*, Lorenzo Ferrarotti sets out from the observation that these dialects show a number of traits, both at the phonetic and at the morphological level, which not only sets them apart from the urban variety spoken in Novara, the main city in the area, and from Lombard (and Milanese) dialects, but are also unique among Romance languages more generally. These features include "hardening" of word-final [ŋ] > [k], preservation of final vowels (which also entails preservation of richer inflectional paradigms in the nominal domain), and generalized enclisis of weak object pronouns in all syntactic contexts. Viewed in their Romance context, these traits strike as rather unusual, and could be dismissed as oddities. Instead, Ferrarotti argues that a better understanding of these traits can be achieved once these are considered in a more general context. In particular, following Trudgill (2011a), he argues that these traits represent more *complex* strategies with respect to neighboring dialects and Romance languages more generally, and that these processes of complexification can only take place due to the specific social and geographic settings in which these dialects are spoken.

In a similar vein, in the chapter *On typological shift in Inner Anatolian Greek*, Kostantinos Sampanis takes a look at variation in dialects of Greek spoken in Anatolia (Inner Anatolian Greek) through a typological lens. These dialects show a number of morphosyntactic peculiarities with respect to Modern Greek and to dialects spoken in Greece, which have traditionally been explained as the result of intensive contact with Turkish (contact among these varieties is such that some scholars have also analyzed Inner Anatolian Greek as a mixed Greek and Turkish language, an analysis which, however, the author of the chapter refutes). As Sampanis points out, these peculiarities may be better understood if placed in a typological perspective, as these include the agglutinative nominal morphology, with separate case and number endings, and a tendency towards left-branching structures at the phrasal and sentence level. In other words, in these domains, one may consider Inner Anatolian Greek as displaying a distinct typological profile from that of other Greek varieties. Crucially, the typological divergence between Inner Anatolian and Modern Greek is to a large extent triggered by contact with Turkish, but, as the author observes, different traits have developed under different social settings. In particular, one may imagine that the reshaping of nominal paradigms in a more agglutinative-like direction is the result of a long-standing contact scenario within a bilingual society, whereas left-branching structures may have been more readily introduced, even within the span of a generation, due to the pressure of dominant Turkish upon local Greek varieties.

The notion of mixed language also plays a key role in the chapter by Anja Hasse and Guido Seiler. In this chapter, Hasse and Seiler discuss this notion in light of data from Amish Shwitzer. Amish Shwitzer is a language spoken by a group of Old Order Amish in Adams County, Indiana (US), which, as the author argue, has emerged as a result of language contact between Bernese Swiss German and Pennsylvania Dutch. By framing their analysis within a more general typology of mixed languages and the possible socio-cultural conditions that may favor their emergence, the authors argue that Amish Shwitzer is to be considered an intertwined language. In particular, the authors single out two socio-historical factors as crucial in determining the rise (and success) of this language: the role of mixed marriages and the role of this language as a marker of identity, as it constitutes a means whereby speakers differentiate themselves not only from American majority society but also from Non-Swiss Amish communities and from Non-Amish Swiss communities. Interestingly, the two factors are linked to two distinct stages in the history of Amish Shwitzer: while mixed marriage (and the consequent incomplete adult L2 acquisition of Bernese Swiss German by Pennsylvania Dutch-speaking Amish) are the main reason why the new mixed lect emerged, its success within the community is mostly linked to its function as a marker of identity. In doing so, this chapter makes a compelling case that distinct socio-historical factors might account for different stages of language change, namely actuation and diffusion.

The main lesson that sociolinguistics has taught typology concerns the need to take into account intra-linguistic variation and its underlying extra-linguistic factors, along two lines. The first line of research focuses on the interaction between language-internal and cross-linguistic variation. On a methodological level, what typologists may learn from sociolinguistics is the opportunity to consider, for languages with a complex sociolinguistic situation, (also) non-standard varieties, often neglected in the practice of building typological samples. This point is well illustrated in the chapter by Sampanis, where remarkable typological differences among dialects of Greek are discussed. In addition, the comparison between non-standard, typically oral, varieties may reveal the existence of common features even across typologically distant languages (cf. e.g. Auer 1990; Auer and Maschler 2013; Ballarè and Inglese 2022) and show patterns of variation that cannot be observed taking into consideration standard varieties only (Bossong 1985, 1991 and more recently, Filppula et al. 2009; Murelli and Kortmann 2011; Kortmann and Lunkenheimer 2013; Seiler 2019; Grandi 2021).

The second line of research, exemplified by Trudgill (2011), aims at integrating non-linguistic factors in understanding and explaining linguistic diversity, much in the same vein as sociolinguistics looks at extra-linguistic factors to explain intra-linguistic variation. While non-linguistic factors investigated by sociolinguistics generally pertain to individual speakers within a speech community, the focus of typological studies evidently lies in how the distribution of language structures is shaped by factors that instead pertain to population structure and more generally the ecology of speech communities as a whole (see Di Garbo et al. 2021 and Becker et al. this volume for an overview).

Among the factors that have been proposed, one might mention demographic factors such as the structure of social networks (open vs. close-knit) within communities (Wray and Grace 2007; Trudgill 2011b), marriage practices in terms of endogamy vs. exogamy (Pakendorf et al. 2021), population size and number of linguistic neighbors (Lupyan and Dale 2010), as well proportion of L2 speakers in a community (Bentz and Winter 2013), but also non-social factors, including environmental and climatic considerations (Everett et al. 2015). Factors of various kinds may also be combined: for example, Urban (2020) discusses the way in which environmental constraints affect social and demographic structures in mountainous areas, and the consequences for the structure of languages spoken in these areas. As also remarked by Grandi (2021), such considerations also have non-negligible methodological consequences, for example on the guidelines for building typological samples. More generally, over time, also thanks to the development of typological atlases (Section 3.2), it has become increasingly clear how geographic and areal considerations must be accounted for in explaining the distribution of linguistic traits (see Nichols 1992; for an overview see Bickel 2017). As Becker et al. (this volume) remark, one of the reasons why socio-historical factors have not yet systematically been taken into account in typological studies is a practical one. As already remarked by Trudgill (2011b), quantitative studies aiming at establishing correlations between cross-linguistic distributions of linguistic traits and socio-cultural factors have predominantly relied on population size as a predictor. This is essentially a practical choice, as population size is relatively easy demographic data to access, but there is in principle no reason to assume that this factor indeed displays a higher explanatory power. Building on these premises, in the chapter *Socio-linguistic effects on conditional constructions: A quantitative typological study*, Laura Becker, Matías Guzmán Naranjo, and Samira Ochs try to assess, by means of fine-grained quantitative analyses, the impact of various social factors on the inventory of conditional markers in a sample of the languages of the world. Their finding is that population size remains the better predictor, in the sense that languages with a higher number of speakers will also likely have more than conditional markers. Other factors, such as use of the language in education and existence of a written tradition do not appear to be as informative, partly due the fact that they often correlate with population size, but also partly because this is data that is more difficult to come by in a detailed enough way to measure its relevance with quantitative techniques. Therefore, the chapter makes a compelling point that language description and documentation constitutes the crucial missing link between typology and sociolinguistics: the more grammar writers include socio-cultural information in their description, the more typologists will be able to take these into account when investigating language diversity.

Conditionals are also the topic of the chapter authored by Alessandra Barotto, Simone Mattiola and Caterina Mauri, titled *Counterfactual conditionals: linguistic variation in Italian and beyond*. The aim of this chapter is two-fold. On the one hand, the authors investigate the strategies to express counterfactual conditional in different varieties of Italian. To this aim, adopting a sociolinguistic perspective, they conduct a corpus analysis of counterfactuals in a spoken corpus of Italian and find that the symmetric strategy involving the imperfective past tense (*imperfetto*) in both the protasis and the apodosis is more likely to occur in non-formal situations and is favored by less educated speakers. This sociolinguistic investigation, which highlights patterns of intralinguistic variation, is then connected to a cross-linguistic investigation of counterfactuals in a sample of 203 languages. Cross-linguistic data shows the widespread use of symmetrical constructions, especially those involving past habitual forms. This means that the strategy most frequently found in non-standard Italian is in fact the manifestation of a recurrent cross-linguistic type. This raises the issue whether such symmetric counterfactuals are in fact typical of non-standard spoken varieties cross-linguistically. In this respect, the authors echo Becker et al. (this volume) and remark that, unless cross-linguistic data also comes with detailed metadata on the sociolinguistic context of the variety recorded, bridging studies of inter- and intra-linguistic variation remains a difficult task.

It must be remarked that, in some cases, the sociohistorical factors that have been so far explored remain to some extent *distal* to the mechanisms underpinning language variation (and change). An attempt to bridge this gap takes center stage in the chapter by Bert Cornillie and Malte Rosemeyer, *Syntactic elaboration in the domain of periphrasticity: evidence from Spanish*. The authors focus on diamesic variation, and frame their analysis from the perspective of the contrast between communicative distance vs. immediacy, as developed in Romance linguistics. Based on quantitative analyses of extensive historical documentation from Spanish, the authors compellingly show that periphrastic verb constructions, especially those of Latinate origin, are more likely to occur in texts that belong to the real of communicative distance. In particular, they establish a correlation between a higher percentage of clause linking strategies, which are typical of written texts in a communicative distance setting, and occurrences of verbal periphrases. In doing so, they offer clear evidence of how the distribution of a particular typological trait, that is, analytic verbal strategies, may be the historical result of a precise socio-cultural setting. This contrasts with the rise of analytic strategies in other contexts, such as in pidgin and creole languages, which is rather motivated by the need for clarity in contexts of communicative immediacy. These findings offer further evidence that even the same typological trait may arise for different reasons in different languages, thus corroborating the findings of source-oriented diachronic typology.

The lines of research mentioned in this section, as well as the chapters presented in this volume, show that a lot has already been achieved in the direction of integrating sociolinguistic and typological approaches to variation, but that much is yet to be done. Understanding the link between sociohistorical and typological variation ultimately requires a twofold effort, which future research will have to take into account: on the one hand, conducting in-depth studies of language evolution and change and of the role of contact and language ecology in the dynamics of language; on the other hand, using evidence from these studies to develop new methods and variables for large-scale comparisons of language structures, social structures and interactions thereof.

Acknowledgements: This book collects some of the papers presented at the workshop "Integrating sociolinguistic and typological perspectives on language variation" which took place (online) during the 54th annual meeting of the *Societas Linguistica Europaea* (31 August – 3 September 2021). We would like to express our gratitude to the participants to the workshop, and especially to our co-convenors, Francesca Di Garbo and Eri Kashima, whose ideas also largely inspired this introductory chapter. We also thank Chiara Gianollo and Daniel Van Olmen for having encouraged us to submit this volume to the TiLSM series, as well as Barbara Karlson for her kind assistance during the editorial process. Finally, we thank all the authors who have contributed to the current volume for believing in our editorial project and all the anonymous reviewers for their invaluable help. Silvia Ballarè acknowledges that this contribution is the result of the research carried out within the PRIN 2017 UniverS-Ita project Written Italian of university students: sociolinguistic framework, typological trends, didactic implications (ERC SH4, Prot. 2017 LAP429).

Reference

Alfieri, Luca, Giorgio Francesco Arcodia & Paolo Ramat (eds.). 2021. *Linguistic Categories, Language Description and Linguistic Typology*. Amsterdam/Philadelphia: John Benjamins.

Arkadiev, Peter & Marian Klamer. 2018. Morphological theory and typology. In Jenny Audring & Francesca Masini (eds.), *The Oxford Handbook of Morphological Theory*, 436–454. Oxford: Oxford University Press.

Auer, Peter. 1990. Einige umgangssprachliche Phänomene der türkischen Syntax und Möglichkeiten ihrer Erklärung aus 'natürlichen' Prinzipien. In Norbert Boretzky, Werner Enninger & Thomas Stolz (eds.), *Spielarten der Natürlichkeit–Spielarten der Ökonomie. Beiträge zum 5, Essener Kolloquium, vol. 2*, 271–298. Bochum: Brockmeyer.

Auer, Peter & Yael Maschler. 2013. Discourse or grammar? VS patterns in spoken Hebrew and spoken German narratives. *Language Science* 37. 147–181.

Ballarè, Silvia & Guglielmo Inglese (eds.). 2021 *Tipologia e sociolinguistica: verso un approccio integrato allo studio della variazione. Atti del Workshop SLI 2020*. Milano: Officinaventuno.

Ballarè, Silvia & Guglielmo Inglese. 2022. The development of locative relative markers. From typology to sociolinguistics (and back). *Studies in Language* 46(1). 220–257. https://doi.org/10.1075/sl.20013.bal

Barbiers, Sjef, Hans Bennis, Gunther de Vogelaer, Magda Devos & Margreet van der Ham. 2005. *Syntactische Atlas van de Nederlandse Dialected, Deel I*. Amsterdam: Amsterdam University Press.

Bentz, Christian & Bodo Winter. 2013. Languages with more second language learners tend to lose nominal case. *Language Dynamics and Change* 3. 1–27.

Berruto, Gaetano. 2007 [1995]. *Fondamenti di sociolinguistica*. Rome/Bari: Laterza.

Berruto, Gaetano. 2009. Περί συντάξεως. Sintassi e variazione. In Angela Ferrari (ed.), *Sintassi storica e sincronica dell'italiano. Subordinazione, coordinazione, giustapposizione, Atti del X Congresso della Società Internazionale di Linguistica e Filologia italiana* (Basilea, 30 giugno-3 luglio 2008), 21–58. Firenze: Cesati.

Berruto, Gaetano. 2010. Identifying dimensions of linguistic variation in a language space. In Peter Auer & Jürgen Erich Schmidt (eds.), *Language and Space, Part I: Theories and Methods. An International Handbook of Linguistic Variation*, 226–241. Berlin/New York: De Gruyter Mouton.

Bickel, Balthasar. 2010. Grammatical relations typology. In Jae Jung Song (ed.), *The Oxford Handbook of Linguistic Typology*, 399–444. Oxford: Oxford University Press.

Bickel, Balthasar. 2017. Areas and universals. In Raymond Hickey (ed.), *The Cambridge Handbook of Areal Linguistics*, 40–55. Cambridge: Cambridge University Press.

Bisang, Walter, Andrej Malchukov & the Mainz Grammaticalization Project team (Iris Rieder, Linlin Sun, Marvin Martiny, Svenja Luell). 2020. *Position paper: Universal and areal patterns in grammaticalization*. In Walter Bisang & Andrej Malchukov (eds.), *Grammaticalization Scenarios: Cross-linguistic Variation and Universal Tendencies*, 1–88. Berlin/New York: De Gruyter Mouton.

Blevins, Juliette. 2004. *Evolutionary phonology: the emergence of sound patterns*. Cambridge: Cambridge University Press.

Bossong, Georg. 1985. *Empirische Universalienforschung. Differentielle Objektmarkierung in den neuiranischen Sprachen*. Tübingen: Narr.

Bossong, Georg. 1991. Differential Object Marking in Romance and Beyond. In Douglas Kibbee & Dieter Wanner (eds.), *New Analyses in Romance Linguistics*, 143–170. Amsterdam/ Philadelphia: John Benjamins.

Brigada Villa, Luca & Guglielmo Inglese. 2021. Inferring Morphological Complexity from Syntactic Dependency Networks: A Test. *Proceedings of the Third Workshop on Computational Typology and Multilingual NLP, 10 June 2021*, 10–22. Association for Computational Linguistics. Available at <https://aclanthology.org/2021.sigtyp-1.pdf>

Cameron, Richard & Scott Schwenter. 2013. Pragmatics and variationist sociolinguistics. Robert Bayley, Richard Cameron & Celi Lucas (eds.), *The Oxford Handbook of Sociolinguistics*, 464–483. Oxford: Oxford University Press.

Cerruti, Massimo. 2009. *Strutture dell'italiano regionale. Morfosintassi di una varietà diatopica in prospettiva sociolinguistica*. Frankfurt am Main: Lang.

Cerruti, Massimo. 2011. Il concetto di variabile sociolinguistica a livello del lessico. *Studi italiani di linguistica teorica e applicata* 40(2). 211–231.
Cerruti, Massimo. 2021. Variazione sociolinguistica e processi di grammaticalizzazione. In Silvia Ballarè & Guglielmo Inglese (eds.), *Tipologia e sociolinguistica: verso un approccio integrato allo studio della variazione. Atti del Workshop SLI 2020*, 53–80. Milano: Officina 21.
Chambers, Jack K. 2003. *Sociolinguistic theory: linguistic variation and its social significance*. Oxford: Blackwell Publishers.
Choi, Hee-Soo, Bruno Guillaume & Karën Fort. 2021. Corpus-based language universals analysis using universal dependencies. In Radek Čech & Xinying Chen (eds.), *Proceedings of the Second Workshop on Quantitative Syntax (Quasy, SyntaxFest 2021)*, 33–44. Sofia: Association for Computational Linguistics.
Corbett, Greville G. 2000. *Number*. Cambridge: Cambridge University Press.
Corbett, Greville G. 2010. Implicational hierarchies. In Jae Jung Song (ed.), *The Oxford Handbook of Linguistic Typology*, 43–68. Oxford: Oxford University Press
Coseriu, Eugenio. 1973. Sulla tipologia linguistica di Wilhelm von Humboldt: contributo alla critica della tradizione linguistica. *Lingua e stile* 8. 235–266.
Cristofaro, Sonia & Fernando Zúñiga. 2018. Synchronic vs. diachronic approaches to typological hierarchies. In Sonia Cristofaro & Fernando Zúñiga (eds.), *Typological hierarchies in synchrony and diachrony*, 4–27. Amsterdam/Philadelphia: John Benjamins.
Cristofaro, Sonia. 2003. *Subordination*. Oxford: Oxford University Press.
Cristofaro, Sonia. 2013. The referential hierarchy: Reviewing the evidence in diachronic perspective. In Dik Bakker & Martin Haspelmath (eds.), *Languages Across Boundaries: Studies in the Memory of Anna Siewierska*, 69–93. Berlin/New York: De Gruyter Mouton.
Cristofaro, Sonia. 2019. Taking diachronic evidence seriously: Result-oriented vs. source-oriented explanations of typological universals. In Karsten Schmidtke-Bode, Natalia Levshina, Susanne Maria Michaelis & Ilja A. Seržant (eds.), *Explanation in typology: Diachronic sources, functional motivations and the nature of the evidence*, 25–46. Berlin: Language Science Press.
Cristofaro, Sonia. 2021. Towards a source-oriented approach to typological universals. In Peter Arkadiev, Jurgis Pakerys, Inesa Šeškauskienė & Vaiva Žeimantienė (eds.), *Studies in Baltic and Other Languages*, 97–117. Vilnius: Vilniaus Universiteto Leidykla.
Croft, William. 2000. *Explaining language change: an evolutionary approach*. Harlow: Pearson Longman.
Croft, William. 2003. *Typology and universals*. Cambridge: Cambridge University Press.
Croft, William. 2016. Comparative concepts and language-specific categories: Theory and practice. *Linguistic Typology* 20(2). 377–393.
Croft, William. 2022. *Morphosyntax. Constructions of the World's Languages*. Cambridge: Cambridge University Press.
Cysouw, Michael & Bernhard Wälchli. 2007. Parallel texts: Using translational equivalents in linguistic typology. *Sprachtypologie und Universalienforschung (STUF)* 60(2). 95–99.
Dahl, Östen. 1985. *Tense and Aspect Systems*. Oxford: Blackwell.
Daniel, Michael. 2010. Linguistic typology and the study of language. In Jae Jung Song (ed.), *The Oxford Handbook of Linguistic Typology*, 43–68. Oxford: Oxford University Press.
de Benito Moreno, Carlota. 2022. *The Middle Voice and Connected Constructions in Ibero-Romance: A Variationist and Dialectal Account*. Amsterdam/Philadelphia: John Benjamins.
Di Garbo, Francesca, Eri Kashima, Ricardo Napoleão de Souza & Kaius Sinnemäki. 2021. Concepts and methods for integrating language typology and sociolinguistics. In Silvia Ballarè & Guglielmo Inglese (eds.), *Tipologia e sociolinguistica: verso un approccio integrato allo studio della variazione. Atti del Workshop SLI 2020*, 143–176. Milano: Officina 21.

Dryer, Matthew S. & Martin Haspelmath (eds.). 2013. *The World Atlas of Language Structures Online*. Leipzig: Max Planck Institute for Evolutionary Anthropology (wals.info).

Evans, Nicholas. 2020. Introduction: Why the comparability problem is central in typology. *Linguistic Typology* 24(3). 417–425.

Everett, Caleb, Damián E. Blasi & Seán G. Roberts. 2015. Climate, vocal folds, and tonal languages: connecting the physiological and geographic dots. *PNAS* 112. 1322–1327.

Filppula, Markku, Juhani Klemola & Heli Paulasto (eds.). 2009. *Vernacular Universals and Language Contacts. Evidence from Varieties of English and Beyond*. New York: Routledge.

Gerdes, Kim, Sylvain Kahane & Xinying Chen. 2021. Typometrics: From Implicational to Quantitative Universals in Word Order Typology. *Glossa: a journal of general linguistics* 6(1). 17.

Ghyselen, Anne-Sophie & Gunther De Vogelaer. 2018. Seeking systematicity in variation: theoretical and methodological considerations on the "variety" concept. *Frontier in psychology* 9. 385.

Giacalone Ramat, Anna, Caterina Mauri & Piera Molinelli (eds.). 2012. *Synchrony and Diachrony. A dynamic interface*. Amsterdam/Philadelphia: John Benjamins.

Gil, David. 2016. Describing languoids: When incommensurability meets the language-dialect continuum. *Linguistic Typology* 20(2). 439–462.

Grandi, Nicola. 2014. *Fondamenti di tipologia linguistica*. Roma: Carocci.

Grandi, Nicola. 2018. Su alcune possibili interazioni tra tipologia e sociolinguistica. In Chiara Gianollo & Caterina Mauri (eds.), *CLUB Working Papers in Linguistics*, 257–265. Bologna: Alma Mater Studiorum – Univesità di Bologna.

Grandi, Nicola. 2021. Fattori sociolinguistici e costruzione del campione tipologico. Su alcune possibili interazioni tra tipologia e sociolinguistica. In Silvia Ballarè & Guglielmo Inglese (eds.), *Tipologia e sociolinguistica: verso un approccio integrato allo studio della variazione. Atti del Workshop SLI 2020*, 81–101. Milano: Officina 21.

Greenberg, Joseph H. 1960. A quantitative approach to the morphological typology of language. *International Journal of American Linguistics* 26(3). 178–194.

Greenberg, Joseph H. 1963. Some universals of grammar with particular reference to the order of meaningful elements. In Joseph H. Greenberg (ed.), *Universals of language*, 73–113. Cambridge: MIT Press.

Greenberg, Joseph H. 1995. The diachronic typological approach to language. In Masayoshi Shibatani & Theodora Bynon (eds.), *Approaches to language typology*, 145–166. Oxford: Clarendon Press.

Haig, Geoffrey, Stefan Schnell & Frank Seifart (eds.). 2021. *Doing Corpus-Based Typology with Spoken Language Corpora: State of the art*. Honolulu: University of Hawai'i Press.

Haspelmath, Martin. 2006. Against markedness (and what to replace it with). *Journal of Linguistics* 42(1). 25–70.

Haspelmath, Martin. 2010. Comparative concepts and descriptive categories in crosslinguistic studies. *Language* 86(3). 663–687.

Haspelmath, Martin. 2011. The indeterminacy of word segmentation and the nature of morphology and syntax. *Folia Linguistica* 45(1). 31–80.

Haspelmath, Martin (ed.). 2014-. *Studies in Diversity Linguistics*. Berlin: Language Science Press.

Haspelmath, Martin. 2016. Universals of causative and anticausative verb formation and the spontaneity scale. *Lingua Posnaniensis* 58(2). 33–63.

Haspelmath, Martin. 2018. How comparative concepts and descriptive linguistic categories are different. In Daniël Van Olmen, Tanja Mortelmans & Frank Brisard (eds.), *Aspects of linguistic variation*, 83–114. Berlin/New York: De Gruyter Mouton.

Haspelmath, Martin. 2019. Can cross-linguistic regularities be explained by change constraints? In Karsten Schmidtke-Bode, Natalia Levshina, Susanne Maria Michaelis & Ilja A. Seržant (eds.), *Explanation in typology: Diachronic sources, functional motivations and the nature of the evidence*, 1–23. Berlin: Language Science Press.

Haspelmath, Martin. 2021. Explaining grammatical coding asymmetries: Form-frequency correspondencies and predictability. *Journal of Linguistics* 57(3). 605–633.

Haspelmath, Martin, Matthew S. Dryer, David Gil & Bernard Comrie (eds). 2005. *The World Atlas of Language Structures*. Oxford: Oxford University Press.

Hinskens, Frans & Gregory R. Guy (eds.). 2016. *Coherence, covariation and bricolage. Various approaches to the systematicity of language variation*. Amsterdam: Elsevier. [= Special issue of *Lingua* 172/173].

Heine, Bernd & Heiko Narrog (eds.). 2018. *The Oxford Handbook of Grammaticalization*. Oxford: Oxford University Press.

Hopper, Paul. 1991. On some principles of grammaticalization. In Elizabeth C. Traugott & Bernd Heine (eds.), *Approaches to grammaticalization, Vol. 1, Theoretical and methodological issues*, 17–35. Amsterdam/Philadelphia: John Benjamins.

Hopper, Paul J. & Elizabeth Closs Traugott (eds.). 2003. *Grammaticalization*. 2nd edn. Cambridge: Cambridge University Press.

Hudson, Richard A. 1980. *Sociolinguistics*. Cambridge: Cambridge University Press.

Iannàccaro, Gabriele. 2000. Per una semantica più puntuale del concetto di 'dato linguistico'. *Quanderni di semantica* 21(1). 51–79.

Keenan, Edward & Bernard Comrie. 1977. Noun phrase accessibility and Universal Grammar. *Linguistic Inquiry* 8. 63–99.

Keenan, Edward & Bernard Comrie. 1979. Noun phrase accessibility revisited. *Language* 55(3). 649–664.

Koptjevskaja-Tamm, Maria. 2012. New directions in lexical typology. *Linguistics* 50(3). 373–394.

Koptjeskaja-Tamm, Maria, Ekaterina Rakhilina & Martine Vanhove. 2015. The semantics of lexical typology. In Nick Riemer (ed.), *The Routledge Handbook of Semantics*, 434–454. London: Routledge.

Kortmann, Bernd (ed.). 2004a. *Dialectology Meets Typology: Dialect Grammar from a Cross-Linguistic Perspective*. Berlin/New York: De Gruyter Mouton.

Kortmann, Bernd. 2004b. Introduction. In Bernd Kortmann (ed.), *Dialectology Meets Typology: Dialect Grammar from a Cross-Linguistic Perspective*. Berlin/New York: De Gruyter Mouton.

Kortmann, Bernd & Krestin Lunkenheimer. 2013. *The Mouton World Atlas of Variation in English*. Berlin/New York: De Gruyter Mouton.

Kortmann, Bernd, Krestin Lunkenheimer & Katharina Ehret (eds.). 2020. *The Electronic World Atlas of Varieties of English* (https://ewave-atlas.org/).

Kuteva, Tania, Bernd Heine, Bo Hong, Haiping Long, Heiko Narrog & Seongha Rhee. 2019. *World lexicon of grammaticalization*. 2nd, extensively revised and updated edition. Cambridge: Cambridge University Press.

Labov, William. 1972. *Sociolinguistic patterns*. Philadelphia: University of Pennsylvania Press.

Labov, William. 2001. *Principles of Linguistic Change. Vol. II. Social Factors*. Oxford: Blackwell.

Labov, William. 2004. Quantitative reasoning in linguistics. In Ulrich Ammon, Norbert Dittmar & Klaus J. Mattheier (eds.), *Sociolinguistics/Soziolinguistik: An International Handbook of the Science of Language and Society*. Volume 1, 6–22. Berlin/New York: De Gruyter Mouton.

Labov, William, Sharon Ash & Charles Boberg. 2006. *The Atlas of North American English: Phonetics, phonology and sound change*. Berlin/New York: De Gruyter Mouton.

Lameli, Alfred. 2010. Linguistic Atlases – traditional and modern. In Peter Auer & Jürgen Erich Schmidt (eds.), *Language and Space, Part I: Theories and Methods. An International Handbook of Linguistic Variation*, 567–592. Berlin/New York: De Gruyter Mouton.
Lavandera, Beatriz. 1978. Where does the sociolinguistic variable stop? *Language in Society* (7)2. 171–182.
Lehmann, Christian. 1985. Grammaticalization: Synchronic variation and diachronic change. *Lingua e Stile* 20. 303–318.
Lehmann, Christian. 2015 [1995]. *Thoughts on grammaticalization*. 3rd edn. Berlin: Language Science Press.
Levshina, Natalia. 2019. Token-based typology and word order entropy: A study based on Universal Dependencies. *Linguistic Typology* 23(3). 533–572.
Levshina, Natalia. 2021. Corpus-based typology: applications, challenges and some solutions. *Linguistic Typology* 26(1). 129–160.
Lupyan, Gary & Rick Dale. 2010. Language structure is partly determined by social structure. *PLOS one* 5(1). 1–10.
Luraghi, Silvia. 2010. Causes of language change. In Silvia Luraghi & Vit Bubenik (eds.), *Continuum Companion to Historical Linguistics*, 354–366. London – New York: Continuum.
Malchukov, Andrej. 2005. Case pattern splits, verb types and construction competition. In Mengistu Amberber & Helen de Hoop (eds.), *Competition and variation in natural languages: The case for case*, 73–117. Amsterdam: Elsevier.
Meyerhoff, Miriam, Erik Schleef & Laurel MacKenzie. 2015. *Doing sociolinguistics. A practical guide to data collection and analysis*. London: Routledge.
Michaelis, Susanne Maria, Philippe Maurer, Martin Haspelmath & Magnus Huber (eds.). 2013. *Atlas of Pidgin and Creole Language Structures Online*. Leipzig: Max Planck Institute for Evolutionary Anthropology. (http://apics-online.info).
Miestamo, Matti. 2005. *Standard negation: the negation of declarative verbal main clauses in a typological perspective*. Berlin/New York: De Gruyter Mouton.
Mithun, Marianne. 2018. Deconstructing teleology: The place of synchronic usage patterns among processes of diachronic development. In Sonia Cristofaro & Fernando Zúñiga (eds.), *Typological hierarchies in synchrony and diachrony*, 111–128. Amsterdam/Philadelphia: John Benjamins.
Moran, Steven & Daniel McCloy (eds.). 2019. *PHOIBLE 2.0*. Jena: Max Planck Institute for the Science of Human History. https://phoible.org/
Moravcsik, Edith A. 2010. Explaining language universals. In Jae Jung Song (ed.), *The Oxford Handbook of Linguistic Typology*, 69–89. Oxford: Oxford University Press.
Moravcsik, Edith A. 2016. On linguistic categories. *Linguistic Typology* 20(2). 417–425.
Murelli, Adriano & Bernd Kortmann. 2011. Non-standard varieties in the areal typology of Europe. In Bernd Kortmann & Joan van der Auwera (eds.), *The Languages and Linguistics of Europe. A Comprehensive Guide*, 525–544. Berlin/New York: De Gruyter Mouton.
Muysken, Pieter, Harald Hammarström, Olga Krasnoukhova, Neele Müller, Joshua Brichall, Simon van de Kerke, Loretta O'Connor, Swintha Danielsen, Rik van Gijn & George Saad. 2016. *South American Indigenous Language Structures (SAILS) Online*. Jena: Max Planck Institute for the Science of Human History. (http://sails.clld.org).
Narrog, Heiko. 2017. Typology and grammaticalization. In Alexandra Aikhenvald & R. M. W. Dixon (eds.), *The Cambridge Handbook of Linguistic Typology*, 151–177. Cambridge: Cambridge University Press.
Nevalainen, Terttu & Minna Palander-Collin. 2011. Grammaticalization and sociolinguistics. In Bernd Heine & Heiko Narrog (eds.), *The Oxford Handbook of Grammaticalization*, 118–128. Oxford: Oxford University Press.

Nichols, Johanna. 1992. *Linguistic Diversity in Space and Time*. Chicago: University of Chicago Press.
Paschen, Ludger, François Delafontaine, Christoph Draxler, Susanne Fuchs, Matthew Stave & Frank Seifart. 2020. Building a time-aligned cross-linguistic reference corpus from language documentation data (DoReCo). *Proceedings of the 12th Conference on Language Resources and Evaluation (LREC 2020)*, 2657–2666. Marseille: European Language Resources Association. http://www.lrec-conf.org/proceedings/lrec2020/pdf/2020.lrec-1.324.pdf
Paschen, Ludger, Susanne Fuchs & Frank Seifart. 2022. Final Lengthening and vowel length in 25 languages. *Journal of Phonetics* 94. 101179. https://doi.org/10.1016/j.wocn.2022.101179.
Pakendorf, Brigitte, Nina Dobrushina & Olesya Khanina. 2021. A typology of small-scale multilingualism. *International Journal of Bilingualism* 25(4). 835–859.
Pichler, Heike. 2013. *The structure of discourse-pragmatic variation*. Amsterdam/Philadelphia: John Benjamins.
Poplack, Shana. 2011. Grammaticalization and linguistic variation. In Bernd Heine & Heiko Narrog (eds.), *The Oxford Handbook of Grammaticalization*, 209–224. Oxford: Oxford University Press.
Poplack, Shana. 2021. Le corpus comme portail pour l'étude de la variation (socio)linguistique. *Corpus* [en ligne] 22.
Rickford, John R. 2002. Implicational scale. In Jack K. Chambers, Peter Trudgill & Natalie Schilling-Estes (eds.), *The Handbook of Language Variation and Change*, 142–167. Oxford: Blackwell.
Round, Erich R. & Greville G. Corbett. 2020. Comparability and measurement in typological science: The bright future for linguistics. *Linguistic Typology* 24(3). 489–525.
Sanga, Glauco. 1991. I metodi della ricerca sul campo. *Rivista Italiana di Dialettologia* 15. 165–181.
Sankoff, Gillian. 1972. Above and beyond phonology in variable rules. In Charles-James Bailey & Roger W. Shuy (eds.), *New ways of analyzing variation in English*, 44–61. Washington: Georgetown University Press.
Sansò, Andrea. 2018. Explaining the diversity of antipassives: Formal grammar vs. (diachronic) typology. *Language and Linguistics Compass* 12(6). e12277.
Sansò, Andrea. 2020. *I segnali discorsivi*. Roma: Carocci.
Sapir, Edward. 1921. *Language. An Introduction to the Study of Speech*. New York: Harcourt, Brace & World.
Saussure, Ferdinand de 2016 [1916]. *Cours de linguistique générale*. Edited by Charles Bally & Albert Sechehaye. Paris: Payot & Rivages.
Schneider. Klaus P. & Anne Barron (eds.). 2008. *Variational pragmatics*. Amsterdam/Philadelphia: John Benjamins.
Seiler, Guido. 2018. Synchrony and diachrony: two outdated dimensions? In Martin Glessgen, Johannes Kabatek & Harald Völker (eds.), *Repenser la variation linguistique. Actes du Colloque DIA IV à Zurich (12–14 sept. 2016)*, 77–96. Strasbourg: Éditions de linguistique et de philologie.
Seiler, Guido. 2019. Non-Standard Average European. In Andreas Nievergelt & Ludwig Rübekeil (eds.), *'athe in palice, athe in anderu sumeuuelicheru stedi'. Raum und Sprache. Festschrift für Elvira Glaser zum 65 Geburtstag*, 541–554. Heidelberg: Winter.
Skirgård, Hedvig et al. 2023. Grambank reveals the importance of genealogical constraints on linguistic diversity and highlights the impact of language loss. *Science Advances* 9(16). eadg6175. doi: 10.1126/sciadv.adg6175.
Siegel, Jeff, Benedikt Szmrecsanyi & Bernd Kortmann. 2014. Measuring analyticity and syntheticity in creoles. *Journal of Pidgin and Creole Languages* 29(1). 49–85.
Song, Jae Jung. 2010. Word order typology. In Jae Jung Song (ed.), *The Oxford Handbook of Linguistic Typology*, 253–279. Oxford: Oxford University Press.
Stassen, Leon. 1985. *Comparison and Universal Grammar*. Oxford: Blackwell.

Stassen, Leon. 2010. The Problem of Cross-Linguistic Identification. In Jae Jung Song (ed.), *The Oxford Handbook of Linguistic Typology*, 90–99. Oxford: Oxford University Press.

Stave, Matthew, Kilu von Prince & Frank Seifart. 2021. A usage-based approach to morphological typology. Paper presented at the *Societas Linguistica Europaea (SLE) 2021. Workshop: Integrating sociolinguistic and typological perspectives on language variation*, 30 August – 3 September 2021, online.

Tagliamonte, Sali A. 2000. The grammaticalization of the present perfect in Eglish: Tracks of change and continuity in a linguistic enclave. In Olga Fischer, Anette Rosenbach & Dieter Stein (eds.), *Pathways of Change: Grammaticalization in English*, 329–354. Amsterdam/Philadelphia: John Benjamins.

Tagliamonte, Sali A. 2005. So who? Like how? Just what? Discourse markers in the conversations of young Canadians. *Journal of Pragmatics* 37(11). 1896–1915.

Tagliamonte, Sali A. 2006. *Analysing sociolinguistic variation*. Cambridge: Cambridge University Press.

Tagliamonte, Sali A. 2012. *Variationist sociolinguistics. Change, observation, interpretation*. Malden: Wiley-Blackwell.

Torres Cacoullos, Rena. 2011. Variation and Grammaticalization. In Manuel Díaz Campos (ed.), *The Handbook of Hispanic Sociolinguistics*, 148–167. Oxford: Blackwell.

Trudgill, Peter. 2011a. *Sociolinguistic typology*. Oxford: Oxford University Press.

Trudgill, Peter. 2011b. Social structure and phoneme inventories. *Linguistic Typology* 15(2). 155–160.

Tsunoda, Tasaku. 1985. Remarks on transitivity. *Journal of Linguistics* 21. 385–396.

Urban, Matthias. 2020. Mountain linguistics. *Language and Linguistics Compass* 14(9). e12393.

Velupillai, Viveka. 2012. *An introduction to linguistic typology*. Amsterdam/Philadelphia: John Benjamins.

Viberg, Åke. 1984. The Verbs of Perception: a Typological Study. *Linguistics* 21. 123–162.

Weiner, Judith & William Labov. 1983. Constraints on the agentless passive. *Linguistics* 19. 29–58.

Weinreich, Uriel, William Labov & Marvin I. Herzog. 1968. Empirical foundations for a theory of language. In Winfred P. Lehmann & Yakov Malkiel (eds.), *Directions for historical linguistics: A symposium*, 95–188. Austin: University of Texas Press.

Witzlack-Makarevich, Alena. 2019. Argument Selectors. A new perspective on grammatical relations: An introduction. In Alena Witzlack-Makarevich & Balthasar Bickel (eds.), *Argument Selectors: A new perspective on grammatical relations*, 1–38. Amsterdam/Philadelphia: John Benjamins.

Wray, Alison & George W. Grace. 2007. The consequences of talking to strangers: Evolutionary corollaries of socio-cultural influences on linguistic form. *Lingua* 117(3). 543–578.

Zeman, Daniel, Joakim Nivre et al. 2020. *Universal Dependencies 2.6*. LINDAT/CLARIAH-CZ digital library at the Institute of Formal and Applied Linguistics (ÚFAL), Faculty of Mathematics and Physics, Charles University. Available at: http://hdl.handle.net/11234/1-3226. See also http://universaldependencies.org.

Lorenzo Ferrarotti

2 Isolation, complexification, and development of unusual features: A case study from some Gallo-Italian dialects of Northern Italy

Abstract: One of the main tenets of sociolinguistic typology is that complexification typically occurs in isolated varieties. While typologically well-known, even within the Romance domain, complexification patterns have not yet been described in Northern Italian dialects. This paper discusses peculiar cases of complexification that take place in some Gallo-Italian dialects spoken in Eastern Piedmont. These varieties display a substantial array of phonological, morphological, and syntactic innovations, along with some considerably conservative features. These innovations are mostly idiosyncratic and unique compared not only to neighboring dialects but also to the Gallo-Italian group and possibly to the Romance languages as a whole. Some of these unusual features have already been described *per se*, but they can be more profitably understood together as increasing the morphophonological opacity and syntactic eccentricity of the dialects under scrutiny, as well as their overall linguistic complexity. As will be argued, these features arise in closed societies as a result of low adult language contact, small community size, and stable social networks.

1 Introduction

1.1 Societal vs. linguistic types and the issue of complexity

Within the framework of sociolinguistic typology, Trudgill (2011, 2020) hypothesizes that different types of societies are related to different types of languages and language changes. This tendential correlation implies a deterministic approach to language change already present in the author's seminal works on dialect contact and koineization (Trudgill 1986, 2004), by which the initial input of a language contact setting and the subsequent output are bound by a cause-effect relationship: there-

Lorenzo Ferrarotti, University of Bergamo, e-mail: lorenzo.ferrarotti@unibg.it

fore, the knowledge of the first makes the second in some ways predictable. More specifically, Trudgill observes, drawing on typological data gathered from a broad sample of languages in several sociolinguistic contexts, that two opposed tendencies can be identified: *simplification* and *complexification* of languages.

Simplification (Trudgill 2011: 20–26) can be intended in several ways, such as the regularization of irregularities and the increase in lexical and morphological transparency, as well as the loss of syntagmatic and paradigmatic redundancy. Some examples of simplification are the change from a synthetic linguistic type to an analytic one, the reduction of morphological categories or grammatical agreement, and the increase in regularity and transparency. Diachronic processes of this kind seem to develop mainly in specific social settings. Indeed, they seem to be correlated to some specific factors in a social context of heavy language contact: high rate of short-term, adult, second language learning type of contact ("interrupted transmission" in McWhorter 2007), societal instability (e.g., social upheavals, rapid demographic growth, immigration), presence of bigger and looser social networks.

On the other hand, *complexification* can be intended, according to Trudgill (2011: 26–33; 62–63), as a general irregularization of linguistic forms, an increase in opacity or syntagmatic redundancy, and the addition of morphological categories.[1] These processes, too, seem to be correlated to specific social factors. In this case, low rate of short-term adult second language learning (that equals social contexts with few "newcomers"), societal stability, and tight smaller social networks can be linked to linguistic complexification. In general, intra-group languages tend to have more complex features, being low-contact communities where the preservation and development of complexity (called "spontaneous complexification" by Trudgill) can occur more easily due to socio-demographic factors. These complexifying dynamics, or "mature phenomena" (Dahl 2004: 103–118), can manifest at several levels of analysis. The general categories that Dahl (2004: 114–115) lists, drawing on typological (Comrie 1992, McWhorter 1998, 2001) evidence, are generally linked to some degree of "non-linearity":

- complex word structure (inflectional and derivational morphology, incorporating constructions).
- lexical idiosyncrasy (grammatical gender, inflectional classes, idiosyncratic case marking).
- syntactic phenomena dependent on inflectional morphology (agreement and, partially, case marking).
- word order rules over and above internal ordering of sister constituents.

---

[1] These features are often paired with conservatism: for instance, isolated dialects show a more faithful transmission of morphological irregularity (Andersen 1988: 61).

– specific marking of subordinate clauses.
– morpheme and word-level features in phonology.

However, the concept of linguistic complexity (and thus, complexification) has been highly debated, especially in the morphological domain.[2] Several criteria have been proposed to evaluate the degree of complexity in languages. Miestamo (2008: 23–25) underlines that McWhorter's (2001, 2007) and Dahl's (2004) approach to complexity is definable as an *absolute* approach, according to which the more parts a linguistic system is composed of, the more it is complex. Another approach is a *relative* one, which defines complexity in terms of usage and users, i.e., how difficult to process or learn a system is (e.g., the approach of Kusters 2003, 2008). This notion is very hard indeed to define and measure: for this reason, Miestamo (2008: 33), who contends that absolute approaches to linguistic complexity are preferable, has proposed a two-criteria definition of complexity based on 1) the "Fewer Distinctions" principle and 2) the "One-Meaning-One-Form" principle (cf. Langacker 1977). According to 1), languages that display fewer grammatical distinctions within a functional domain can be deemed simpler than languages with more of them, while 2) refers to the one-to-one correspondence of form and function, both paradigmatically and syntagmatically: an exact correspondence between the two entails less complexity. If we consider Kusters' (2003, 2008) three criteria for evaluating morphological complexity, we can see that his principle of *transparency* coincides with the One-Meaning-One-Form principle, as Miestamo (2008: 32) notes, and involves how categories are expressed: instances of allomorphy, homonymy, fusion, and fission are interpretable as cases of complexity. Kusters' *economy* refers to the number of categories that are expressed, such as the overt marking of verbal categories such as tense, mood, aspect, or agreement. At the same time, *isomorphy* regards the order of morphological elements that should follow an ideal cross-linguistic semantic-pragmatic hierarchy of features ordered along the dimension of relevance to the verb stem (Kusters 2003: 21, 30–32). McWhorter's (2007: 21–50, 2008) framework encompasses three criteria as well, namely *overspecification, structural elaboration*, and *irregularity*. *Overspecification* refers to how much languages overtly and obligatorily encode semantic distinctions morphologically that, in many languages, are instead left to context, *structural elaboration* is the number of rules required to generate surface forms in a given language, and *irregularity* refers generically to irregularities in grammar (such as suppletion).

---

2 See in general Arkadiev & Gardani (2020), Dahl (2020) for the contrast between "minimum description" approaches (as the one which is fundamentally adopted here) and markedness-based "canonical" approaches to linguistic complexity.

Even in such different approaches, some clear consensus on what is not complex can be identified: fewer overtly expressed categories, fewer distinctions, fewer morphological irregularities, and a consequent stricter form-function correspondence mean less complexity.

Another critical question is whether the overall complexity of a language can be measured. Miestamo (2008: 29–-32) sees representativity (i.e., the fact that not all the aspects of grammar can be meaningfully measured) and comparativity (i.e., that different aspects of grammar can be difficult to compare) as the central issues in the evaluation of the global complexity of a language. He suggests that the attention should be focused on a local comparison for those aspects of grammar that are effectively comparable cross-linguistically.

1.2 A case study from Northern Italy

The object of this study will be a peculiar linguistic area in which some kinds of morphological complexification seem to have occurred, along with the development of typologically unusual features and the retention of important archaisms. It is composed of middle and small-sized towns in the Novara province (Figure 1), Piedmont, namely Cameri, Trecate, Galliate, Romentino, Cerano (all neighboring Novara to the east), Borgomanero (30 km north of Novara) and Quarna Sotto (lying on a hill northwest to the Orta Lake, about 60 km north of Novara, nowadays in the Verbano-Cusio-Ossola province). The local dialects are considered part of the Gallo-Italian dialects, which are structurally separated from Standard Italian,[3] even if they have been historically influenced by it. Moreover, the dialects of this part of the Novara province are somehow misunderstood by the current dialectological classification, as they are classified as "Lombard" dialects that lie very close to the Piedmontese ones. The local (socio-)linguistic setting is peculiar indeed: if the local middle city, Novara, shows a variety that is quite influenced by the prestige dialect of Milan, the local rural and small-town varieties are in a strong continuum with the neighboring Valsesia, whose dialect is today classified as Piedmontese (see Ferrarotti 2020, 2022). This is related to the historical ties between these areas, as they have been part of the States of Milan and the Novara diocese since the late Middle Ages. Eventually, they were annexed to the Savoy States (Piedmont-Sardinia at that time) only later, during the first half of the 18th century.

---

3 See Bossong (2008), Benincà, Parry and Pescarini (2016), Bossong (2016), Regis (2020) for the linguistic diversity between Northern Italian Dialects and Standard Italian, and Central and Southern dialects.

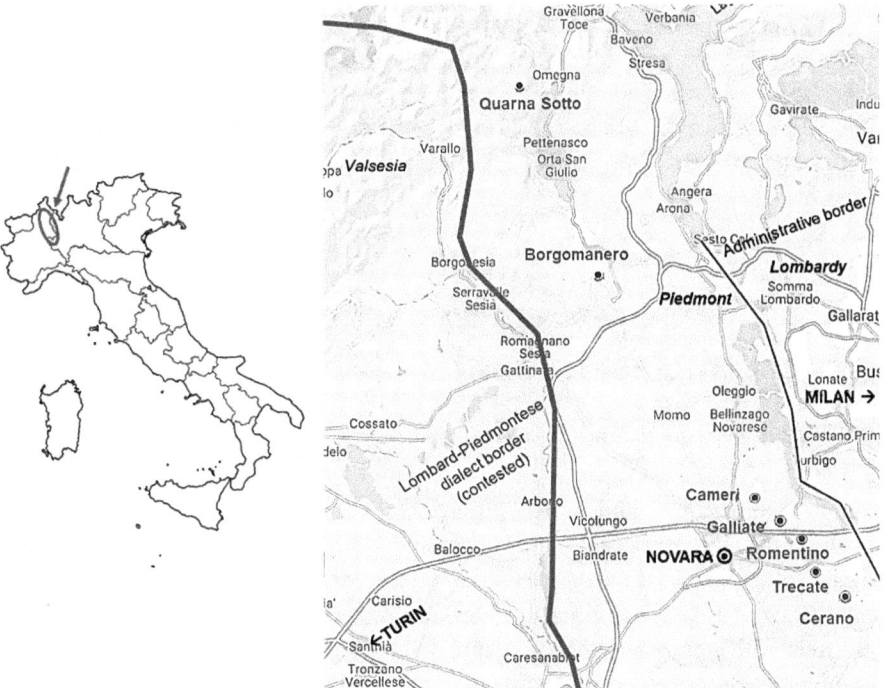

Figure 1: The Novara province and the centers examined here.

Some studies are available for these varieties, namely Tortora (2014) for the syntax of Borgomanero and Manzini and Savoia (2005), who report a great deal of linguistic data for many of these varieties. However, the most relevant for the aim of the present paper are those by Tuttle (1992a, b; 1993). He noticed that a phonetic feature of these dialects (see §2.2) is truly uncommon, and its origin can be linked to their sociolinguistic setting. This perspective, which will be expanded here, will form the basis of the present analysis.[4] The data employed here will be drawn mainly from grammars, descriptive works, and linguistic atlases (AIS, ALI, VIVALDI). Observations will be primarily historical in focus and qualitative, as it is difficult to evaluate the contemporary use at the present stage by quantitative means, mainly because these varieties find themselves in a state of strong language attrition. In fact, local dialects are actively spoken only by older people (60 years old or more), as is common for dialects in northwestern Italy (ISTAT 2015).

---

[4] A first partial observation about the eccentricity of this area in relation to the neighboring ones is in Ferrarotti (2022, 243, 245–247, 250–253).

The main goal of this paper is to highlight the overlap of several unusual features in this area and to link linguistic structures and changes to specific sociolinguistic and historical settings. Firstly, the development of unusual features and complexification will be observed (§2) and, secondly, how it can often occur with unusual archaisms (§3–4). Lastly, some sociohistorical hypotheses will be put forward (§5).

2 Development of unusual features and complexification

2.1 "General enclisis" of object clitics

Many Piedmontese (and some Val d'Aosta Francoprovençal) dialects exhibit enclitic (postverbal) Object Clitics (direct and indirect object, viz. accusative and dative clitics) on past participles in compound tenses as the result of clitic doubling (Parry 1995). The original pre-verbal climbed clitic can be kept, or, eventually, omitted, with significant variation among dialects: *a m'à dacc* > *a m'à dami* > *a l'à dami* 'he gave me'. Even if Portuguese and Galician exhibit the enclisis of Object Clitics (OCs) on simple tenses, but just in main clauses (Tortora 2004: 88), this is otherwise uncommon in other Romance languages. Contemporary Italian shows the enclisis only on the infinitive in subordinate clauses (e.g., *mangiarlo* 'to eat it'), while medieval Italian (and often the literary and formal language until the 19th century) had this kind of enclisis in some other contexts: it was almost obligatory if the verb was clause-initial or if it appeared after some conjunctions (the so-called "Tobler-Mussafia Law", see Benincà 1994), as in *domandollo allora l'ammiraglio* ('the admiral then asked it' Boccaccio, *Decameron* I 6; vs. contemporary Italian = *lo domandò* 'asked it'). Moreover, Salvioni (1903) already noted that in old Italian and old Venetian the enclisis of OCs could be found on elements that are not verbs, such as adverbs or lexicalized Prepositional Phrases: old Italian *addossogli* 'on him', old Venetian *drioghi* 'behind him' (as in the contemporary Italian *eccolo* 'there it is').

In this context, some of the Novarese varieties mentioned above are characterized by a *generalized enclisis* of OCs (as defined by Tortora 2004: 86). Simply put, no proclitic OCs at all are attested in these dialects, even in simple tenses. This is unique in the context of Romance languages. If something similar, as seen above, is or was common in some of them in a context-constrained fashion, in these dialects there are no syntactic constraints (main/embedded clause, etc.) to this phenomenon. It is attested (Figure 2) in Quarna Sotto, Borgomanero, Galliate, Romentino, Trecate, and Cerano (Cameri is excluded).

Figure 2: Presence of the generalized enclisis of object clitics (dark shade).

Moreover, this kind of enclisis often leads to peculiar morphological developments due to clitic fusion. Examples (1) to (6) (data from Manzini and Savoia 2005: III 518–525) show cases of simple enclisis in which the verb is preceded by a subject clitic (SC) and followed by one or two OCs (SC=V=OC; SC=V=OC$_{DAT}$=OC$_{ACC}$). It can be seen that, when two OCs combine, they are fused and often no longer immediately recognizable, as in (1c), (4c), (5c), (6c) and, in some cases, even a single OC is fused with the verb ending, as in (2b) and (6a). This kind of morphophonemic reductions and fusions is probably related to the phonotactic properties of the word in these varieties that, as is common in most Piedmontese and Emilian dialects (Ferrarotti 2022: 68–71), tend to reduce the weight of the unstressed syllables. In this case, there is a strong tendency to reduce the weight of posttonic syllables in words stressed on the pre-penultimate.

(1) Borgomanero
 a. [i ˈlavami] 'I wash myself' < [i ˈlavi] 'I wash' + [mi] 'me'
 b. [at ˈvøŋgami] 'you see me' < [at ˈvøŋgi] 'you see' + [mi] 'me'
 c. [al ˈdagːu] 'he gives it to them' < [al da] 'he gives' + [gi]$_{DAT}$ 'to them' + [lu]$_{ACC}$ 'it'

(2) Galliate
 a. [i ˈvødru] 'I see him' < [i ˈvøda] 'I see' + [ru] 'him'
 b. [ti ˈvømːi] 'you see me' < [ti ˈvøda] 'you (sg.) see' + [mi] 'me'
 c. [a ˈdavji] 'he gives them to him' < [a da] 'he gives' + [v]$_{DAT}$ 'to him' + [i]$_{ACC}$ 'them'

(3) Quarna Sotto
   a. [iɐ 'vɔgːɐy] 'I see him' < [i 'vɔg] 'I see' + [ɐy] 'him'
   b. [ɐd 'lɛvɐt] 'you wash yourself' < [ɐd 'lɛv] 'you (sg.) wash' + [ɐt] 'you' (sg.)
   c. [ɐu̯ 'datɐy] 'he gives it to you' < [ɐu̯ da] 'he gives' + [ɐt] $_{DAT}$ 'to you (sg.)' + [ɐy]$_{ACC}$ 'it'

(4) Trecate
   a. [a 'tʃamːa] 'he calls me' < [a 'tʃama] 'he calls' + [ma] 'me'
   b. ['jevaru] 'I had it' < [j 'eva] 'I had' + [ru] 'it'
   c. [a 'damru] 'he gives it to me' < [a da] 'he gives' + [ma]$_{DAT}$ 'to me' + [lu]$_{ACC}$ 'it'

(5) Cerano
   a. [i 'tʃamal] 'I call him' < [i 'tʃama] 'I call' + [al] 'him'
   b. [a 'tʃamal] 'he calls him' < [a 'tʃama] 'he calls' + [al] 'him'
   c. [i 'denvu] 'they give it to you' < [i 'dena] 'they give' + [av]$_{DAT}$ 'to you (pl.)' + [u]$_{ACC}$ 'it'

(6) Romentino
   a. [i 'tʃamu] 'I call him' < [i 'tʃama] 'I call' + [u] 'him'
   b. [ti tʃa'mevma] 'you called me' < [ti tʃa'meva] 'you (sg.) called' + [ma] 'me'
   c. [i 'denvu] 'they give it to you' < [i 'dena] 'they give' + [av]$_{DAT}$ 'to you (pl.)' + [u]$_{ACC}$ 'it'

For comparison, the normal proclisis is attested in Novara (Turri 1973: 86–91), the closest middle town (the main local administrative and religious center): [ti la 'pɔrti] 'you bring it', [i ga 'stʃapi] 'I break it to him'.

The enclisis is possible even on postverbal elements ("other than the verb" cf. Salvioni 1903). An important class in which this can occur is negative adverbs. These six dialects split in two as far as this kind of enclisis is concerned: just Borgomanero, Galliate and Quarna Sotto, as in (7) to (9), exhibit the enclisis on the negative adverb, while the other show the "normal" enclisis on the verb, as in (10) to (12) (data from Manzini and Savoia 2005: III 518–525).

(7) Borgomanero
   [i 'tʃami 'milːu] < [i 'tʃami] 'I call' + ['mia] 'not' + [lu] 'him' 'I don't call him'

(8) Galliate
   [i 'vøda 'mei̯ru] < [i 'vøda] 'I see' + ['meja] 'not' + [ru] 'him' 'I don't see him'

(9) Quarna Sotto
[iɐ vɔg 'miɐn] < [iɐ vɔg] 'I see' + ['mia] 'not' + [en] 'him' 'I don't see him (any of them)'

(10) Trecate
[a 'tʃamːa 'mia] < [a 'tʃama] 'he calls' + [ma] 'me' ['mia] 'not' 'he doesn't call me'

(11) Cerano
[a 'tʃamum ɲent] < [a 'tʃamu] 'they call' + [m] 'me' + [ɲent] 'not' 'they don't call me'

(12) Romentino
[i 'tʃamenu 'mia] < ['tʃamen] + [u] + ['mia] 'not' 'they don't call me'

This variation is even more remarkable with other elements such as nouns, other adverbs such as non-negative adverbs, as in (13) and (14), or adverbs and prepositional phrases that can be considered part of the VP (i.e., in phrasal verbs), as in (15) and (16) (data from Manzini and Savoia 2005: III 518–525).

(13) Galliate - Modal adverb *ben* 'well'
[a='vøda   'bej=ti]
SC.3SG=see-3SG well=OC.2SG.DAT
'he sees you well'

(14) Trecate - Place adverb *là* 'there'
[j= øk   la=r]
SC.3PL=have.3PL there=OC.3SG.M.ACC
'they have it there'

(15) Borgomanero - Phrasal verb with adverb
[i='bytːi   'mia   'sɔra=lu]
SC.1SG=put-1SG NEG   over=OC.3SG.M.ACC
'I don't put it over'

(16) Trecate - PP *(a) cà* 'at home'
[a='pɔrta   (a) ka=ma]
SC.3SG=bring-3SG (at) home=OC.1SG.ACC
'he brings me (at) home'

This gives rise to potentially long (and not always predictable) clitic strings, as when nouns part of the VP are phonetically reduced (17, data from Belletti et al. 1978: 102) or OCs fuse with the ending causing the voicing of the consonantal segment of the latter and a different vocalization of the two clitics: [ma] + [na] = [amna] (18, data from Leone et al. 2000: 154).

(17) Galliate - noun in the VP
 [a=sta 'mia 'miz=mi]
 SC=stay-3SG NEG friend=OC.1SG.DAT
 'he's no friend to me' (['mizmi] < [a'mizu] 'friend' + [mi] 'to me')

(18) Trecate - dative and partitive clitic cluster
 [lo i = parla'røg = am = na]
 PRO.3PL.they SC=speak-FUT-3PL=OC.1SG.DAT=OC.PART
 'They will tell me about it' ([parla'røk]⁵ 'they will tell' + [ma] 'to me' + [na] 'of it')

As has already been seen, OCs are often fused, and the resulting clitic string can be ambiguous or even fused with the lexical root. A good example of non-transparent fusion is mentioned by Tortora (2004: 177–178), who shows that in Borgomanero postverbal *mu* may underlie both *mi* (DAT.1SG) + *nu* (PART) and *mi* (DAT.1SG) + *lu* (ACC.3SG.M). Again, due to clitic fusion, in the Galliate dialect the presence of an OC can be assessed only by a consonantal lengthening (Belletti et al. 1978: 100): [par'lena] 'they talk' vs. [par'len:a] 'they talk about it (of it)' < [par'lena] 'they talk' + [na] 'of it'.

A further step towards morphological opacity is seen when the vocalic segment of inflectional morphemes (in unstressed endings) changes with unexpected patterns when OCs follow them. In Borgomanero (see Tortora 2014: 180–191, Cardinaletti 2015), two strategies of vowel change are attested that are not entirely predictable and used interchangeably: 1) the *vowel reduplication strategy*, whereby the originally word-final ending takes the vowel quality of the vowel of the OC: [i 'məndʒi] 'I eat' vs. [i 'məndʒu=nu_PART] 'I eat any some of it'. 2) the *change to [a] strategy*, whereby the same ending takes an unrelated [a] vowel: [i ka'pisi] 'I understand' vs. [i ka'pisa=ti_ACC] 'I understand you'. However, this does not occur with every unstressed ending, in an unpredictable way (see the analysis in Cardinaletti 2015), and, in contrast, it happens not exclusively with inflected verbs but even with past participles and non-verbal elements of phrasal verbs: [i 'byt:i 'dentulu]

---

5 [parla'røk] is a form originated from *[parla'rɜŋ] < *[parla'raŋ] and exhibits the "hardening" of the velar nasal described at §2.2 in this chapter.

'I put it inside' (cf. ['denti] 'inside'). Something similar is attested for Trecate (Leone et al. 2000: 151) in the form of vowel metathesis: in some cases, the vowel [u] of the ending and the final vowel [a] of the word (i.e., of the OC) are swapped and then the morpheme boundary is blurred by syncope and consonant lengthening, e.g. 'they see you' [i 'vødu̱] 'they see' + [ta̱] 'you' > [i 'vøda̱tu̱] > [i 'vøt:u̱].

The most extreme case of this kind of enclisis is attested in Quarna Sotto (Manzini and Savoia 2005: 520–521, Barone et al. 2009). Here OCs can appear optionally after various kinds of adverbs of time and aspect (19) and, crucially, after the NP direct object (20), even if, in this case, the "ordinary" generalized verbal enclisis is possible (21).

(19) Enclisis on temporal adverb
      [iɐ=vɔɣ   ɐ'dmɐn=ɐɣ]
      SC.1SG=see.1SG   tomorrow=OC.3SG.ACC
      'I see him tomorrow'

(20) Enclisis on the direct object (NP)
      [iɐ=daį̱   əų̱='libər=ɐt]
      SC.1SG=give.1SG DET.SG.M=book=OC.3SG.DAT
      'I give you the book'

(21) Enclisis on the verb in the same type of sentence as (20)
      [iɐ=daį̱=ɐt   əų̱='libər]
      SC.1SG=give.1SG=OC.3SG.DAT   DET.SG.M=book
      'I give you the book'

In many of the examined cases, various morphological and morphophonemic processes are at play, such as clitic fusion, development of consonant lengthening with phonemic value, not entirely predictable word clippings, and unpredictable vowel alternations triggered by cliticization. All this generally results in an affix-like behavior of OCs and, for this reason, in something that could be seen as heavier inflectional patterns that often directly involve OCs. Examples (13) to (18) and especially (19), (20) show that a significant change of the word structure is present, in which the cliticization of OCs on elements such as nouns or adverbs (that come after the verb) follows a seemingly incorporating word pattern (an essential clue of complexification according to Dahl 2004), as they behave as one complex word group to which the enclitic is attached.

In any case, the presence of these phenomena, which are typologically unusual for Romance languages, can be interpreted as a decrease in linearity and transparency (see §1.1) and a corresponding increase in opacity and the so-called "word level" features (Dahl 2004). At the same time, it can be taken as a violation of the "One-Meaning-One-Form" principle, especially in those cases where clitic boundaries are blurred. In fact, the relation between the base form of verbs plus clitic elements in isolation (including cliticized NPs) and the final form of the verb and clitic elements combined is not always predictable, namely when the surface form requires several *sandhi* and deletion rules before being spelled out from the underlying form (an attribute of *structural elaboration* in McWhorter 2007, see §1.1). The development of these features could therefore be interpreted as an actual increase in complexity, at least from a morphological perspective.[6]

One might wonder about the possible origins and causes of such uncommon changes. From a morphophonemic point of view, as has already been observed, clitic fusion is driven by word structure. In these varieties, the stressed syllable is heavier, and this causes the reduction of the unstressed ones (see above and Ferrarotti 2022: 68–71). From a syntactic point of view, the generalized enclisis was evidently unstable diachronically: for example, in earlier written sources (end of 19th – early 20th century), OCs could be found in other contexts (e.g., after different types of adverbs, v. Tortora 2014: 209), so it is difficult to fully understand its extent. It is also difficult to reconstruct its origin: Tuttle (1992a) is skeptical of a possible connection to the "Piedmontese" enclisis (on the past participle in compound tenses, see above and fn. 6), of which the "general" enclisis would be a sort of extension or generalization (in other words, it could be defined as an extremization). The structural conditions that possibly led to this radical change are not clear: for this reason, only some circumstantial external evidence can be considered, at least as far as the historical and sociolinguistic context is concerned. Undeniably, the varieties that show the "generalized" enclisis are in strong areal contiguity with dialects that show past participle and adverb enclisis, as those of neighboring Valsesia (Salvioni 1903: 101–102). At the same time, the dominant urban variety of Novara (along with the less conservative rural varieties) has no such feature and tends to

---

6 It might be questioned whether this morphological complexification due to the general enclisis of all OCs after the VP has some effects on the complexity of the syntax, i.e., if morphological complexification is counterbalanced by syntactic simplification (Berruto 1990: 21). Given that the stage preceding the generalized enclisis of OCs is not attested for these dialects, we can assume that, if OCs were mainly preverbal (as in the urban dialect of Novara and Italian), in this case, the generalized enclisis would constitute a mere displacement. Instead, if they had a diversified placement (preverbal in simple tenses, pre- and postverbal or only postverbal in compound tenses), as in neighboring Valsesia and Piedmontese varieties, it could be seen as an instance of simplification (i.e., a generalization of a single syntactic position for OCs). Nevertheless, it must be noted (see Parry 1995) that the origin of postverbal OCs in compound tenses was probably related to transparency issues, i.e., when preverbal OCs (mainly direct 3SG OCs) were no longer clearly identifiable by number or gender.

spread the general proclisis of OCs as an innovation, which is probably a Milan dialect-influenced prestige feature. In this regard, the varieties exhibiting general enclisis seem to have undertaken an opposite change, almost as a reaction (see also §5). From the areal point of view, the distribution of the generalized enclisis is puzzling too, because Borgomanero is 30 km north of the Eastern Novarese centers that exhibit this feature, and Quarna Sotto is an isolated center. For this reason, it is not clear whether this feature was once more widespread or whether some centers developed it independently from one another.

2.2 Hardening/enhancement of the final velar nasal

In Trecate, Cameri, and historically in Borgomanero, a "hardening" or "enhancement" (in Tuttle's 1992b, 1993 words) of final -[ŋ] to -[k] is attested (Figure 3), i.e., a loss of nasality and voicing of the segment that probably took place through unattested stages, in which the nasal articulation was displaced as nasalization on the preceding vowel (which would then have disappeared). To illustrate this, three outcomes of some Latin words containing -N- and three different stressed vowels can be examined. The most singular case is probably PANEM 'bread' > [pan] > [pə̃n] > *[pə̃ŋg] > *[pə̃k] > [pək] ([pøk]), where the stressed vowel changes quality, possibly because of its nasality (a rural feature well attested in the area, see Ferrarotti 2022: 77–81).

Figure 3: Presence of the hardening of final -[ŋ] to -[k] (dark shade).

The same goes, without an alteration of the stressed vowel, in cases as VINUM 'wine' > [vik] and BENE 'well' > [bek].

Tuttle (1992b) observes that this happened only at the end of a word group, at least in origin, because the original nasal sound can be kept in *sandhi* (albeit with structural differences among dialects): Borgomanero [ben 'ditʃu] 'well said', Trecate [ben tʃar] 'well clear'. This change has been well attested since the end of the 19th century (cf. the written texts in Biondelli 1853[7] and Rusconi 1878), and it can be associated with unusual phonetic changes of this kind found in several isolated or peripheral dialects of Europe (of Swiss Romansh, French, Danish, German, Polish, etc.) that Andersen (1988) defined as "exorbitant phonetic developments" (1988: 70) typically found in communities characterized by tightly knit or "dense" social networks (in Trudgill's 2011 terms). For this reason, Tuttle (1992b, 1993) sees a link between "closed" or "endocentric" communities and the development of "more effortful" variants.

In the case of Borgomanero, it can be reconstructed that this "hardening" could had been a stereotype in the Labovian sense (a variable that speakers are aware of and comment on, Labov 1994: 78, 301). Pagani (1918), a native speaker of the Borgomanero dialect himself, reports that speakers were aware of this feature (a sign of covert prestige?), which was even represented in popular sayings.[8] It is worth to be noted that these dialects again contrast starkly with neighboring Lombard varieties, such as the dialect of Milan, that on the contrary have a strong tendency to reduce the word-final nasal to a nasalization on the preceding vowel: [pã] 'bread' < PANEM, [vĩ] 'wine' < VINUM, [bẽ] 'well' < BENE (Sanga 1984: 9, 61). In terms of complexification, this development adds phonological rules to the system, i.e., a series of allophonies in *sandhi* in some not always predictable environments, that can be interpreted as a "word level" feature according to Dahl (2004) and as a sign of *structural elaboration* (see §1.1).

In addition, Pagani's texts in his own dialect seem to reveal something more about this feature, because he seems to hypercorrect it,[9] as it is typical of stere-

---

7 In this case, only partially: see fn. 9.
8 [la 'nɔsta 'leŋgwa 'kume tytʃ i søk l ɛ meju ke l la'tik e ke l tus'køk] 'our language as everybody knows is better than Latin and Tuscan' etc. (Pagani 1918: 3).
9 Tuttle (1992b: 99–100) insightfully shows that Pagani rewrites the translations reported in Biondelli (1853, *The Parable of the Prodigal Son*) and Papanti (1875, *The Tale of the king of Cyprus* from Boccaccio's *Decameron* I 9) by adding the hardening in contexts where it would not be expected, i.e., in *sandhi*: for example, *un di sarvitui* 'one of the servants' becomes *uk di sarvitui* in Pagani's translation. This is particularly relevant in the case of Biondelli's (1853) translation, which exhibits almost no instance of the hardening of the nasal (the only example is *cravicchi* < *cravin = 'kid', 'little goat', that probably represents a [kra'vikʲ]-like pronunciation, quite common in the AIS data, e.g., map 1463 "corn" [mal'gokʰʲ] < *[mal'goŋ]). This is probably an important fact because either

otypes in some stages (cf. Labov 1994: 78). This feature's stereotypical character can also be postulated through the analysis of its later diachronic development. As Labov (1994: 211; 2010: 186) observes, stereotypes can be subjected to folklorization and then to stigmatization (cf. the case of the (oi) variable in New York City), which is probably what happened in Borgomanero. If many older accounts (Pagani 1918, Rusconi 1878) represent this feature in a full-fledged fashion (albeit with significant fluctuations), the contemporary dialect[10] shows no trace of -[ŋ] > -[k]. [køk] 'dog' becomes [køŋ] (restructured [ŋ]) or [køi̯] (modeled on the plural < *cani). Some hints allow us to see that it is possible that this change happened before the 1920s. Data from the linguistic atlases offer a narrow but interesting picture in this regard: the female informant of the AIS (survey point 129), born in 1866 ca., preserves it very regularly, while the male informant of the ALI (survey point 29), born in 1878 ca., exhibits it in a much less significant and very variable way. Texts written between the 20s and 60s of the 20th century by Gianni Colombo (1898–1984) no longer exhibit it, and he even states that it was a feature of the olden dialect spoken at the beginning of the century.[11] From an age group perspective, Colombo's generation was probably the first to have steadily abandoned this feature. It is likely that the industrial development and the demographic expansion of the city in the late 19th century (see §5) led to a greater opening to the exterior[12] and caused an expansion of the speech community, hence the consequent stigmatization and suppression of this feature.[13]

---

the author of the text did not perceive it as a phonemically relevant feature, or it was already being suppressed by some speakers. The author of Biondelli's (1853) translation, as Lomaglio and Lomaglio (1977: 51) point out, was a progressive journalist, musician, and railway advocate: it is possible then that the hardening was already in a state of class-based variation, whereby the upper classes were beginning to suppress it.

10 As documented by the informant born in 1931 of the VIVALDI archive and informants in Tortora (2004).

11 Colombo (1925, 1967) was a native speaker of the Borgomanero dialect and a popular poet and historian. He was aware of Pagani's (1918) works, and, in the grammatical sketch of his native dialect, he portrays as an archaism the hardening of the final velar nasal (Colombo 1967: 18), stating that it was in usage at the beginning of the 20th century ("vi fu un tempo – e ciò ancora al principio del nostro secolo – che invece della *n* era usata la *k* [*poek, groek, coek*]"). This feature nowadays seems to be lost in the main center, but it is preserved in the *frazione* (hamlet) of Santo Stefano di Borgomanero – *Varganbas* (Gregorio Fornara, p.c.).

12 Historical accounts show that Borgomanero was precariously connected with the exterior still at the end of the 18th century due to poor road maintenance (Lomaglio & Lomaglio 1977: 45). The building of the Novara-Borgomanero-Gozzano railway, completed in 1864, led to a fast development and to the birth of an industrial upper middle class (Lomaglio & Lomaglio 1977: 50–53, 110–112)

13 It is remarkable that both Cameri and Trecate never lost this feature, which still survives (see data in Ceffa 2003 and Leone et al. 2000). It must be noted, however, that Borgomanero has

3 Conservation of morphological complexity: Final unstressed vowels and inflectional classes

In several Gallo-Italian dialects (Piedmontese, Lombard, Emilian, Romagnol), final Latin unstressed vowels different from -A tend to drop, e.g., CRUDU(M) > [kry], CRUDA(M) > ['krya] 'raw', while Ligurian and Venetian preserve them to a much greater extent (Rohlfs 1966: 180–189, Benincà, Parry, Pescarini 2016: 187).

So does a relic area of conservation (Figure 4) that encompasses, among the centers discussed here, Borgomanero[14] and Galliate, extending to Busto Arsizio and Legnano to the East beyond the Ticino River (with some structural differences from one town to another: see Ferrarotti 2022: 82–84). Some neighboring dialects (Valsesia, High Novarese) preserve final unstressed vowels in some contexts (e.g., after a consonant cluster), and so do Cameri, Romentino, Trecate, and Cerano (Ferrarotti 2022: 82–84). Note that these dialects are completely surrounded by Piedmontese or Lombard dialects that exhibit the complete fall of final unstressed vowels different from -A.

Figure 4: presence of the preservation of final unstressed vowels (dark shade).

---

always been a bigger center than Cameri and Trecate (§5), and that the presence of unusual features is usually linked to the size of the speech communities (§1.1).

14 This feature was and still is a stereotype in Borgomanero (Pagani 1918: 3) that was kept due to its (covert?) prestige in the community.

The conservation of final unstressed vowels allows these varieties to maintain, in general, a richer inflectional nominal morphology. These dialects, however, often keep some kinds of metaphonic marking of the plural masculine (i.e., a quality change of the stressed vowel conditioned by final unstressed [i], see Maiden 2020), which is a conservative feature too for Gallo-Italian dialects, having been suppressed in most urban centers and in most less-isolated rural ones. In this way, the preservation of unstressed endings, combined with the metaphonic marking of the plural, yields a richer inflectional system. The well-described Galliate dialect can be taken as an example of this inflectional richness[15] at least if it is compared with the neighboring urban variety of Novara (Tables 1 and 2).

Table 1: Part of the Galliate noun classes, according to Belletti et al. (1978).

CLASS	SG	PL	
I (mainly M)	-u	-i	['myru]/ ['myri] 'wall'
II (M)	-u	metaphony + -i	['ratu]/['raj̇ti] 'rat'
III (F)	-a	-i	['dɔna]/['dɔni] 'woman'
IV (M, F)	-V# [+stress]	-Vi	[t͡ʃɔ] / [t͡ʃɔi̯] 'nail'
V (M)	-V# [+stress]	-V[+metaphony]	[fra'dɛ]/[fra'di] 'brother'
VI (M, F)	-Ø	-Ø	[ka't͡sy] 'ladle'

Table 2: The Novara dialect noun classes.

CLASS	SG	PL	
I (M, F)	-Ø	-Ø	[myr] 'wall', [rat] 'rat' , [t͡ʃɔ] 'nail', [ka'syl] 'ladle'
II (F)	-a	-i	['dɔna]/'[dɔni] 'woman'
III (M)	-ɛl	-ei̯	[fra'dɛl]/[fra'dɛi̯] 'brother'

---

15 Note that in the Galliate dialect classes I and III are quite productive and tend to overextend unetymologically and on the basis of grammatical gender e.g. ['kruza] 'cross' < CRUCEM (f.), ['lat͡ʃu] 'milk' < LACTEM (m.). This attempt at regularization is without doubt a sign of simplification in an otherwise complex system. It is quite noteworthy, however, that this does not take place in Borgomanero, where the etymologically expected ['kruzi] and ['lat͡ʃi] are attested (see AIS 790, 1199).

4 A true "isolate": Quarna Sotto

As has been seen, Quarna Sotto shares a significant syntactic feature with Borgomanero (§2.2) and the other centers surrounding Novara, but it is clearly a different case. In fact, it is a much more isolated and demographically less populated center. Its dialect is peculiar too, as several innovations and unusual features can be found in it (Barone et al. 2009).

- The development of unusual sounds, such as [l] > [ɣ] (described as a velar fricative by Manzini and Savoia 2005, but also as retroflex in Barone et al. 2009).
- The development of new phonological oppositions based on consonant lengthening, e.g. [kɐˈʃtɛɲɐ] sg. ~ [kɐˈʃtɛɲːɐ] pl. 'chestnut'; [ˈkuɲɐ] sg. ~ [ˈkuɲːɐ] pl. 'wedge'.
- Unusual allomorphies: e.g., the present infinitive alternates between -/ˈar/ and -/ˈer/ (< Lat. -ARE) in a synchronically not entirely predictable way (Ferrarotti 2022: 54–59).
- Pervasive noun and verb metaphonic marking (see Ferrarotti 2022: 145–147, 162). If the metaphonic marking is common on nouns in that area, the verbal marking is particularly noteworthy here, e.g., es. [ja maɲ] 'I eat', [t mɛɲ] 'you eat', [ja pjɛnd͡ʒ] 'I cry' [t piːnd͡ʒ] 'you cry', [ja mət] 'I put', [t mit] 'you put'.

The other varieties of the Novara province examined here are far less conservative than Quarna Sotto. Even the neighboring "sister" village, Quarna Sopra, does not show these original features (at least on the basis of the data present in Manzini and Savoia 2005). This could mean, again, that the development of uncommon features and the conservation of archaisms seem to depend on physical-geographical isolation to the extent that it has an influence on the sociolinguistic environment (in terms of social network stability).

5 General remarks

To sum up, the most bewildering question concerning the unusual features discussed in Sections 2 to 4 is: why are they geographically distributed in such a way (Figure 5), and how could sociolinguistic factors have a role in their development?

Due to the lack of comprehensive historical data, it is unclear whether the shared unusual features of these dialects are due to a hypothetical earlier linguistic unity (which would have been broken later) or to an independent genesis: the first hypothesis surely holds as far the preservation of unstressed vowels is concerned

- Generalized enclisis of Ocs
- Preservation of unstressed final vowels
- -[ŋ] > -[k]

Figure 5: Peculiarities of the dialects in the Novara province.

(§3), but what about the unusual features in §2? In any case, sociohistorical factors should have been crucial to the development and conservation of these features. If Quarna Sotto is a true "isolate" and a remote community, this is not the case for the other towns or villages. Tuttle's (1992b, 1993) relevant hypothesis about endocentric communities, limited initially to the "hardening" of the final nasal, is probably on the right track and must be expanded. In fact, if geographic isolation is not at play, then social isolation must be the main influencing factor in terms of social stability and endogamy (or, generally, closure to the outside).[16]

From a demographic perspective, Galliate (with Romentino), Trecate (with Cerano), and Borgomanero have always been middle-sized or small towns, founded in the late Middle Ages in a peripheral zone with not much social upheaval. In the past, they were demographically more relevant in comparison with the present day (the bigger being about half the size of Novara before 1861). These facts, com-

---

[16] This should be verified by historical records, which is not always an easy task. Some sort of past prolonged endogamy is attested for Borgomanero in terms of the "family" origin of the neighborhoods. See e.g., the families mentioned in Lomaglio and Lomaglio (1977: 22): each one of them was associated with specific streets of the town.

bined with census data from the 19th -20th century, that shows average growth or no growth at all (Figure 6), could be a sign of the prolonged stability of social networks. It is also likely that the development of these features probably happened before the 19th century, as the earliest historical records of these dialects already show them.

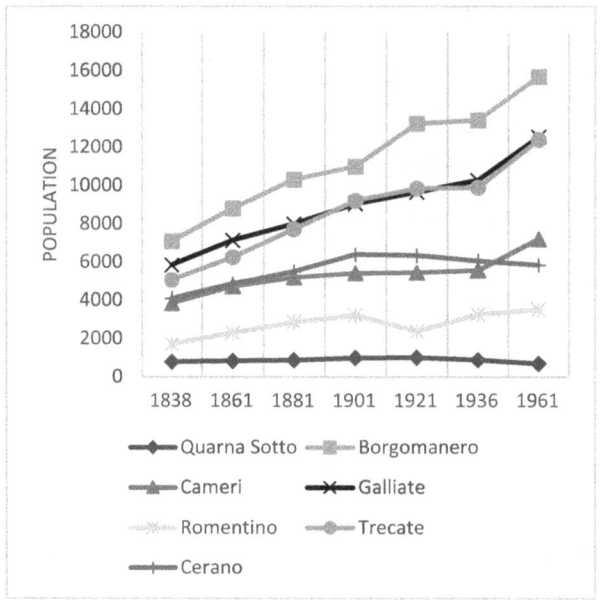

Figure 6: Population growth from 1838 to 1961.

In conclusion, it is safe to assume that the presence of unexpected developments on several levels of analysis is relevant and not due to haphazard linguistic changes. The coexistence of unusual innovative features and archaisms is another sign of the peculiarity of this area: but how did this complexification originate, and how was it preserved?

From a geographical perspective, these dialects occur in two geographical contexts: a small, isolated village (Quarna Sotto) and several not geographically isolated medium-sized towns (Borgomanero, Galliate, Trecate) and villages (Cameri, Romentino, Cerano). They all fit, in a certain sense, the profile of small-sized, low-contact, socially "dense" communities that often develop "mature phenomena" (Trudgill 2011, 2020; Dahl 2004, see §1), the so-called "societies of intimates". It is important to note that they stand quite clearly in opposition to the dominant variety of Novara, which is influenced by the dialect of Milan, a significantly different dialect that lacks these complex developments. It is possible that the contrast with the dominant variety, which is quite different from the local ones, has had a role, also considering that, according to Trudgill's (2011) hypothesis, we should be able to witness a very significative urban-rural divide,[17] as far as complexification processes are concerned. In Trudgill's (1972) "gravity" dialect contact model, the "preexisting similarity" of dialects in contact is a facilitating factor in the diffusion of linguistic features: in our case, we can imagine that the local dialects had been in contact with an urban dialect that was, in fact, quite different linguistically, and this inhibited the suppression of these features or even encouraged[18] their development. An opposite change, probably stimulated by the contact with the urban variety, is visible in one case (§2.2, Borgomanero), where we can see how a marked feature could disappear in a few generations, probably when social stagnation had been broken, and the local community had opened to the exterior due to industrialization and development.

In the study of these phenomena through a historical lens, the interaction between geographical and sociolinguistic determinants is critical because, even if it is difficult to fully comprehend and measure what "complex" is in an absolute fashion, it is sure more feasible to identify a complexified variety in relation to its neighboring dialects. For this reason, a global approach to language contact is beneficial in these cases, where typology and (historical) sociolinguistics interact to reconstruct changes in the past.

---

17 In fact, urban varieties, if they are high-contact ones, should be simpler varieties (poorer phonological inventories, loss of morphological markings, loss of syntactic complexity), especially if they underwent by koineization processes (Trudgill 1986, Trudgill 2004; Regis 2011 for the case of Turin). This seems the case for Novara in relation to the other dialects examined here.

18 This type of dynamics was already noted by Benvenuto Terracini in his studies on the Francoprovençal dialects of Piedmont. In a neo-idealistic framework, he spoke of *linguistic vitality* (*vitalità linguistica*) of marginal but socially tight rural mountain centers in opposition to innovative urban varieties (see Grassi 1969). Even if his conception of language change and diffusion is without doubt outdated, some of his conclusions foreshadow the tenets the sociolinguistic typology: see, e.g., his adage quoted by Tuttle (1992b: 97, in Terracini 1934: 140): "Massima innovazione e massima conservazione sono i tratti caratteristici di ogni zona linguistica più remota dalla cultura... e soprattutto mancante di un centro regolatore. [...]" ("The highest rates of innovation and conservation are the typical features of every linguistic area that is far removed from culture... and above all missing a regulating center. [...]").

References

Ais, Jaberg Karl & Jud Jacob (eds.). 1928–1940. *Sprach- und Sachatlas Italiens und der Südschweiz*, 8 voll., Zofingen: Verlagsanstalt Ringier & Co. Electronic version NavigAIS http://www3.pd.istc.cnr.it/navigais-web/.

Ali, Bartoli, Matteo, Ugo Pellis & Lorenzo Massobrio (eds.). 1995–2018. *Atlante Linguistico Italiano*. Voll. I-IX. Roma: Istituto Poligrafico e Zecca dello Stato (I-VIII), then Torino: Istituto dell'Atlante Linguistico Italiano (IX).

Andersen, Henning. 1988. Center and periphery: adoption, diffusion, and spread. In Jacek Fisiak (ed.), *Historical Dialectology, Regional and Social*, 39–83. Berlin: Mouton de Gruyter.

Arkadiev, Peter & Francesco Gardani. 2020. Introduction: Complexities in morphology. In Peter Arkadiev & Francesco Gardani (eds.), *The Complexities of Morphology*, 1–19. Oxford: Oxford University Press.

Barone, Guido, Giorgio Cecchetti, Erminio Coppi, Iginio Nicolazzi, Mario Nicolazzi & Claudio Zolla. 2009. *Dialetto di Quarna Sotto. Vocabolario – Grammatica – Proverbi e modi di dire – Toponimi – Come vivevano i nostri vecchi*. Quarna Sotto: Associazione Museo di Storia Quarnese Onlus.

Belletti, Angelo, Ezio Bozzola, Angelo Jorio & Alessandro Mainardi. 1978, *Gajà spitascià. Grammatica e antologia del dialetto galliatese*. Vol. 1. Novara: La Moderna.

Benincà, Paola, Mair Parry & Diego Pescarini 2016. The dialects of northern Italy. In Adam Ledgeway & Martin Maiden (eds.), *The Oxford Guide to the Romance Languages*, 185–205. Oxford: Oxford University Press.

Benincà, Paola. 1994. La sintassi dei clitici complemento nelle lingue romanze medievali. In Paola Benincà (ed.), *La variazione sintattica. Studi di dialettologia romanza*, 213–246. Bologna: Il Mulino.

Berruto, Gaetano. 1990. Semplificazione linguistica e varietà sub-standard. In Günter Holtus & Edgar Radtke (eds.), *Sprachlicher Substandard III, Standard: Substandard und Varietätenlinguistik*, 17–43. Tübingen: Niemeyer.

Biondelli, Bernardino. 1853. *Saggio sui dialetti Gallo-Italici*. Milano: Bernardoni.

Bossong, Georg. 2016. Classifications. In Adam Ledgeway & Martin Maiden (eds.), *The Oxford Guide to the Romance Languages*, 63–72. Oxford: Oxford University Press.

Bossong, Georg. 2008. *Die romanischen Sprachen: eine vergleichende Einführung*. Hamburg: Buske.

Cardinaletti, Anna. 2015. Cases of Apparent Enclisis on Past Participles in Romance varieties. *Isogloss* 1. 179–197.

Ceffa, Giuseppe (ed.). 2003., *Dizionario storico linguistico camerese*. Novara: Gruppo dialettale camerese.

Colombo, Gianni. 1925. *'Na misciuronda. Poemetto dialettale borgomanerese*. Borgomanero: Vecchi.

Colombo, Gianni. 1967. *Na bisa bòsa. Poesie in dialetto borgomanerese*. Borgomanero: Lions Club.

Comrie, Bernard. 1992. Before complexity. In Murray Gell-Mann & John Hawkins (eds.), *The evolution of human languages: Proceedings of the Workshop on the Evolution of Human Languages, held August 1989 in Santa Fe, New Mexico*, 193–211. Redwood, California: Addison-Wesley.

Dahl, Östen. 2004. *The Growth and Maintenance of Linguistic Complexity*. Amsterdam/Philadelphia: Benjamins.

Dahl, Östen. 2020. Morphological complexity and the minimum description length approach. In Peter Arkadiev & Francesco Gardani (eds.), *The Complexities of Morphology*, 331–343. Oxford: Oxford University Press.

Ferrarotti, Lorenzo. 2020. Il romanzo di Rimella come varietà di contatto. *Bollettino dell'Atlante Linguistico Italiano* 44(2021). 13–50.
Ferrarotti, Lorenzo. 2022. *I dialetti del Piemonte orientale. Contatto e mutamento linguistico*. Berlin: Mouton de Gruyter.
Grassi, Corrado. 1969. Il concetto di *vitalità* nella linguistica di Benvenuto Terracini. *Revue de linguistique romane* 33. 1–16.
ISTAT = *L'uso della lingua italiana, dei dialetti e delle lingue straniere*. Anno 2015. Roma, Istituto nazionale di statistica, 2015. https://www.istat.it/it/files/2017/12/Report_Usoitaliano_dialetti_altrelingue_2015.pdf
Kusters, Wouter. 2003. *Linguistic Complexity, the Influence of Social Change on Verbal Inflection*. [Ph.D. Diss., University of Leiden]. Utrecht: LOT.
Kusters, Wouter. 2008. Complexity in linguistic theory, language learning and language change. In Matti Miestamo, Kaius Sinnemäki & Fred Karlsson (eds.), *Language Complexity: Typology, contact, change*, 3–22. Amsterdam/Philadelphia: John Benjamins
Labov, William. 1994. *Principles of linguistic change*. Vol. 1: *Internal Factors*. Oxford: Blackwell.
Labov, William. 1972. *Sociolinguistic Patterns*. Philadelphia: University of Philadelphia Press.
Labov, William. 2010. *Principles of Linguistic Change*. Vol. 3: *Cognitive and Cultural Factors*. Oxford: Blackwell.
Langacker, Ronald W. 1977. Syntactic re-analysis. In Charles N. Li (ed.), *Mechanisms of syntactic* change, 57–139. Austin: University of Texas Press.
Leone, Gian Piera, Amos Bigogno, Giovanni Bigogno, Angelo Bolchetti, Vanna Garzoli & Antonio Manfredda. 2000. *Tracà un quai an fa*. Novara: Italgrafica.
Lomaglio, Ernesto & Maria Francesca Lomaglio. 1977. *Borgomanero nell'Ottocento e nel primo Novecento*. Torino: Gribaudi.
Maiden, Martin. 2020. *Interactive Morphonology. Metaphony in Italy*. London: Routledge.
Manzini, Maria Rita & Leonardo Maria Savoia. 2005. *I dialetti italiani e romanci. Morfosintassi generativa*. Alessandria: Edizioni dell'Orso.
McWhorter, John H. 1998. Identifying the creole prototype: Vindicating a typological class. *Language* 74. 788–817.
McWhorter, John H. 2001. The world's simplest grammars are creole grammars. *Linguistic Typology* 5. 125–166.
McWhorter, John H. 2007. *Language Interrupted: Signs of Non-native Acquisition in Standard Language Grammars*. Oxford: Oxford University Press.
McWhorter, John H. 2008. Why does a language undress? Strange cases in Indonesia. In Matti Miestamo, Kaius Sinnemäki & Fred Karlsson (eds.), *Language Complexity: Typology, contact, change*,167–190. Amsterdam/Philadelphia: John Benjamins.
Miestamo, Matti. 2008. Grammatical complexity in a cross-linguistic perspective. In Matti Miestamo, Kaius Sinnemaki & Fred Karlsson (eds.), *Language Complexity: Typology, Contact, Change*, 23–42. Amsterdam/Philadelphia: John Benjamins.
Pagani, Giuseppe. 1918. *Il dialetto di Borgomanero*. Rendiconti dell'Istituto Lombardo di Scienze e Lettere 51(2). 602–611, 919–949.
Papanti, Giovanni. 1875. *I parlari italiani in Certaldo*. Livorno: Vigo.
Parry, Mair. 1995. Some observations on the syntax of clitic pronouns in Piedmontese. In John Charles Smith & Martin Maiden (eds.), *Linguistic theory and the romance language*, 133–160. Amsterdam: John Benjamins.
Regis, Riccardo. 2011. Koinè dialettale, dialetto di koinè, processi di koinizzazione. *Rivista Italiana di Dialettologia* 35(2012). 7–36.

Regis, Riccardo. 2020. Italoromanzo. *Revue de linguistique romane* 84. 5–39.
Rohlfs, Gerhard. 1966. *Grammatica storica della lingua italiana e dei suoi dialetti. Fonetica.* Vol. 1. Torino: Einaudi.
Salvioni, Carlo. 1903. Del pronome enclitico oggetto suffisso ad altri elementi che non sieno la voce verbale. *Rendiconti dell'Istituto Lombardo di Scienze e Lettere* 36(2). 1012–1021.
Sanga, Glauco. 1984. *Dialettologia lombarda.* Pavia: Dipartimento di Scienza della Letteratura, Università di Pavia.
Tortora, Christina. 2014. *A comparative Grammar of Borgomanerese.* Oxford: Oxford University Press.
Terracini, Benvenuto. 1934. Review of Duraffour, Antonin, 1932. *Phénomènes généraux d'évolution phonétique dans les dialèctes franco-provençaux d'après le parler de Vaux-en-Bugey (Ain).* Grenoble, chez l'auteur. *Archivio Glottologico Italiano* 36. 130–144.
Trudgill, Peter. 1972. Linguistic change and diffusion: Description and explanation in sociolinguistic dialect geography. *Language in Society* 3(2). 215–246.
Trudgill, Peter. 1986. *Dialects in Contact.* Oxford: Blackwell.
Trudgill, Peter. 2004. *New-Dialect Formation. The Inevitability of Colonial English.* Edinburgh: Edinburgh University Press.
Trudgill, Peter. 2011. *Sociolinguistic Typology. Social Determinants of Linguistic Complexity.* Oxford: Oxford University Press.
Trudgill, Peter. 2020. *Millennia of Language Change. Sociolinguistic Studies in Deep Historical Linguistics.* Cambridge: Cambridge University Press.
Turri, Carlo. 1973. *Grammatica del dialetto novarese.* Novara: Famiglia Nuaresa.
Tuttle, Edward F. 1992a. Del pronome d'oggetto suffisso al sintagma verbale. In calce a una nota Salvioniana del 1903. *L'Italia Dialettale* 55. 15–63.
Tuttle, Edward F. 1992b. Comunità linguistiche chiuse o endocentriche e l'intensificazione delle nasali finali nel Norditalia. *Rivista Italiana di Dialettologia* 16. 81–180.
Tuttle, Edward F. 1993. Closed communities and nasal enhancement in Northern Italy. In William J. Ashby, Marianne Mithun, Giorgio Perissinotto & Eduardo Raposo (eds.), *Linguistic Perspectives on the Romance Languages*, 139–148. Amsterdam/Philadelphia: John Benjamins.
Vivaldi = *Vivaio Acustico delle Lingue e dei Dialetti d'Italia.* http://www2. hu-berlin.de/vivaldi/.

Konstantinos Sampanis

3 On typological shift in Inner Anatolian Greek

Abstract: The paper investigates whether existing approaches in favor of a typological shift in *Inner Anatolian Greek* (IAG, also known as *Inner Asia Minor Greek*) varieties are justified. It is suggested that the arguments postulating the rise of agglutination in certain IAG varieties and the description of them as a "mixed language" are at least problematic. It is argued that typological shift in IAG is rather realized and manifested in head-complement directionality patterns that differ significantly with respect to Common Modern Greek. The paper proposes a diachronic scenario about how directionality change was triggered and discusses the structural and sociolinguistic implications thereof.

1 Introductory remarks: Inner Anatolian Greek

Inner Anatolian Greek (IAG) is a cover term introduced hereby for a number of related yet distinct Greek varieties spoken until the beginning of the 20th century in landlocked regions of what is today the Asian side of Turkey. IAG comprises three main branches, namely Silliot, the dialect of the settlement of Sílli close to the city of Iconium (modern *Konya*), Cappadocian Greek (CG) spoken in a region defined by the urban centers of Nevşehir and Ürgüp in the north and Niğde in the south, and Pharasiot, spoken in the eastern part of Cappadocia in the citadel of Phárasa and satellite settlements (cf. Figure 1). CG in turn is divided in several (sub)dialects (cf. Figure 2) which differ from each other not only due to dialect-internal developments but also with respect to the Degree of Turkish Influence (DTI) exerted on them. DTI should be understood as a continuum upon which the IAG varieties are placed. In broad

---

Acknowledgements: This publication/paper has been produced benefiting from the 2236 Co-Funded Brain Circulation Scheme2 (CoCirculation2) of TÜBİTAK (Project No: 120C061). However, the entire responsibility of the publication/paper belongs to the owner of the publication/paper. The financial support received from TÜBİTAK does not mean that the content of the publication is approved in a scientific sense by TÜBİTAK. I would like to thank two anonymous reviewers for their valuable comments, Professor Hubert Haider for his feedback on some relevant questions of mine and Professor Sarah Thomason for our discussion during the ICHL25 in Oxford (August 2022). It goes without saying that I am entirely responsible for any lapses or mistakes found in this paper.

Konstantinos Sampanis, University of Vienna, e-mail: konstantinos.sampanis@univie.ac.at

strokes, the Southwest CG (sub)dialects are seen as having been radically reshaped by Turkish whereas the Northeast CG varieties are regarded as the least influenced ones (cf. Table 1).[1] Some of the criteria defining the DTI are displayed below.

IAG varieties are mostly known in the relevant literature as *Asia Minor Greek* (AMG). This nomenclature was introduced as early as in Dawkins' (1916) emblematic work on the Greek (sub)dialects of Inner Anatolia and since then it is the main term used for them. The obvious problem with this definition is that Asia Minor is a wider region including what is today's Asian Turkey (with the exception of the northern part of Mesopotamia) where several Greek varieties were spoken in different locations of the Asia Minor peninsula (cf. Figure 1). To correct this misnomer Manolessou (2019) uses the term *inner Asia Minor Greek* which entails IAG as well as Pontic. We opt for the term *Inner Anatolian Greek* in order to avoid any misinterpretation.[2]

Figure 1: Anatolian Greek (Asia Minor Greek) varieties.

---

1 The Central and Southeast CG varieties are similarly classified as heavily influenced; for details cf. Dawkins (1916: 203, 208–211), Janse (2009a) and (forthc.). Pharasiot exhibits a higher degree of DTI in comparison to Silliot (cf. Dawkins 1916: 203). Both latter dialects can be placed in the lower edge of the DTI continuum (cf. Theodoridi 2017: 531).
2 The term Anatolian seems to be preferred in studies associated with the era after the arrival of the Turks in the region. It is indicative that in Turkish the term *Anadolu* 'Anatolia' appears 1.030.000x in Google Scholar while the term *Küçük Asya* 'Asia Minor' appears 112.000x. It is similarly interesting that Donabédian and Sitaridou (2020) refer to *Anatolia* in the examination of language contact in that region (compare also Mellink 1966 for a parallel usage of both geographical terms in the archaeological domain). Thus, in order to underscore that Turkish is a major parameter in any discussion concerning the Greek dialects of the region the term *Anatolian* is herein preferred. Cf. also Johanson's (2002: passim) reference to *Anatolian Greek*.

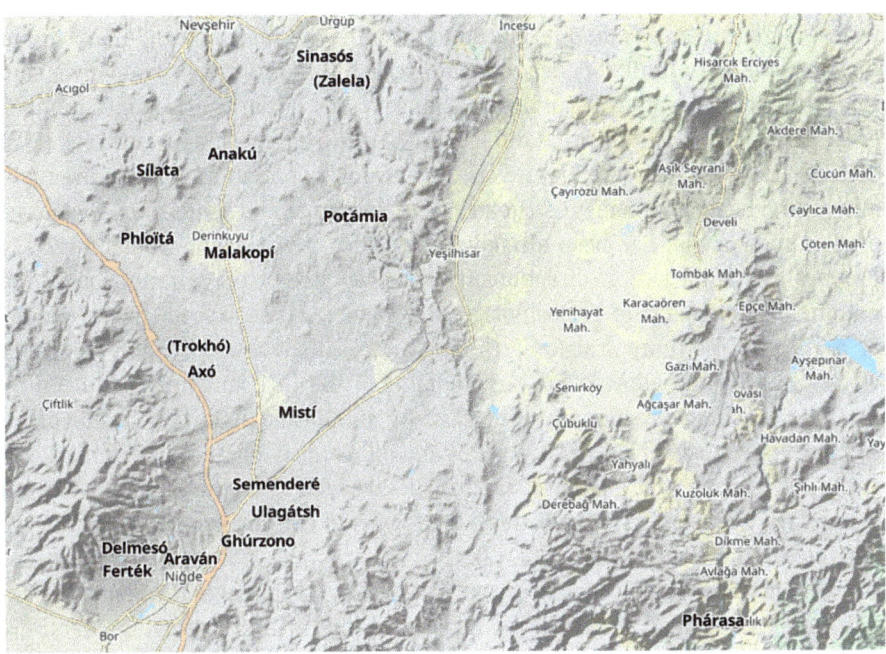

Figure 2: Greek-speaking Cappadocian settlements at the beginning of the 20th century.

Table 1: Cappadocian settlements' dialectal subgrouping.[3]

North CG	
Northwest CG	**Northeast CG**
Anakú, Sílata, Phloïtá, Malakopí	*Delmesó, Sinasós, Potámia*
Central CG	
Axó, Mistí, Trokhó	
South CG	
Southwest CG	**Southeast CG**
Aravan, Ferték, Ghúrzono	*Semenderé, Ulaghátsh*

The general aim of this paper is to discuss whether approaches on the so-called typological shift in IAG are justified or not. I firstly examine the validity of analyses according to which IAG is a "mixed" variety that involves a shift from fusional to agglutinative declension patterns. Contrary to these approaches, I argue that the

---

3 Classification based on Janse (2021: 204).

terms "mixed languages" and "agglutination" cannot be applicable to IAG at least in their stricter sense. Still, the idea of typological shift in IAG is legitimate if we consider the overall architecture of the IAG clause which is characterized by a number of contact-induced features that differentiates IAG from most Modern Greek (MG) dialects. The main of these features is the existence of a left-branching directionality in the head-complement structure of the nominal and prepositional clauses, a phenomenon that has been already observed in the relevant scholarship.[4] My proposal is that the shift in directionality was prompted by the introduction of free grammatical elements of Turkish origin that have a leftward scope over a phrase or a clause. This (untypical for a Greek variety) innovation probably triggered wider changes and allowed for a remodeling of the IAG sentential architecture. The left-branching directionality impact is also manifested in the cliticization of the copular verb in certain CG (sub)varieties and in instances of (arguably unmarked)[5] verb-final clauses. These latter characteristics, as well as the fact that in IAG both VO and OV word orders us are attested, allow us to categorize IAG as a *third-type language* in the sense of Haider (2013).

Should the above diachronic scenario be valid, it challenges the idea that contact-induced typological shifts only take place low in the Borrowing Hierarchy scale. Instead, typological shifts can occur in the first phases of intense language contact under intense pressure of the dominant group and when the speakers of the target language start replicating patterns of the source language or when they adopt free grammatical elements that are readily borrowable yet affect the overall grammatical organization of the borrowing language. In corroboration of this argument, I also make a brief comparison with temporary Istanbul Greek which is close to Common Modern Greek (CMG), yet it clearly replicates Turkish word order patterns because of the extended bilingualism of its speakers.

The article is organized as follows: Sections 2.1. and 2.2. provide a sketch of the theoretical discussion that revolves around IAG while section 2.3. revisits some of the existing theoretical premises. Section 3 is dedicated to a novel approach concerning the typological profile of IAG. In section 4 I indicate how IAG's typology is an indicator about intense language contact between the Greek and the Turkish varieties of Anatolia. Section 5 sums up the results of our analysis.

---

4 On specific aspects of the contact-induced directionality alteration in IAG cf. Melissaropoulou (2017) and (2019), Karatsareas and Georgakopoulos (2016), Georgakopoulos and Karatsareas (2017).
5 Cf. Janse (2006).

2 Approaches on IAG: A critical overview

2.1 IAG as a "mixed language"

Due to the great degree of influence of Turkish elements on Inner Anatolian Greek the latter is often presented as a *par excellence* case of "heavy borrowing" (Thomason and Kaufman 1988: 215–222). In particular, Janse (2009a: 50) describes Cappadocian Greek as a "mixed language" and remarks that "[f]rom a purely linguistic point of view, the Northern dialects remain Greek dialects in the full genetic sense, whereas the Central and especially the Southern dialects are typologically so much closer to Turkish that they have to be considered mixed". In the same vein, Winford (2003: 170–175) refers to IAG as "a Greek Turkish mixture". These designations evoke the question of how we should define a mixed language altogether. In her typology of contact languages Thomason (1997) set four criteria: a. mixed languages emerge in a two-languages contact context, b. extensive bilingualism from at least one part of the contact situation is a presupposition, c. it is relatively easy to discern the origin of the components that make up the linguistic outcome of the "mixture" process and d. a mixed language is not a simplified form of either variety participating in the "mixture". On these grounds, the emergence of a mixed language is regarded as an explicit indication of extensive bilingualism.

The treatment of IAG as a mixed language has been justified on the basis of grammatical features that are typical for Turkic languages and unknown in all Greek varieties outside Anatolia. For instance, Dawkins (1916: 42–43) reports that Turkish-like vowel harmony is found in loan verbs in Silliot. In (1a) the verbal stem follows the usual vocalization of a MG verb with accentuation on the final syllable whereas in (1b) the vocal deviates from the MG pattern due to the influence of the preceding front vowel of the verbal stem. Similar phenomena are also attested in the main CG (sub)dialects (Dawkins 1916: 67–68).

(1)   a. Cappadocian Greek *bašladó* 'to begin' < Turkish *başlamak*
           SG. *bašlad-ó, -ás, -á*
           PL. *bašlad-úmi, -áti, -úši*
    b. Cappadocian Greek *düšündó* 'to think' < Turkish *düşünmek*
           SG. *düšünd-ó, -és, -é*
           PL. *düšünd-ǘmi, -éte, -ǘši*

An equally unusual structure in CG that indicates a strong underlying Turkish influence is the replication of left-branching relative clauses,[6] as in (2a), a structure that clearly differs from the corresponding MG right-branching construction but resembles a Turkish relative clause (2c):

(2)   a.   IAG, CG, Settlement of Axó
            to   írtes   t' méra
            REL (< *the*)   come.2SG.PST.PFV   the_day
    b.   SMG
            ti   méra   pu   írthes
            the.ACC.F.   day   REL   come.2SG.PST.PFV
    c.   Standard Modern Turkish[7]
            gel=diğ=in   gün
            come.POSS.2SG   day
            'The day that you came.' (Cf. Mavrochalyvidis and Kesisoglou 1960: 90)

Yet, according to certain scholars, the most illustrative cases of high DTI on IAG are grammatical phenomena that are described as "agglutinative patterns". In broad strokes, these pertain to nominal declension and verbal conjugation paradigms. The case of "agglutinative" nominal declension in certain (yet not all) CG (sub)dialects has been widely discussed in several publications (Janse 2009b, 2019; Karatsareas 2016a; Revithiadou, Spyropoulos and Markopoulos 2016) and has been presented as an indicator of extensive and intense language contact (e.g. Thomason 2001: 63; Johanson 2002: 79; Matras 2009: 262). The most cited example of an agglutinative-like nominal pattern refers to the declension of the noun *néka* 'woman'. The genitive plural form of this noun is *néc-ez-ju* 'of women', a form which exhibits juxtaposition of two distinct morphemes encoding different grammatical categories, namely plurality (the suffix *-ez* (*-es*), compare the ending of the nominative plural form of Standard Modern Greek (SMG)[8] in (3) below) and case (the suffix *-ju* stemming from the genitive singular suffix of neutral diminutives ending in *-í /-i* in Common Greek[9]). This form clearly differs from the fusional declination of SMG, in which the ending *-ón* in *jinek-ón* conveys information

---
[6] On relative clauses in IAG cf. Janse (1999); Bağrıaçık and Danckaert (2021).
[7] The participle suffix *-DIK* that is attached to the verbal root in this example is used for the formation of relative clauses in Standard Modern Turkish cf. Göksel and Kerslake (2005: 85 and 380–395).
[8] For the methodological distinction between Standard and Common Modern Greek cf. Mertyris and Sampanis (under review).
[9] Cf. Dawkins (1916: 96) and discussion in Janse (2019: 8).

for both plural and genitive case, yet it matches perfectly with the Turkish type *kadın-lar-ın*.

(3)   Ferték / Ulaghátsch CG[10]   Standard MG   Standard Turkısh
   NOM.SG   *néka*   *jinéka*   *kadın*
   GEN.SG   *néka-ju*   *jinéka-s*   *kadın-ın*
   NOM.L   *néc-es*   *jinéc-es*   *kadın-lar*
   GEN.PL   *néc-ez-ju*   *jinek-ón*   *kadın-lar-ın*

The development of agglutinative-like paradigms in IAG is also attested in the verbal conjugation. Dawkins (1916: 142) noted that in several subdialects there are mediopassive forms which he calls "peculiar" due to the persistent extension of the verbal stem with the form *-ton* followed by personal endings. Contrary to the fusional Standard MG paradigm, the Cappadocian case resembles the Turkish pattern. In Turkish the copula verb is enclitic but the past form is *ol-du* in third person singular, with no marking of person. To this form there are attached personal endings: 1SG *ol-du-m*, 2SG *ol-du-n*, 3SG *ol-du-Ø*, 1PL *ol-du-k*, 2PL *ol-du-nuz*, 3PL *ol-du-lar*. In Turkish the suffix *-DI* encodes the past. As Dawkins states (1916: 143, cf. also Janse 2009) the CG forms with the morphological element *-ton* emerged as a case of reanalysis: in the 3Sg. *íç-ton* the ending *-ton* (cf. MG *-tan*) was not interpreted as a fusional morpheme encoding past tense, singular and the third person, but, probably, as a morpheme expressing the past tense outright (i.e. *íç-ton* → *íç-ton-Ø*). Subsequently, the personal endings are attached in a fashion obviously analogous to the Turkish paradigm.[11]

(4)   IAG, CG, Settlement of Axó[12]   Standard Modern Greek
      Present   Past   Present   Past
      (ín)-me   *íç-ton-me*   *í-me*   *í-mun*
      (ín)-se   *íç-ton-se*   *í-se*   *í-sun*
      en / -ne   *íç-ton*   *í-ne*   *í-tan*
      (ín)--meste *íç-ton-meste* *í-maste*   *í-mastan*
      (ín)--ste *íç-ton-ste*   *í-s(a)ste*   *í-sastan*
      (ín)-nde   *íç-tan*   *í-ne*   *í-tan/ í-san*

---

10 The Ferték example in Dawkins (1916: 114), the Ulagátsch one in Kesisoglou (1951: 31 – 33).
11 Regarding the aberrant 3PL form in *-tan* instead of *-ton* Janse (2009: 102) remarks that the 3PL is often irregular in the verbal paradigm (compare e.g. the case of Polish *są* be.PRS.3PL '(they) are'). Moreover, in the Turkish paradigm the 3PL is marked only for plurality with the *-ler/-lar* suffix. Thus, the CG cases may have a limited allomorphy for the 3PL, however, according to Janse this exception should not be seen as a counterexample to the agglutinative profile of this conjugation.
12 Mavrochalyvidis and Kesisoglou (1960: 58).

In a few cases, along with the development of a "more" agglutinative-like paradigm, the IAG varieties also adopted the Turkish endings *per se*. Consider example (5). In the 1PL and 2PL medio-passive tense of the verb *kémi* (cf. 5a) the endings -*k* and -*niz* are pleonastic exponents of the respective person adopted directly from Turkish (cf 5.b.). Janse (2009: 103–107) argues that these borrowings must constitute a case of code-switching triggered by the phonological similarity of the personal suffix -*misti* and -*sti* with the temporal suffix -*mIştI*. The same insertion of the Turkish endings is found in the dialect of Silliot (Dawkins 1916: 59), a fact that Janse links to the vowel-raising phonology of both varieties.[13]

(5)[14] a. IAG, CG, Settlement of Semenderé, verb: *kémi* 'to lie'[15]
Imperfect

Person:	1st	2nd	3rd
Singular	ké-tun-mi	ké-tun-si	ké-tun
Plural	ké-tun-misti-k	ké-tun-sti- niz	ké-tan

b. Standard Modern Turkish
Imperfect

Person:	1st	2nd	3rd
Singular:	gel-iyor-du-m	gel-iyor-du-n	gel-iyor-du-
Plural:	gel-iyor-du-k	gel-iyor-du-nuz	gel-iyor-du-lar

In light of the afore-mentioned phenomena - drawn by varieties showing high DTI – one can easily realize that the grammatical profile of several IAG (sub)dialects was molded under the intense linguistic contact of Greek varieties with the dominant Turkish ones.[16] In turn, this intense linguistic contact was the outcome of the cultural, political and social pressure that speakers of Turkish exerted on speakers of Greek. This may sound as a truism yet it is far from clear how contact-induced

---

13 In my view it is remarkable that the direct adoption of the Turkish endings occurs in the first and second plural. Although the main trigger for the adoption should be the phonological affinity, I surmise that pragmatic factors should be in play here (a 'we' versus 'you' (PL) antithesis which must have been prominent in the bilingual repertoire of the IAG speakers.
14 Cf. Dawkins (1916: 142) and discussion in Janse (2009a: 42 – 44).
15 Cf. Janse (2009: 103). The Ancient Greek κεῖμαι *keĩmai* is also found as a learned lexeme in Standard MG (i.e. κείμαι *kíme*). In some CG subdialects is preserved in the meaning of 'exist', cf. Dawkins (1916: 608).
16 For an overview of the distribution of various grammatical phenomena on IAG one can also consult the most informative interactive dialectal atlas of the Cappadocian dialects of the "Digitizing the Cappadocian Dialectal Landscape" project (DiCaDLand) accessible on http://cappadocian. upatras.gr/en/node/10 (27.12.2022) in Greek.

grammatical changes and extralinguistic causation interrelate. As we will see below there is no clear-cut answer to this issue.

2.2 Contact-induced changes as sociolinguistic and extralinguistic indicators

Thomason and Kaufman (1988) were not only the first who discussed IAG within the framework of contemporary language contact studies but also developed a model that attempted to associate social conditions and what they called *Language Contact Intensity* (LCI) with the borrowability of grammatical features in a language contact situation, which they called *Borrowing Hierarchies* (BH). The analysis Thomason and Kaufman (1988: 74–75) introduced (summarized in Table 2 below) captures – but also challenges – previous insights about the borrowability of grammatical categories in LC situations. For instance, Jakobson (1962 [1938]: 241) postulated the constraint that languages in a LC context adopt grammatical features that correspond to inherent tendencies of the borrowing language. Contrary to this approach, Thomason and Kaufman'a analysis predicts that when the LCI is fairly high (when the cultural pressure is "very strong" or "overwhelming" as they stated) there are virtually no boundaries in what can be adopted by a language under pressure, therefore imposing borrowability constraints appears to be erroneous (cf. also similar remarks in De Angelis 2017: 135).

Table 2: Correlation of Language Contact Intensity stages and the corresponding Borrowing Hierarchies according to Thomason and Kaufman (1988: 74–76).

Language Contact Intensity	Borrowing Hierarchies
I. "Casual Contact" →	Lexical borrowing limited to content words
II. "Slightly more intense contact" →	Minor changes in phonology or syntax, borrowing of free function words. No typological disruption.
III. "More intense contact" →	Adoption of derivational affixes, adpositions, basic lexicon (pronouns, low numerals)
IV. "Strong cultural pressure" →	Little typological change but extensive word order changes, new distinctive features (or loss thereof) in phonology, inflectional affixes may be borrowed
V. "Very strong cultural pressure" →	Considerable changes in typology and in all grammatical domains, development of new morphosyntactic categories

IAG is portrayed in Thomason and Kaufman (1988: 93 – 94) as belonging to the fifth category: several IAG varieties bear witness to minor or major typological shifts, a fact which is an indicator of the "pervasive" character of the Turkish cultural pressure. Additionally, Thomason (2002: 63–64) explicitly refers to the rise of the nominal paradigms in IAG we examined in (4) as a counterexample to Meillet's (1921: 87) claim that grammatical interference in LC is restricted to typologically similar languages, thus in her account the "fusion to agglutination" argument implies an overcoming of typological constraints.[17]

In what follows, I will not contend either the importance of the examination of the restructuring of the declension system in certain IAG varieties nor with the idea of overall typological shift *per se*. Nevertheless, I explain why I take issues with the designation "agglutination" and why I support the idea that typological shift in IAG is traceable even in phenomena which are usually placed high in the BH.

2.3 "Mixed languages" and "agglutinative patterns": A critical approach with respect to IAG

In the previous section the terms "mixed language" and "agglutination patterns" were critically analyzed. In this section I am going to argue that both terms are problematic with respect to IAG for a number of reasons. Let us begin with the former term. The very definition as to what "mixed" implies is quite vague. Matras (2009: 288) states that "[w]hile there is no uniform view of what precisely constitutes a mixed language, it is generally understood that mixed languages show mixtures that are distinct, either qualitatively or quantitatively, from other cases of contact-induced change." This is of course a barely helpful definition; it is however indicative of the difficulty we encounter to figure out what the term really applies to. Thomason and Kaufman (1988) associate mixed languages with what they call a "non-genetic development", a breach in the "normal" typological transmission of a language from a stage to another. Thomason (2003: 196–197) asserts that all mixed languages share the property of having grammatical subsystems that do not derive from a single language. In the same vein, Velupillai (2015: 69) defines mixed languages as "languages with split ancestry" which emerge in cases of communal bilingualism.

Myers-Scotton (2002: 246–253) rejects the term "mixed" due to its negative connotations and instead proposes the designation "split languages" which she defines as a "Matrix Language turnover". In cases of bilingual convergence, the source of the matrix of a sentence (i.e. a CP, a Complementizer Phrase, in Myers-Scotton's analysis) is not a single source language. When convergence goes a step further

---

17 Cf. also discussion in Johanson (2002: 36–37).

the CP matrix is based not on the source language that provides most of the (core) lexicon but on another source language which gradually determines more and more grammatical compartments of the sentential frame. Some of the most representative mixed/split languages discussed in the relevant bibliography are a) Michif, a language spoken in Western Canada and in the USA (North Dakota and Montana) within which the French noun system and Cree verb phrases are combined (cf. Bakker 1997) and b) Ma'a (also referred to as *Mbugu*) spoken in Tanzania, a variety comprising Cushitic lexicon and Bantu grammar (cf. Mous 2003).

Evidently, notwithstanding the difficulties in defining what a mixed language is, the study thereof is well-established in the literature. Still, there are opinions questioning the usefulness of the term. For instance, Versteegh (2017) refers to the "myth of the mixed languages" and cites Backus (2003: 263) who similarly expresses a note of concern whether it is really interesting to draw a distinction between what he calls a "mixed lect", an unstable mixed language with high degree of variability, and a stable mixed language, a term used for mixed languages with low degree of variability and stability in its usage (on stable mixed languages cf. Thomason 2003). Matras and Bakker (2003:1) also state that the set of languages corresponding most closely to their definition of mixed languages, namely "a bilingual mixture, with split ancestry" applies to a small set of languages. Interestingly, IAG is not mentioned in the Matras and Bakker's set and neither is it so in Velupillai's account on mixed languages (2015: 69–74).

Despite the problems we encounter while dealing with defining a mixed language, the goal of this article is not to rebut the usage of the term "mixed language" altogether. Instead, we are mostly interested in why the application of the term on IAG may be deemed erroneous. The main argument against a mixed language analysis for IAG is the absence of compartmentalization (see Matras 2000a) of these varieties, i.e. the absence of a clear-cut distinct "Turkish" grammatical subsystem versus "Greek" grammatical subsystems, in a system similar to the way Michif has been compartmentalized. While it is beyond any doubt that some structures, such as the relative clauses or word order, have been remodeled towards getting more Turkish-like, the formation of the various varieties of IAG has to do with the gradual convergence of the Greek dialects spoken in Anatolia with the local Turkish varieties. It is true that the degree of convergence is impressively significant, yet the idea of IAG being a mixed language would imply a lexicalization of Turkish structures with (largely Turkified) Greek lexicon, however this is not the case. Instead, we see how Greek dialectal structures "struggle" to fit into a sentential Matrix heavily shaped under Turkish influence. Thus, convergence and "mixing" should be seen as two different operations, and contact-induced changes in IAG pertain to the former kind.

Additionally, the theoretical corollary of our argumentation above is that a mixed-language analysis for IAG implies a merging process of varieties of different ancestry, namely Greek and Turkish ones in the case under examination. Such a view undermines a synchronic analysis of IAG in its own rights and as a system the profile of which was shaped not merely due to lexical/grammatical borrowing or structural replication but also due to the combined dynamics of language contact and internal developments. This last remark is clearly pointed out by Karatsareas (2016a) with respect to the nominal flexion of various IAG (sub)dialects and the development of the so-called agglutinative patterns.

As already stated above, the "agglutination" argument has been focal in the discussion about a contact-induced typological shift. Yet, similarly to the case of *mixed languages*, *agglutination* is a term that seems to be problematic in the description of the IAG nominal system for a number of reasons. As we saw in (4), the nominal system of certain IAG, and in particular CG, varieties is rearranged in a fashion which bears a striking resemblance to Turkish. There are two main approaches regarding the rise of the CG nominal system. The first one is put forward by Karatsareas (2011, 2016a) who advocates the idea that not (only) language contact but (also) internal developments in CG led to the remodeling of the nominal system. Karatsareas (2011: 266–270, 2016a: 34) appears to be highly skeptical towards the usage of the term *agglutination* and the proposal that the CG nominal paradigm constitutes a case of a large-scale typological shift. Janse (2019) in turn proposes an elaborate scenario concerning the emergence of the agglutinative traits in CG and supports the idea of pattern replication from Turkish.

Irrespective of which of these two analyses of diachronic development is valid, it is interesting that both works reach conclusions indicating that the usage of the designation *agglutinative* is erroneous for the following two reasons:

a. In several CG subdialects the genitive plural is either absent (e.g. CG subdialect of Potámia: *lík-os* NOM.SG 'wolf' versus *lík-jú* GEN.SG 'wolf's, of a wolf' but no genitive plural is attested; cf. Dawkins 1916: 96) or, more rarely, the genitive singular and plural share a syncretic form marked in both cases by the mono-exponential genitive marker *-ju* (e.g. *papá-s* NOM.SG '(Orthodox) priest', *papá* and *papa-jú* GEN.SG 'priest's, of a priest' and *papa-jez-jú* and *papa-jú* GEN.PL 'priests', of the priests'; cf. Mavrochalyvidis and Kesisoglou 1960: 39, and discussion in Janse 2019: 12).

b. As Karatsareas (2016a: 40) observes, the "agglutinative" genitive forms in *-ju/-jú* attested in CG of the *néc-ez-ju* type we saw in (4) all occur after the plurality suffix *-es* (> *-ez*) which is linked to animate nouns that correspond to non-neutral nouns in most Modern Greek varieties.[18] The more generalized CG *-ja* plurality suffix is never combined with the *-ju* genitive but in a unique dubious

---

[18] Cf. Nom.Pl. *jinéc-es* of Standard MG presented in ex. (4) above.

case[19] and, clearly, the very existence of (at least) two different plural suffixes challenges the agglutination argument.[20]

In our view, the reference to "agglutinative declension" is problematic not only due to the reasons we discussed above but also from a wider terminological and typological point of view. For instance, Haspelmath (2009) doubts that the terms agglutination and fusion are theoretically legitimate. They have been employed as descriptive tools for clear-cut cases (such as Latin, a fusional language or Turkish, an agglutinative one) but they fail to describe every linguistic system. As Haspelmath (2009: 15) observes that "linguistics should move beyond Latinocentrism and Turkocentrism and try to do justice to each language, to describe and characterize it in its own terms, or in truly universal terms". In the same vein – and specifically on IAG – Johanson (2002, 64) notices: "Thomason and Kaufman (1988: 93–4) depict Turkish influence on certain Anatolian Greek dialects as extremely strong. However, a number of phenomena resulting from Turkish influence, as reported by Dawkins (1916), are actually only sparsely attested in the texts. Hovdhaugen (1976: 149) therefore rejects the notion of Turkish having deeply influenced these varieties."

From a comparative perspective, we know that a few IE languages developed non-inherited cases due to the influence of neighboring "agglutinative" languages: Finnic had an impact on the Old Lithuanian nominal system, Kartvelian on Ossetic, Turkic or Uralic on Tocharian (cf. Fortson 2004: 102; specifically on Tocharian cf. Fortson 2004: 357 and Peyrot 2019). In IAG on the other hand there is no evidence of the emergence of new cases that are found in Turkish. The semantic roles of LOCATION, GOAL or SOURCE (which in Turkish are expressed by means of the Locative, Dative and Ablative case respectively) are instantiated through adpositional phrases across all IAG varieties (cf. Karatsareas 2016b). On these grounds, it is rather paradoxical to talk about agglutination in IAG, not only due to the problems we encounter in defining what agglutination actually means, but also because IAG's nominal system differs considerably with respect to the Turkish one. The novel

---

19 Sasse (1992: 66) reports the attestation of the form *atropoz-ja-ju* GEN.PL 'men's, of men' uttered by one of the last surviving CG speakers from the settlement of Ulaghátsch, cf. discussion in Karatsareas (2011: 256) and Janse (2019: 18).
20 Janse (2019:46–47) also admits that, strictly speaking, the CG nominal paradigm cannot be analyzed as genuinely agglutinative, yet he wonders whether the [j] of the plural endings *-j-ús* [ACC.PL] / *-j-ú(n)* [GEN.PL] in some CG declension classes was becoming a mono-exponential market of plurality. In terms of diachronic morphophonology this is an interesting analysis which however does not justify the usage of the term "agglutinative" because it does not seem to apply to all declension classes of the CG nominal system (cf. *nec-ez-ju* for instance) and it is not synchronically valid since [j] is never attested as a stand-alone plurality marker.

nominal system that IAG developed due to internal developments (as proposed by Karatsareas 2011, 2016a) and the Turkish influence is a case of convergence (cf. Myers-Scotton 2002: 101–102), not a case of structural replication thus, the term *agglutination* is a misnomer for the contact-induced changes that occurred in IAG.

3 The typological profile of IAG

3.1 Beyond "agglutination": Gradual typological shift in Inner Anatolian Greek

If we refute the agglutination argument, can we still support an idea of typological shift for Inner Anatolian Greek? Yes, but for different reasons than the ones normally discussed in the relevant literature. In this section we put forward a scenario about how the Turkish impact on IAG led to a new typological profile of these Greek varieties. The premise of our argumentation is simple: Turkish free grammatical elements that easily entered IAG (in code-switching contexts for instance) gradually triggered word order and head-dependent directionality changes. Along broad strokes, we postulate that these changes were instantiated in the following steps:

i) "Thetical" elements (especially sentential particles, interjections, "expressives" etc.) Theticals constitute a wide category of lexemes and phrases which occur parenthetically or peripherally to a sentence and do not intertwine syntactically with the sentence they disrupt or precede or follow (cf. Kaltenböck, Heine and Kuteva 2011). In our account below, we focus on borrowed lexical elements adjacent to a Complementizer Phrase (CP) which however enter the utterance after the complete formation of a complete sentence. Consider the examples in (6a) and (6b), both sharing the same meaning:

(6) a. SMG
ma   ti   na   káno?
EXPR what   SUBJ.PRT   do.1SG.
Compare: **ti   na   káno   ma?*
b. Istanbul Greek
ti   na   káno   ya?
what   SUBJ.PRT   do.1SG   EXPR
'What should I do then?'

The particle *ma* is of Italian origin, is found in Common and Standard Modern Greek and expresses a feeling of light discouragement or dismay in (rhetoric) questions. Being borrowed from Italian, the element is used at the initial position of a clause and its omission would not influence the grammaticality of the rest of the "main" sentence. Similarly, *ya* is an element of Turkish origin, attested in the speech of Istanbul Greeks in Istanbul and the diaspora, and can readily be interpreted as a distinctive identity marker of the speakers of that community. Following the Turkish pattern, the element *ya* is attached to the right periphery of the CP.

One may argue that synchronically both *ma* and *ya* partake in the sentential structure as pragmatic markers. There are however two reasons why it may be preferable to describe them as *theticals*: a. from a contact perspective the borrowed elements entered an already well-formed proposition and b. the borrowed elements convey meanings associated with what Langacker (2008: 475) called *expressives*, which are closer to theticals than to fully embedded modality particles (therefore we also glossed these elements as EXPR for *expressives*). In my account, I prefer to talk about theticals in order to underscore the fact that these elements were adjusted to a sentence through language contact and (probably) code-switching.

As we observe, the *ma* and *ya* sentential "particles" entered Greek varieties due to language contact. Their presence at the periphery of a CP does not cause any changes to the internal structure of the sentence. Nevertheless, contrary to *ma*, the *ya* particle occurs in a position which is untypical for Common Greek, namely the final one. For instance, a Greek interjection thetical typically precedes the "main" sentence, cf e.g. (7):

(7) Standard Modern Greek
    po   po   ti   su   ípe
    INTERJ INTERJ what you.GEN say.PST.3SG
    literally: "oh oh, what did s/he tell you" > "how bad s/he insulted you!"
    *ti su ípe po po

So, I suggest that the adjunction of theticals of Turkish origin was structurally unproblematic since these elements do not interact with the (rest of) CP in terms of syntax. However, because of their left-branching scope over the sentence, they probably presented a first peculiarity in the syntax of the Greek varieties and is a good indicator of how theticals of Turkish origin entered utterances of IAG speakers in code-switching situations. In IAG, *ya* is found in several (sub)dialects in a function similar to the one of Istanbul Greek, cf. e.g. (8):

(8) IAG, CG, Settlement of Axó
   Ti   na   ta   bíko?
   what SUBJ.PRT they.ACC.PL.N do. PFV.1SG
   De   na   ta   fáyo   ya.
   NEG FUT.PRT[21] they.ACC.PL.N eat.PFV.1SG EXPR
   "What can I do with them? I cannot eat them indeed" (Dawkins 1916: 396)

ii) Function words

According to the analysis on borrowing hierarchies captured in Table 2 above the free grammatical elements category is the most susceptible to be borrowed in a language contact situation. The free grammatical elements category comprises a wide set of function words that are not all readily borrowed from one language into another. Therefore, while the function words are generally regarded as being high in the borrowing hierarchy scale as a whole, there is variation in how prone each subcategory of function words is to be borrowed.[22] This is obvious when we compare CMG and IAG: In CMG, despite the large number of borrowed Turkish lexical words, there is a limited number of adopted function words categories, mostly conjunctions used in emphatic contexts such as the enumerating *em...em* < Turk. *hem...hem* as in (9):

(9) Common Modern Greek
   em   δen   xéris,   em   milás
   CONJ NEG know.2SG CONJ talk.2SG
   "You are talking (about this topic) without having any idea"

As expected, function words in IAG are abundant. Yet, what is of interest for us in this study are the borrowed function words that occur at the end of a CP and have a leftward scope. Consider ex. (10):

(10) IAG, Silliot
    ǰaní=m,   A-Yóryis   mu,
    life = POSS.PRON.1SG Saint George mine
    írtis   ro   m'   ki?
    come.2SG.PST here Q EMPH.PART
    "My dear Saint George, did you really come here?" (Kostakis 1968: 116)

---

21 The particle *na* in GK is a marker not only of the subjunctive, as in SMG, but also of the future tense. For Axó (cf. Mavrochalyvidis and Kesisoglou 1960: 63).

22 This variation has been examined for instance in Stolz and Stolz (1996) and Matras (2000b). For IAG cf. Melissaropoulou and Ralli (2020).

In this sentence we observe the accumulation of two function words of Turkish origin, the question particle *mi* < Turk. *mI* and the emphatic particle *ki* < Turk. *ki* at the end of the sentence.[23] The combined occurrence of these elements complies with Turkish patterns and the most interesting feature is that both elements have scope over the preceding sentence. As with theticals, the incorporation of these function words is straightforward because they appear at the periphery of the sentence and can easily be incorporated into the CP. Still, the adoption especially of the Turkish question particle gives rise to new grammatical rules that are not found but in the Greek varieties of Anatolia.[24]

At face value, the previous example does not seem to constitute a case of typological shift. However, it should be examined along with parallel developments in IAG. Consider example (11):

(11) IAG, Silliot
Vavás čis   éršiti, náftši ta ksíla   op'   čin iréan
father her   comes   lights   the wood(N).ACC.PL from the idea(F).ACC.SG
óči   kóri   apés'   tun   éni   deyí
that   daughter   inside these is   SUBORD
"Her father comes, he sets light to the wood, thinking that his daughter is inside." (Dawkins 1916:284)

The borrowed function word in (11) is *deyí* < Ottoman Turkish *deyü* (Standard Modern Turkish: *diye*). According to Göksel and Kerslake (2005: 354) Modern Turkish *diye* is analysed as a subordinator although its syntactic properties are so "versatile" that this designation may be somehow restrictive (cf. Gündoğdu 2017).

The *deyí* subordinator explains why the "father sets lights to the wood", it has a causal meaning and has a leftward scope. Within this adverbial clause there is

---

23 On microvariation in the distribution of the adopted question particle in CG cf. Bağrıaçık (2013). Bağrıaçık suggests that diachronically the question particle was initially attached to the VP [Verb Phrase], not the CP, layer, in compliance with the source language, namely Turkish. For ex. *Sano ne mi ito do xerifos?* [crazy is Q this the man] 'Is this man crazy?' (Ulaghátsh, Kesisoglou 1951: 156 apud Bağrıaçık 2013: 31). In my opinion it is highly hypothetical to postulate that in the "prehistory" of the CG with Turkish this element was directly associated with VP rather than the CP layer in all CG subvarieties. In either case the crux here is the introduction of a left-scope element into the sentential structure of a Greek variety.
24 Recently, I myself heard a young L2 Greek speaker, member of the Greek-orthodox community of Istanbul, who used the Turkish question particle *mI* by applying vowel harmony on it after a well-formed Greek sentence: *tha érthi o kírios Yórgos mu?* 'Will Mr. Yorgos come?'. This formation, suggestive as it may be, does not seem to be systematic in the speech of Istanbul Greeks though. The particle is also found in Pontic Greek (cf. Papadopoulos 1961: 45).

another subordinator, namely *óči* (cognate to AG *hóti*, MG *óti*) introducing the complement of the propositional phrasal *op' čin iréan óči* (lit. "from the idea that" i.e. "thinking that") which has a rightward scope. Thus, in a single IAG sentence there is a cooccurrence of both right-branching (*óči*) and left-branching (*deyî*) subordinators. The former complies with subordination patterns of Greek while the latter introduces a novel syntactic structure by following the directionality of the source language, namely of Turkish. Hence, the introduction of a single borrowed function word creates a syntactic "anomaly" whereby two directionalities, a right-branching and a left-branching co-exist.[25] In our view, contexts like the one above may have been the trigger for a typological shift of IAG.

iii) Copular cliticization and other phenomena in IAG
The rise of left-branching structures into IAG through the introduction of function words with leftward scope may have caused – or at least is linked to – wider changes in the typological profile of IAG that revolve around the directionality parameter. Some related phenomena have been already discussed singly in the relevant literature, e.g. the persistent postposition of spatial adverbs[26] as in (12), the occurrence of prenominal relative clauses[27] as in (13) and the left-branching directionality in nominal clauses as in (14a), which differs from respective nominal head-dependent MG structures as in (14b):

(12) IAG, CG, Settlement of Mistí
      Píyi   so   danís   kundá
      go.PST.PFV.3SG to   sea   close
      "(He) went close to the sea" (Dawkins 1916: 386)

---

25 An anonymous reviewer observes that this is not a novel idea. Indeed, as mentioned in footnote 5, the co-occurrence of contrastive directionalities has been discussed with respect to specific grammatical phenomena. What is however new in my account is not only the explicit reference to the concept of *directionality* but also the proposal that the introduction of function words could have given rise to left-branching structures. Additionally, as discussed further below, the directionality shift could have been the cause for the copular cliticization and the varying head-complement order of the verbal phrase. All these features in combination, examined along with the radical remodeling of the IAG grammatical system, could reveal more about the overall typological type of IAG.
26 cf. Karatsareas (2016b) who refers to *postpositions*. Cf. Holton et al. (2012: 454–458) for comparison with MG.
27 Cf. also example (2b) and fn. 6 above.

(13) IAG, CG, Settlement of Delmesó
ke   ðíxni   sas
and   show.3SG   to.you
to   istedízete   to   xorjó
which(< the)   want.2PL   the   village
"...and she shall show you the village you wish" (Dawkins 1916: 322)

(14) a. IAG, CG, Settlement of Ulaghátsh)
    írte   'na   devjú   manajú=t   to   spit
    come.PST.PFV.3SG   a   giant.GEN mother.GEN=POSS.2SG   the   house
  b. "He came to the house of the mother of a giant." (Dawkins 1916: 378)[28]
    SMG
    írθe   sto   spíti   tis   mánas   tu   yíyanda
    come.AOR.3SG   to=the   house   the   mother.GEN   the   giant.GEN
    "S/he came to the house of the mother of the giant."

Another IAG feature, which has not attracted much attention, is the enclitization of reduced forms of the copular verb which can be cliticized after nouns/adjectives or adverbials (see Janse forthc.). Compare examples (15) and (16) below:

(15) IAG, CG, Settlement of Axó)
    to   mo   vavá=m   énan   geró   vašiljós=ton
    the   my_own   father=POSS.1SG a   time.ACC   king=was
    "My father was once a king" (Mavrochalyvidis and Kesisoglou 1960: 218)

(16) IAG, CG, Settlement of Phloitá
    íben   "hanum, eðó   péra   pu   ímeste?"
    say.PST.PFV.3SG   lady   here that_side where   be.PRS.1SG
    ke   to   hanum   íben   "so   xapíz =meste".
    and   the   lady   say.PST.PFV.3SG   in   prison=be.PRS.1SG
    "'(He) said 'Lady where are we?' and the lady said 'we're in the prison'."
    (Dawkins 1916: 434)

Cliticization of the third person of the copular verb is possible in CMG. However both examples in (15) and (16) are unusual with respect to the common modern variety. In (15) the past form is encliticized even after a consonant (therefore in that case we probably have no vowel deletion), while in (16) the non-encliti-

---

[28] Cf. also discussion in Theodoridi (2017: 489).

cized form *ímeste* occurs along with the clitic form *'meste*. This "reduced" forms are only possible in MG when a vowel precedes. It is crucial to notice that the copular verb is at the final position of the sentence. Although IAG (sub)dialects are not verb-final, the final position seems to be preferred while in MG the default position of the copular verb would rather precede the predicate.[29]

In accordance with the Turkish pattern the copular verb can be also cliticized after a negator, as in (17):

(17) IAG, Silliot
 enéka   yráfi   tu   vaván   jis   ki
 woman   write.PRS.3SG the   dad   hers   that
 'kóri   su   kalí   kóri   re=ni,   skrófa=ne
 daughter   yours   good   daughter not=be.PRS.3SG harlot= PRS.3SG
 "The woman writes to the girl's father 'Your girl is not a good girl; she is a harlot. . .'" (Dawkins 1916: 300)

The encliticization of the copular verb does not only indicate that IAG replicates the Turkish structure but also indicates that before becoming a clitic the copular verb occurred in the final position of a phrase. IAG is far from being a genuine OV language, at least on the "surface" level, yet the final position of the copular verb and its subsequent encliticization is suggestive about word order tendencies. We discuss these tendencies in the next section.

3.2 Ongoing typological changes as a theoretical challenge

In the previous section we placed emphasis on directionality patterns in IAG and we suggested that free function words may have been the cause for the rise of a typological profile that differentiates IAG from other MG dialectal varieties on which impact of Turkish has not been that intense. Admittedly, it is difficult to confirm our analysis in terms of diachronic corpus research, since we do not have access to extensive IAG before the 19th c. Nevertheless, implicationally, it is reasonable to put forward that even minor contact-induced changed gradually led to a significant shift in the typological properties of IAG. The typological shift is traceable in all phenomena we examined above, so "agglutination", i.e. the radical reconstruction of IAG's nominal

---

29 Clearly a statistic approach on the IAG corpus would be illuminating at that point.

system is but "epiphenomenal"³⁰ of those changes in the sense that it occurred within a system already distinct in comparison to most MG dialects out of Inner Anatolia.

The discussion concerning the left-branching directionality begs the following question: is IAG an OV language altogether? At face value, no. After some consideration, still no (at least in the consistent way Turkish is an OV language). The matrix predicates do not exclusively emerge at the final position of a sentence (as in Turkish) in any IAG (sub)dialect, thus the pattern replication observed in the case of copular verbs does not apply here. Still, there are some indications that point to a tendency towards an OV structuring. For instance, Janse (2006) postulates that the OV order is the unmarked one whenever the objects are definite and present what he calls a "given information", as in (18) and (19):³¹

(18) IAG, CG, Settlement of Delmesó
  χerífos [*ta fšáχa*]ᵢ *píren*   *da*ᵢ
  man.NOM children.ACC take.PST.PFV.3SG CL.3PL
  "The man took the children." (Dawkins 1916: 318 *apud* Janse 2006: 120)

(19) IAG, CG, Settlement of Axó
  To *méya* *to* *koríč* "*mána,*
  the eldest the girl "mother
  na *po*   *na* *to* *pšáso*"   *ípen*
  SUBJ.PRT go.PFV.1SG SUBJ.PRT it.ACC look.after.PFV.1SG say.PST. PFV.3SG
  "The eldest girl said 'Mother I will go to catch him'." (Dawkins 1916: 390)

---

30 This statement here should be taken with a pinch of salt. It is hard to establish a direct connection between the directionality shift and the reshaping of the nominal system (yet cf. Fenk-Oczlon 1983 for an attempt to correlate word order and flexion). An anonymous reviewer is also right to remark that the reshaping of the IAG nominal system should be examined in conjunction with further changes such as the loss of gender distinctions. The same reviewer also points out that changes in the morphological component may have occurred autonomously. Undoubtedly, these are reasonable counterarguments which should be seriously considered. Yet, it is hard to believe that in a system within which several "catastrophic" (in the sense of Lightfoot 1979, 1997) changes take place in parallel that changes do not really occur at the interfaces of the linguistic system. Clearly, this issue should be further investigated.

31 Cf. also Janse (1998) and the relevant discussion in DiCaDLand (accessible on http://cappadocian.upatras.gr/atlas/el/syntax-060/mi-markarismeni-seira-oron-i-ar, 27.12.2022) on the diagnostic of the verb-preceding full personal pronoun in object position (e.g. *eyó séna filáttu=su* I you.ACC guard.PRS.1SG=CL.2SG. "(if you will marry me) I will keep you safe", Dawkins 1916: 286 and Janse 1998: 525). I am rather skeptical about analyzing these structures as "unmarked" (as DiCaDLand does in interpreting Janse although the latter does not use this term in this context).

The placement of the main verb in a final position, after the quotative phrase and with a preposed subject would be only marginally accepted in MG and is definitely not the default one. It is similarly true however that this configuration is not frequent and, generally, the IAG verb position seems to align with the rest of the MG dialects with only minor "peculiarities", i.e. a bent towards left-branching structures not only in nominal but also verbal clauses. Compare example (20):

(20) IAG, CG, Settlement of Ulaghátsh
Do néka épe ki "na
the woman say.PST.PFV.3SG that SUBJ.PRT
fotíš" deyí "to sardó" épe
light_up.3SG SUBORD it wind.PRS.1SG say.PST.PFV.3SG
"The woman said 'with the intent that it may give light I am winding it' said she." (Dawkins 1916: 356)

The repetition of the main verb of saying *épe* in the CG (sub)dialect of Ulaghátsh is recurring. The first *épe* is followed by right-branching *ki*, an element of Persian origin which introduces[32] quotative and complement clauses and cooccurs with left-branching *deyí*. The final *épe* has scope over the whole quotative phrase. A tentative explanation is that the final-positioned verb moves to the left because of *ki*, which is found in this position due to replication from Turkish in quotative contexts. Indeed, out of 38 attestations of double or even triple *épe* iteration in Dawkins (1916: 347 – 384) there is only one case in which the "first" *épe* is not followed by *ki* while the second (or third) verb of saying always follows the quotation in direct speech. If we postulate that in some IAG varieties verbs of saying occur in a final position following the quotation as in (20), then we can similarly propose a movement from the final position leftwards without deletion of the element in situ. And even if this is a replication of a Turkish pattern, it is still indicative about the typology of the Ulaghátsh (sub)dialect.

Dryer (2007) (in the light of grammatical properties from a verb-final language, namely Lezgian) enumerates some further characteristics of an OV language. Some of them are reminiscent of IAG: the usage of postpositions and the precedence of genitives modifying a nominal head. So, why are IAG varieties not exclusively OV? If we see the big picture, the typological profile of languages the directionality of which is left-branching in nominal and relative clauses what we observe is that actually "everything goes": A Genitive-Noun configuration can be a feature

---

32 It is questionable whether *ki* should be treated as a complementizer, a quotative or a discourse marker (cf. Kesıcı 2013, Griths and Güneş 2015).

of either a VO or an OV language. Similar is the case of Relative Clause – Noun structure, although in this case the preponderance of the OV word order is striking. In both cases the directionality of the nominal and relative clauses is statistically significant which means that right-branching correlates with OV. Consider Tables 3 and 4 below:[33]

Table 3: The position of geneitive modifiers in OV vs. VO languages.

	SVO	SOV
Noun – Genitive	249	26
Genitive-Noun	106	398

$\chi2 = 346.615$ (Yates correction 343.8182), $p < 0,00001$, significant at $p < 0.5$

Table 4: The position of relative clauses in OV vs. VO languages.

	SVO	SOV
Noun-Relative Clause	293	87
Relative Clause – Noun	4	113

$\chi2 = 201.983$ (Yates correction 198.9304), $p < 0,00001$, significant at $p < 0.5$

So, how can we deal with these facts? There are two ways:

a. The IAG varieties are in fluctuation and constant change. The population exchange interrupted the persistent Turkish influence. Should this influence have gone on then the natural tendency would be for IAG to become OV so that the varieties become uniformly left-branching. Hypothetical as this may sound there is still persuasive evidence, as we saw, in the case of the copular verb encliticization and in examples (18)–(20) above.

b. The IAG syntactic system applies both directionalities, a right-branching for the verbal phrase and a left-branching one for nominal, relative and some adverbial sentences. This could then be accounted for in terms of theoretical approaches similar to Haider's *Third Type*, a type "of phrasal architecture in which the head of the verb phrase is directionally unconstrained" (Haider and Szucsich 2022: 1, cf. also Haider 2013) or the *Final-over-Final Condition*

---

[33] Data retrieved from The World Atlas of Language Structures (WALS) accessible on https://wals.info/ (29.12.2022).

(cf. Sheehan et al. 2017) according to which a head-final phrase cannot immediately dominate a head-initial phrase while it is possible for a head-initial phrase (the verb phrase in IAG) to dominate a head-final phrase (a nominal phrase in IAG for instance).

Needless to say, the concept of an "ongoing change" and a "third type" typology are not incompatible analyses. However, the crux of our analysis above is that IAG differs typologically from other Greek varieties that have not been exposed to that extent of Turkish impact not because of its "agglutinative" traits but because of an overall reorganization of its phrasal architecture.

4 The extralinguistic perspective

Contact-induced changes leading to typological disruptions are casually interpreted as indicators of a sociocultural context within which bilingualism between a prestigious and politically hegemonic language and one having a weaker status. As already stated by Myers-Scotton (2002: 101) "[t]the motivation for convergence is clear: the influence of one language on another reflects generally asymmetrical sociopolitical relations between the native speakers of the languages involved, with the language that is influenced often in the less dominant role".

It is a truism to attribute the high degree of Turkish influence on IAG in the historical conditions that were established in Anatolia after the arrival of the Turkish tribes in 11th c. A.D and the subsequent geographical and political separation of IAG from the Greek-speaking continuum.[34] Nonetheless, there are but few attempts to reconstruct the linguistic ecology of the IAG area and to precisely define the extralinguistic conditions that facilitated the influx and the replication of Turkish structures into the Greek varieties of Inner Anatolia.[35] It is beyond the scope of this paper to deal with the extralinguistic parameters of the contact-induced changes in IAG altogether. Nevertheless, it is tantalizing to discuss what the typological shift of IAG may reveal about the Greek-speaking communities of Anatolia and what

---

[34] For a historical overview cf. Vryonis (1971). On the so called "Byzantine residue" of IAG cf. Janse (2021).
[35] Theodoridi (2017) and Karantzola, Theodoridi and Sampanis (2021) provide a first account about the causation of the uneven DTI on the CG settlements. Sampanis and Karantzola also suggested that the IAG (sub)dialects should be regarded as "endolects", namely varieties confined to the boundaries of the settlement with a very specific repertoire, a fact that explains the fragmentation thereof.

aspects of the correlation between socio- and extra-linguistic and borrowing hierarchies can be possibly revisited by the relevant scholarship.

It is well documented that the once Greek-speaking Orthodox population of Anatolia rapidly shifted into Turkish after the Turkish conquest of the region (cf. Tsalikoglou 1970, Vryonis 1971). As soon as the 14th c. there are reports about the extensive usage of Turkish even among the Orthodox clergy.[36] In more recent centuries, and just before the population exchange between Greece and Turkey in 1923, the existence of a large body of Turkish literature written in the Greek alphabet (known as *karamanlídhika*) was similarly a testimony of the presence of a population that used Turkish as a vehicle to express its distinct Orthodox identity.[37] Remarkably, even in the IAG settlements Turkish was often the language of (a part of) the liturgy, a fact that shows that due to the absence of any ethnolinguistic self-identification until the 19th c. these populations would easily shift into adopting Turkish for cultural activities, preserving their religion as a distinctive identity marker.

Against this backdrop it is reasonable to hypothesize that due to the political disarray brought by the arrival of the Turks in Anatolia the rise of bilingualism among Greek populations of the region was rather an abrupt process, a hypothesis which is corroborated by chronographic reports, as stated above. If this is true, then the gradual development of both sociolinguistic conditions and borrowing hierarchies depicted in Table 2 is challenged by the fact that the "very strong cultural pressure" can be straightforwardly established upon a dominated society leading inexorably to extensive bilingualism within a single generation. In that case the strong sociolinguistic pressure can occur without evidence of "development of new morphosyntactic categories", a process which surely demands time and a stepwise language change. On the other hand, minor changes such as the borrowing of function words which introduce novel typological traits with respect to the directionality of the head-dependent relationship may be revealing of strong cultural pressure although they theoretically correspond to stage II of the Language Contact Intensity scheme in Table 2. While the "agglutinative" traits, i.e. the restructuring of the IAG nominal system, are indeed an indicator of language contact intensity there are several other "low-profile" features that may similarly reveal that the

---

36 Cf. the statement of a famous memorandum of 30 July 1437 (Anonymous 1910: 366; στο Καratsareas 2011: 16): *Notandum est, quod in multis partibus Turcie reperiuntur clerici, episcopi et arciepiscopi, qui portant vestimenta infidelium et locuntur linguam ipsorum et nihil aliud sciunt in greco proferre nisi missam cantare et evangelium et epistolas. Alias autem orationes dicunt in lingua Turcorum.*
37 On *karamanlídhika* written tradition and the identity of the people who made use of it see Balta and Kappler (2010) and Balta (2011).

dominant language exerts pressure on forcibly bilingual speakers. This is not only obvious in the documented IAG but also in today's Istanbul Greek speech, a Greek variety which entails many Turkish loanwords but only a few function words. Yet, the high degree of language contact intensity with Turkish is not revealed by means of "ostentatious" grammatical remodeling but merely by its word order. Compare example (21):

(21) Istanbul Greek
s=ton   Kósta   dípla   eyó   na   kátso   θélo
to=the   Kostas   next   I   SUBJ.PRT   sit.PERF.1SG   want.1SG
"I want to sit next to Kostas."

Example (21) is perfectly grammatical MG but with a twist: this would never be the default order, firstly because the adverb *dípla* would precede the prepositional phrase and secondly because the finite complement *na kátso* would rather be placed after the matrix verb *θélo*. Also, *eyó* would be at the beginning of the sentence, so that the default word order (i.e. without Focus or Topicalizations) would be *eyó θélo na kátso dípla ston Kósta*. These are differences between MG and Istanbul Greek which would pass rather unnoticed.[38] However, in my view, they are quite revealing about the degree of bilingualism within the Greek-speaking community in Istanbul and the pressure on the speakers of this Greek variety.

5 Summing up

In this article we put forward four intertwined analyses: a. the usage of certain terms such as *agglutination* and *mixed language* with respect to IAG is imprecise and therefore descriptively confusing; b. bringing up the "agglutination argument" in order to argue in favor of a typological shift of IAG is not only infelicitous due to the vague content of "agglutination" but also redundant since IAG exhibits typological patterns that differentiate it from the rest of most MG varieties; c. IAG

---

38 Modern Istanbul Greek should be examined not only in the light of their contact with Istanbul Turkish since the 15th c. but also as a Greek variety that on the one hand emerged as a Koine of the Greek-Orthodox population of the former Ottoman capital, on the other hand as a system being in contact with higher ecclesiastical and educational registers of the Greek-Orthodox community and, nowadays, with SMG. All these parameters would impede the development of grammatically radical changes in Istanbul Greek germane to the ones observed for IAG. Nevertheless, I suggest that the frequent replication of OV structures by competent bilinguals reveals the pressure of the dominant Turkish language.

is a language with consistent left-branching nominative, adverbial and relative clauses but with unconstrained directionality of the verbal phrase, despite the fact that there are some indications of a tendency for left-branching structures in certain verbal phrases; d. these observations challenge the strictly linear correlation of language contact intensity parameters and the corresponding grammatical features.

It goes without saying that these observations should be backed up by rigorous statistical measurements and refined intra-dialectal comparison. To this goal the development of "Asia Minor Greek in Contact" (AMGiC, cf. Sampanis and Prokopidis 2021), a Universal Dependencies treebank that comprises annotated IAG sentences entailing contact-induced phenomena will provide a more solid basis for gaining better insights on the typological characteristics of the varieties we examined herein.

Abbreviations

Linguistic varieties

CMG	Common Modern Greek
CG	Cappadocian Greek
DTI	Degree of Turkish Influence
IAG	Inner Anatolian Greek
SMG	Standard Modern Greek

In the Glosses section below there are enlisted only those abbreviations not found in the corresponding list of *The Leipzig Glossing Rules* (available on https://www.eva.mpg.de/lingua/resources/glossing-rules.php, retrieved on 20.12.2022).

Glosses and grammatical terms

CL	clitic
CP	Complementizer Phrase
CONJ	conjunction
EMPH	emphatic
EXPR	expressive
Q	question particle
SUBORD	subordinator
SUBJ.PRT	subjunctive particle

References

De Angelis, Alessandro. 2017. Between Greek and Romance: Competing Complementation Systems in Southern Italy. In Piera Molinelli (ed.), *Language and Identity in Multilingual Mediterranean Settings: Challenges for Historical Sociolinguistics*, 135–156. Berlin/New York: De Gruyter Mouton.

Backus, Ad. 2003. Can a mixed language be conventionalized alternational codeswitching? In Yaron Matras & Peter Bakker (eds.), *The Mixed Language Debate: Theoretical and Empirical Advances*, 237–270. Berlin/New York: De Gruyter Mouton.

Bakker, Peter. 1997. *A language of our own. The genesis of Michif – the mixed Cree-French language of the Canadian Métis*. Oxford: Oxford University Press.

Bağrıaçık, Metin. 2013. Marking polar questions in Cappadocian: IntP as a root clause phenomenon. In Mark Janse, Brian Joseph, Angela Ralli & Metin Bagriacik (eds.), *MGDLT5: Proceedings of the Fifth International Conference on Modern Greek Dialects and Linguistic Theory (Ghent, Belgium, September 20–22, 2012)*. Proceedings of International Conference of Modern Greek Dialects and Linguistic Theory, 19–34. Patras: University of Patras.

Bağrıaçık, Metin & Lieven Danckaert. 2021. Raising and matching in Pharasiot Greek relative clauses: A diachronic reconstruction. *Journal of Linguistics* 58(3). 495–533.

Balta, Evangelia. 2011. *Beyond the Language Frontier Studies on the Karamanlis and the Karamanlidika Printing*. New Jersey: Gorgias Press.

Balta, Evangelia and Matthias Kappler (eds.). 2010. *Cries and whispers in Karamanlidika books: proceedings of the first International Conference on Karamanlidika Studies (Nicosia, 11th-13th September 2008)*. Wiesbaden: Harrassowitz.

Braune, Wilhelm. 2004. *Althochdeutsche Grammatik I: Laut- und Formenlehre* (15th ed. revised by Ingo Reiffenstein). Berlin/Boston: Max Niemeyer Verlag.

Costakis, Athanasios P. 1968. *To ghlosikó idhíoma tis Síllis*. [In Greek: Τὸ γλωσσικὸ ἰδίωμα τῆς Σίλλης – "The dialect of Silli"]. Athens: Centre for Asia Minor Studies.

Dawkins, Richard M. 1916. *Modern Greek in Asia Minor: A Study of the Dialects of Sílli, Cappadocia and Phárasa with Grammar, Texts, Translations and Glossary*. Cambridge: Cambridge University Press.

Donabédian, Anaïd & Ioanna Sitaridou. 2020. Anatolia. In Evangelia Adamou & Yaron Matras (eds.), *The Routledge Handbook of Language Contact*, 404–433. London/New York: Routledge.

Dryer, Matthew S. 2007. Word order. In Timothy Shopen (ed.), *Clause Structure, Language Typology and Syntactic Description*, Vol. 1, 61–131. 2nd ed. Cambridge: Cambridge University Press.

Fenk-Oczlon, Gertraud. 1983. Ist die SVO-Wortfolge die „natürlichste"? *Papiere zur Linguistik* 29. 23–32.

Fortson, Benjamin W. 2004. *Indo-European Language and Culture: An Introduction*. Malden/Oxford/Carlton: Blackwell.

Georgakopoulos, Thanasis & Petros Karatsareas. 2017. A diachronic take on the Source–Goal asymmetry: evidence from inner Asia Minor Greek. In Silvia Luraghi, Tatiana Nikitina & Chiara Zanchi (eds.), *Space in Diachrony*, 179–206. Amsterdam/Philadelphia: John Benjamins.

Göksel, Aslı and Celia Kerslake. 2005. *Turkish: A comprehensive grammar*. London/New York: Routledge.

Griths, James & Güliz Güneş. 2015. Ki issues in Turkish: Parenthetical coordination and adjunction. In Marlies Kluck, Dennis Ott & Mark de Vries (eds.), *Parenthesis and ellipsis: Cross-linguistic and theoretical perspectives*, 173–218. Berlin/New York: De Gruyter Mouton.

Gündoğdu, Hilal Yıldırım. 2017. *The Structure of Diye Clauses in Turkish*. Instanbul: Boğaziçi University MA thesis.

Haider, Hubert. 2013. *Symmetry breaking in syntax*. Cambridge: Cambridge University Press.

Haider, Hubert & Luka Szucsich. 2022. Slavic languages – "SVO" languages without SVO qualities? *Theoretical Linguistics* 48. 1–39.
Haspelmath, Martin. 2009. An empirical test of the Agglutination Hypothesis. In Sergio Scalise, Elisabetta Magni & Antonietta Bisetto (eds.), *Universals of language today*, 13–29. Dordrecht: Springer.
Haugen, Einar. 1950. The analysis of linguistic borrowing. *Language* 26. 210–231.
Hovdhaugen, Even. 1976. Some aspects of language contact in Anatolia. *Working papers in linguistics from the University of Oslo* 7. 142 – 160.
Jakobson, Roman. 1962 [1938]. Sur la théorie des affinités phonologiques entre les langues. In *Selected writings*, vol. 1, 234–246. The Hague: Mouton.
Holton, David, Peter Mackridge & Irene Philippaki-Warburton. 2012. *Greek: A Comprehensive Grammar*. 2nd edn. Revised by Vassilios Spyropoulos. London/New York: Routledge.
Janse, Mark. 1999. Greek, Turkish, and Cappadocian relatives revis(it)ed. In Georgios Babiniotis (ed.), *Greek linguistics 97: Proceedings of the 3rd International Conference on Greek Linguistics*, 463–452. Athens: Elinika Gramata.
Janse, Mark. 2006. Object Position in Cappadocian and Other Asia Minor Greek Dialects. In Mark Janse, Brian D. Joseph & Angela Ralli (eds.), *Proceedings of the 2nd International Conference of Modern Greek Dialects and Linguistic Theory*, 115–129. Patras: University of Patras Press.
Janse, Mark. 2009a. Greek-Turkish language contact in Asia Minor. *Études Helléniques/Hellenic Studies* 17. 37–54.
Janse, Mark. 2009b. Watkins' Law and the development of agglutinative inflections in Asia Minor Greek. *Journal of Greek Linguistics* 5. 3–26.
Janse, Mark. 2019. Agglutinative Noun Inflection in Cappadocian. In Angela Ralli (ed.), *The Morphology of Asia Minor Greek*, 66–115. Leiden: Brill.
Janse, Mark. 2021. Back to the future: Akritic light on diachronic variation in Cappadocian (Asia Minor Greek). In Klaas Bentein & Mark Janse (eds.), *Varieties of Post-classical and Byzantine Greek*, 201–240. Berlin/New York: De Gruyter Mouton.
Janse, Mark. Forthc. I Kappadokiki dialektos [The Cappadocian dialect]. In Christos Tzitzilis (ed.), *Neoelinikes dialekti [Modern Greek dialects]*. Thessaloniki: ILNE.
Johanson, Lars. 2002. *Structural factors in Turkic language contacts*. Richmond: Curzon.
Kaltenböck, Gunther, Bernd Heine & Tania Kuteva. 2011. On thetical grammar. *Studies in Language* 35(4). 848–893.
Karantzola, Eleni, Anatoli Theodoridi & Konstantinos Sampanis. 2021. The Interplay of External and Sociolinguistic Factors in Contact-Induced Language Change: Cappadocian Greek as a Case Study. *Mediterranean Language Review* 28. 21–63.
Karatsareas, Petros. 2016a. Convergence in word structure: Revisiting agglutinative noun inflection in Cappadocian Greek. *Diachronica* 33. 31–66.
Karatsareas, Petros. 2016b. The Asia Minor Greek Adpositional Cycle. A Tale of Multiple Causation. *Journal of Greek Linguistics* 16. 47–86.
Karatsareas, Petros & Thanasis Georgakopoulos. 2016. From syntagmatic to paradigmatic spatial zeroes: The loss of the preposition *se* in inner Asia Minor Greek. *STUF–Language Typology and Universals* 69. 309–340.
Kesıcı, Esra. 2013. Ki-clauses in Turkish: A paratactic analysis. *Coyote Papers: Working Papers in Linguistics* 21. Available at https://repository.arizona.edu/handle/10150/271012.
Kesisoglou, Ioannis I. 1951. *To ghlosikó idíoma tu Ulaghátsh*. [In Greek: Τὸ γλωσσικὸ ἰδίωμα τοῦ Οὐλαγάτς – French Cover title: *Le dialecte d'Oulagatch*). Athens: Institut Français d'Athènes.
Langacker, Ronald W. 2008. *Cognitive Grammar: A Basic Introduction*. Oxford: Oxford University Press.

Lightfoot, David W. 1979. *Principles of diachronic syntax*. Cambridge: Cambridge University Press.
Lightfoot, David W. 1997. Catastrophic change and learning theory. *Lingua* 100(1–4). 171–192.
Manolessou, Io. 2019. The historical background of the Asia Minor dialects. In Angela Ralli (ed.), *Morphology of the Asia Minor Greek dialects*, 20–65. Leiden: Brill.
Matras, Yaron. 2000a. Mixed languages: a functional-communicative approach. *Bilingualism: Language and Cognition* 3(2). 79–99.
Matras, Yaron. 2000b. How predictable is contact-induced change in grammar? In Colin Renfrew, April McMahon & Larry Trask (eds.), *Time Depth in Historical Linguistics*, 563–583. Cambridge: McDonald Institute for Archaeological Research.
Matras, Yaron. 2009. *Language Contact*. Cambridge: Cambridge University Press.
Matras, Yaron & Peter Bakker. 2008. The study of mixed languages. In Yaron Matras & Peter Bakker (eds.), *The Mixed Language Debate: Theoretical and Empirical Advances*, 1–20. Berlin/New York: Mouton de Gruyter.
Mavrochalyvidis, Georgios & Ioannis I. Kesisoglou. 1960. *To ghlosikó idhíoma tis Axú*. [In Greek: Τὸ γλωσσικὸ ἰδίωμα τῆς Ἀξοῦ – French Cover title: *Le dialecte d'Axos*]. Athens: Institut Français d'Athènes.
Meillet, Antoine 1921. *Linguistique historique et linguistique générale*. Paris: Champions.
Melissaropoulou, Dimitra. 2017. On the role of language contact in the reorganization of grammar: a case study on two Modern Greek contact induced dialects. *Poznan Studies in Contemporary Linguistics* 53(3). 449–485.
Melissaropoulou, Dimitra. 2019. Morphological pattern replication phenomena as instances of typological shift. In Karla Grammatiki, Ioanna Manolessou & Nikolaos Pantelidis (eds.), *Volume in honor of the director of the Research Centre for Modern Greek Dialects- I.L.N.E. Christina Mpasea-Mpezantakou*, 317–340. Athens: Book Institute-Kardamitsa.
Melissaropoulou, Dimitra & Angela Ralli. 2020. Revisiting the Borrowability Scale(s) of Free Grammatical Elements: Evidence from Modern Greek Contact induced Varieties. *Journal of Language Contact* 12(3). 707–736.
Mellink, Machteld J. 1966. Anatolia: Old and New Perspectives. In *Archaeology: Horizons New and Old (Proceedings of the American Philosophical Society* Vol. 110, No. 2), 111–129. Philadelphia: American Philosophical Society.
Mertyris, Dionysios & Konstantinos Sampanis. Under review. Πρότυπη και Κοινή Νέα Ελληνική: μια μεθοδολογική διάκριση. [=Standard and Common Modern Greek: a methodological distinction]. To appear in *Proceedings of the 2nd International Conference on the Koine, koines, and the formation of Standard Modern Greek, Manolis Triandaphyllidis Foundation, Aristotle University of Thessaloniki – Teloglion Fine Arts Foundation, November 5th-6th, 2021*.
Mous, Maarten. 2003. *The making of a mixed language. The case of Ma'a/Mbugu*. Amsterdam/Philadelphia: John Benjamins.
Myers-Scotton, Carol. 2002. *Contact Linguistics: Bilingual Encounters and Grammatical Outcomes*. Oxford: Oxford University Press.
Papadopoulos, Anthimios. 1961. *Istorikón lexikón tis pontikís dhialéktu III*. [In Greek: Ἱστορικὸν Λεξικὸν τῆς ποντικῆς διαλέκτου – 'Historical dictionary of the Pontic dialect']. Athens: Epitropi Pontiakon Meleton.
Peyrot, Michaël. 2019. The deviant typological profile of the Tocharian branch of Indo-European may be due to Uralic substrate influence. *Indo-European Linguistics* 7(1). 72–121. doi: https://doi.org/10.1163/22125892-00701007.
Revithiadou, Anthi, Vassilios Spyropoulos & Giorgios Markopoulos. 2017. From fusion to agglutination: The case of Asia Minor Greek. *Transactions of the Philological Society* 115. 297–335.

Sampanis, Konstantinos & Prokopis Prokopidis. 2021. Asia Minor Greek in Contact (AMGiC): Towards a dialectal treebank comprising contact-induced grammatical changes. In *Proceedings of the 20th International Workshop on Treebanks and Linguistic Theories (TLT, SyntaxFest 2021)*, 86–95. Sofia (Bulgaria): Association for Computational Linguistics.

Sampanis, Konstantinos & Eleni Karantzola. 2022. Cappadocian Greek as an endolect/microlect in the light of archival, historical and linguistic research. Paper presented at *HiSoN Conference 2022*, University of Murcia, Spain 1st – 3rd June 2022.

Sasse, Hans-Jürgen. 1992. Language decay and contact-induced change: Similarities and differences. In Matthias Brenzinger (ed.), *Language death: Factual and theoretical explorations with special reference to East Africa*, 59–80. Berlin: Mouton de Gruyter.

Spears, Arthur & Donald Winford (eds.). 1997. *The Structure and Status of Pidgins and Creoles*. Amsterdam/Philadelphia: Benjamins.

Sheehan, Michelle, Theresa Biberauer, Ian Roberts & Anders Holmberg. 2017. *The Final-Over-Final Condition. A Syntactic Universal*. Cambridge (Massachusetts): The MIT Press.

Stolz, Christel & Thomas Stolz. 1996. Grammatical Hispanisms in Amerindian and Austronesian languages. The other kind of Transpacific isoglosses. *Amerindia* 21. 137–160.

Theodoridi, Anatoli. [Θεοδωρίδη, Ανατολή]. 2017. Καππαδοκικές διάλεκτοι και φαρασιωτική: κοινωνιογλωσσικά και δομικά στοιχεία της γλωσσικής επαφής τους με την τουρκική [= *Cappadocians dialects and Pharasiotika: sociolinguistic and structural aspects of their contact with Turkish*]. Mitilini: University of the Aegean dissertation.

Thomason, Sarah G. 1997. A typology of contact languages. In Arthur K. Spears & Donald Winford (eds.), *The Structure and Status of Pidgins and Creoles*, 71–88. Amsterdam/Philadelphia: John Benjamins.

Thomason, Sarah G. 2003. Social factors and linguistic processes in the emergence of stable mixed languages. In Yaron Matras & Peter Bakker (eds.), *The Mixed Language Debate: Theoretical and Empirical Advances*, 21–39. Berlin/New York: De Gruyter Mouton.

Thomason, Sarah G. 2008. Contact-induced typological change. In Martin Haspelmath, Ekkehard König, Wulf Oesterreicher & Wolfgang Raible (eds.), *Language Typology and Language Universals*. 2. Halbband / Vol 2, 1640–1648. Berlin/New York: Mouton de Gruyter.

Thomason, Sarah Grey & Terrence Kaufman. 1988. *Language Contact, Creolization, and Genetic Linguistics*. Berkeley: University of California Press.

Tsalikoglou, Emmanouil I. 1970. Πότε καὶ πῶς ἐτουρκοφώνησεν ἡ Καππαδοκία [= When and how Cappadocia turned to a Turkish-speaking region]. *Mikrasiatika Chronika* 14. 9–30.

Velupillai, Viveka. 2015. *Pidgins, creoles & mixed languages: An introduction*. Amsterdam/Philadelphia: John Benjamins.

Versteegh, Kees. 2017. The myth of the mixed languages. In Benjamin Saade & Mauro Tosco (eds.), *Advances in Maltese Linguistics*. 217–238. Berlin/New York: De Gruyter Mouton.

Vryonis, Speros Jr. 1971. *The decline of medieval hellenism in Asia Minor and the process of islamization from the eleventh through the fifteenth century*. Berkeley: University of California Press.

Winford, Donald. 2003. *An introduction to contact linguistics*. Oxford: Blackwell.

Anja Hasse and Guido Seiler
4 Social factors in mixed language emergence: Solving the puzzle of Amish Shwitzer

Abstract: Mixed languages are stable languages stemming from at least two parental languages from which they inherit larger parts of their linguistic system, e.g. grammatical structure from one parental language and lexicon from another parental language. Amish Shwitzer, spoken by a group of Old Order Amish in Adams County, Indiana (US), is such a mixed language: The lexicon is derived from Bernese Swiss German (the language spoken by the ancestors of this group of Amish) but the grammar from Pennsylvania Dutch (the language spoken by most other Old Order Amish). Mixed languages emerge under specific sociolinguistic circumstances, and they are markers of a distinct identity. In this article, we will contextualize Amish Shwitzer in the existing frameworks of mixed languages and their emergence. In particular, we will use known mechanisms of mixed language emergence in order to reconstruct how and why Amish Shwitzer emerged and became the way it is today. We will argue that Amish Shwitzer expresses a new (rather than an old) identity and a threefold separation, namely from the American majority society, from Non-Swiss Amish communities and from Non-Amish Swiss communities. The specific mixed structure of Amish Shwitzer emerged first as an L2 variety spoken by Non-Swiss Amish whose native language was Pennsylvania Dutch. This variety was nativized by their children and was adopted ultimately by the Adams County Swiss Amish community as a whole.

1 Introduction

Amish Shwitzer is a West Germanic language spoken by a group of very conservative Old Order Amish of Swiss descent in Adams County, Indiana (US). There are remarkable cultural differences between the various Old Order Amish communities across the US. Yet, most of them speak Pennsylvania Dutch. One of the exceptions is the Swiss Amish of Adams County. They are a linguistic minority within the Old Order Amish world.

Anja Hasse, University of Zurich, e-mail: anja.hasse@ds.uzh.ch
Guido Seiler, University of Zurich, e-mail: g.seiler@ds.uzh.ch

https://doi.org/10.1515/9783110781168-004

The language itself can be characterized as a mixed language with a predominantly Bernese Swiss German lexicon, and predominantly Pennsylvania Dutch grammar, cf. Section 3.4. The aim of this article is to explore how typologies of mixed languages can be used to reconstruct the initial contact scenario which ultimately led to the emergence of Amish Shwitzer. In doing this, we do not propose a new typology of mixed languages. Rather, we extract existing hypotheses from theories on mixed languages, apply them to modern Amish Shwitzer data and describe to which extent they can account for the linguistic makeup of Amish Shwitzer. While we have data on Amish Shwitzer collected during fieldwork trips of the authors in 2021 and 2022, we do not have any accounts of the earliest stages of Amish Shwitzer. Our approach is to explore which sociolinguistic factors, which are reported to play a role in the formation of a mixed language, such as identity, might have shaped the sociolinguistic setting in which Amish Shwitzer arose.

Section 2 discusses the notion of mixed languages. Our emphasis lies on three well established approaches that all take a macro-level view by analyzing either the linguistic system or the speech community as a whole. Additionally, we consider approaches that focus on the pragmatic function of mixed languages. These models are presented in Sections 2.1 and 2.2. In the first of these sections, we focus on the emergence of mixed languages, in the second on the role of mixed languages as markers of identity.

In Section 3, we first present shortly the linguistic roots of Amish Shwitzer (Section 3.1), followed by remarks on the data (Section 3.2) and a profile of the modern (socio)linguistic situation of Amish Shwitzer (Section 3.3). In Section 3.4, we illustrate the linguistic makeup of Amish Shwitzer and show which features are inherited from Bernese Swiss German and which ones from Pennsylvania Dutch.

In Section 4, we explore how Amish Shwitzer might have emerged. Drawing from the hypotheses on the emergence of mixed languages, as presented in Section 2, we discuss what could have been the initial contact setting in which Amish Shwitzer evolved. There are three paths we follow. In Section 4.1, we discuss whether the identity expressed by Amish Shwitzer evolved as a new identity or whether the use of the language enabled the speech community to retain an already existing identity. In Section 4.2, we map the distinction of heritage vs. adoptive languages to the parental languages of Amish Shwitzer in order to define their roles in the initial contact scenario. In Section 4.3, we focus on mixed marriages as a driving force of the emergence of mixed languages and discuss to which extent they might have existed between speakers of Bernese Swiss German and Pennsylvania Dutch. After having characterized possible scenarios in which Amish Shwitzer might have evolved in the first place, we pursue the question how the language might have spread. Even though Amish Shwitzer most probably emerged among single speakers or small groups of speakers, it has ultimately become the community norm of the Swiss Amish. Nowadays it is an astonishingly homogenous linguistic system and the only language used within the community.

2 Mixed languages

Within contact linguistics, the study of mixed languages is comparably recent. There is a number of definitions of mixed languages, and each definition yields a new list of mixed languages. Every classification of a language as belonging to the group of mixed languages, or every typology of mixed languages distinguishing different subtypes is risky since "mixed languages are anything but a coherent or uniform language type" (Matras 2000: 80). Nonetheless, "they offer opportunities to identify a complexity of processes of contact-induced change" (Matras 2000: 80). In the following, we do not aim to give a comprehensive overview of the research on mixed languages. Rather, we choose a number of typologies of mixed languages and use them as sources of hypothetical scenarios in which Amish Shwitzer might have evolved. Thus, the article is a thought experiment on how competing approaches could contribute to sketching possible scenarios that might have led to the emergence of Amish Shwitzer.

For present purposes, we define a mixed language as a language (i) with at least two parental languages whose contributions to the linguistic makeup of the mixed language are relatively clearly distinguishable and (ii) of a relatively symmetrical share, whereby (iii) the mixed language is relatively stable and therefore (iv) acquired as such by speakers as L1.

2.1 Emergence of mixed languages

There are various approaches to the classification of mixed languages and the situations in which they arise. In the following, we pick four approaches that are well established.

Firstly, Thomason (2001: 197) defines the typical contact situation of a mixed language as one with widespread bilingualism, thus, distinguishing it from scenarios in which pidgins and creoles evolve. She outlines two possible scenarios for such a contact situation with widespread, "though usually one-way, not mutual, bilingualism" (Thomason 2001: 197).[1] In the first scenario, we see increasing "inter-

---

[1] Cf. Bakker (1997) for an example of an abrupt process (Michif), and Meakins (2011) for a gradual process (Gurindji Kriol) of the emergence of a mixed language.

ferences in a language from the dominant group's language in the receding group's language" (Thomason 2001: 205). In this scenario, only the lexicon of the receding group's language is retained because of its higher salience as compared to grammatical subcomponents of language (cf. Thomason 2001: 208). The second scenario is a an "abrupt creation by people who are active bilinguals in both languages" (Thomason 2001: 205). Such a scenario is only feasible if the newly emerged language serves as a "symbol of new ethnic identity", and in situations of "intimate cultural and linguistic contact between two other ethnic groups" (Thomason 2001: 205–206).

Secondly, Bakker (2003) groups mixed languages according to specific structural patterns, which he then correlates with different types of speech communities. Intertwined languages, on the one hand, show a split between lexicon and grammar and can be attributed to two groups based on their sociolinguistic setting: "those spoken by mixed ethnic groups, and those spoken by former nomads" (Bakker 2003: 110). Examples given by him are Angloromani and Ma'a/Mbugu. Angloromani has been classified as both a variety of English and of Romani, and Ma'a/Mbugu as both a Bantu and a Cushitic language (cf. Bakker 2003: 113–115 for an extensive list of references). In such intertwined languages, the language of the surrounding population contributes the grammar to the mixed language. A converted language, on the other hand, develops when a "language uses lexical and/or morphological material from one language (let us call it A) and maps them onto semantic and grammatical categories of another language (B) in B word order" (Bakker 2003: 110). This type of mixed languages is much less frequent than intertwined languages. Bakker's and Thomason's approaches have in common that they model the formation of mixed languages at the level of the linguistic systems involved in language contact.

Thirdly, most linguists agree that it is a specific property of mixed languages that they do not serve solely communicative purposes, but also function as a marker of identity. This feature is crucial for Croft's (2003) typology of mixed languages (cf. Section 2.2. in more detail). In his typology, the contribution of the input languages to a mixed language correlates with the status of the languages of the speech communities in contact as either being the heritage or the adoptive language. All of these three approaches take a macro-level view on mixed languages and on the speech communities involved in the formation of them.

The fourth perspective on mixed languages and their emergence is speaker-based (cf. Auer 1999, 2014; Auer and Hakimov 2021; Matras 2021). Auer (2014: 294) defends the view that "there is nothing special or extraordinary about mixed languages from a grammatical point of view", such that mixed languages (or, in Auer's terms, fused lects) are the products of heavy borrowing into a matrix language, namely insertion of lexical material into a matrix language. This can, but does not have to include grammatical markers. Mixed languages are the extreme pole of a continuum from rather casual codeswitching via language mixing to (fixed) language fusion. The basic structural mechanisms are very widespread, yet what makes mixed languages special indeed is the sheer amount of borrowing in phases of codeswitching and language mixing, and the fact that the mixed speech is conventionalized to such a degree that "[i]n a fused lect, the speakers no longer have a choice; they speak one, new language" (Auer 2014: 314). Lexical insertion is the source for grammar-lexicon mixed languages, and insertion of lexical material accompanied by grammatical markers for mixed languages with splits e.g. between the nominal and the verbal domains (cf. Auer 2014: 297). By contrast, Matras (2021: 363) claims that mixed languages "should be treated as a distinct language type that is not situated at the far end of a continuum of structural borrowing". What makes mixed languages unique structurally is that finite predication grammar from one language is combined with larger parts from another, a type of combination that is usually not met in 'normal' borrowing situations. Matras further argues mixed languages are the result of conventionalization of performative speech acts, whereby "the performative effect is achieved by explicitly defying the conventions on language mixing (or everyday repertoire management in bilingual settings), giving rise to mixed utterances that stand out even in an environment that is already accustomed to language mixing" (Matras 2021: 363). Both Matras' and Auer's approaches have in common that communicative practices in a high-contact situation with a certain pragmatic function may become conventionalized in such a way that the mixing practice loses its pragmatic function.

The mixed language to be discussed in the present contribution is a stable bilingual mixed language. We follow Thomason's (2003: 24) definition that the "only uncontroversially stable bilingual mixed languages are those that are now spoken outside of the bilingual context in which they arose". As will be discussed in Section 3.5, Amish Shwitzer can be classified as an intertwined language – when following Bakker's (2003) dichotomy – and it can be attributed to the second scenario in Thomason's (2001) dichotomy, i.e. abrupt creation of a language that serves as a marker of identity.

2.2 Mixed languages as markers of identity

As mentioned in Section 2, there is not one unified definition containing a fixed bundle of intra- and extra-linguistic features that captures all languages which so far have been discussed as potentially being a mixed language. One crucial feature, though, which is shared among these languages, is that they do not only serve as means of communication, but also as markers of a distinct identity. As Bakker and

Mous (1994: 10) state, "mixed languages did not come into being because of communication needs (with possible exceptions like Stedsk), as its speakers also had or have other languages in common." Thomason (2001: 198) agrees with this and sees the motivation for creating a mixed language in "a desire, or perhaps even a need, for an in-group language". Croft (2003: 45) emphasizes that identity is the primary mechanism by which speakers select a specific variant out of their linguistic repertoire in any linguistic contact, i.e. contact within and across speech communities. When analyzing mixed languages, Croft (2003: 50) distinguishes between the heritage society, i.e. the society of the speakers' ancestors with their corresponding language(s), and the adoptive society, "the society with which the speakers have come into contact with, and to some extents have socially identified with". If the speakers do not identify with any other society than their heritage society, their language does not undergo any significant language mixture processes. If they no longer identify with their heritage society, they stop using their heritage language. The first scenario leads to language maintenance, the second to language shift. Yet, as for language mixture, Croft (2003) outlines three scenarios in which mixture between the heritage and the adoptive languages may occur:

Scenario I: "basic vocabulary of the heritage language is retained, with perhaps some grammatical substance linguemes [= linguistic structures as defined in Croft (2000: 28)], while the rest of the grammatical structures are of the adoptive language" (Croft 2003: 55), with examples being Ma'a/Mbugu, Para-Romani and languages with extreme borrowing, such as Asia Minor Greek or Kormatiki Arabic (cf. Croft 2003: 52–55).

Scenario II: "the vocabulary is that of the adoptive society's language, while many grammatical inflections [. . .] and most grammatical constructions [. . .] are at least in part those of the native language society" (Croft 2003: 55), as it is found in Media Lengua (cf. Croft 2003: 55–57).

Scenario III: mixed languages due to a considerable number of mixed marriages. These mixed marriages lead to the emergence of a new society with which the speakers identify. Croft (2003: 59) characterizes this scenario as "the most intimate possible contact between speakers" and gives two examples: Mednyj Aleut and Michif, both languages with a split within the grammatical system with the verbal system being inherited from one parental language, and the nominal system from the other (cf. Croft 2003: 57–60).[2]

Croft's (2003) classification is comparable – to a certain degree – to Velupillai's (2015) distinction between mixed languages as markers of a retained identity and mixed languages as markers of a new identity. In the first case – mixed languages as

---

[2] For a different analysis of Michif cf. Gillon and Rosen (2018).

markers of a retained identity – the mixed language emerges "as a consequence of outside pressure from some other, dominating group" (Velupillai 2015: 79; similar: Auer 2014: 297) as in the case of languages such as Gurindji Kriol, Ma'a/Mbugu or Bilingual Navajo. The second scenario – mixed languages as markers of a new identity – is particularly frequent in situations with a high number of mixed marriages "where the descendants form a new ethnic identity" (Velupillai 2015: 78). The most cited examples for such languages are Michif and Mednyj Aleut. The dichotomy found in Velupillai (2015) can be linked directly to the two scenarios of mixed language emergence as defined by Thomason (2001), cf. Section 2.1. If, on the one hand, a mixed language evolves gradually, the non-dominant language is increasingly influenced by the language of the culturally dominant group. The speakers of this changing language, however, retain their lexicon along with their identity. The abrupt creation of a mixed language, on the other hand, coincides with the formation of a new ethnic group and a new ethnic identity.

To close this section, let us very briefly summarize the central criteria that are considered in the typologies of mixed languages mentioned above. We give this summary in the form of a 'checklist' of (partially overlapping) aspects discussed in the literature reviewed above:
- the role of widespread bilingualism
- the role of mixed marriages
- gradual vs. abrupt emergence of mixed languages
- the roles of the heritage society vs. the adoptive society
- the nature of the relationship between the dominating vs. the receding group
- the pragmatic functions of mixed speech as a predecessor for mixed languages
- the role of mixed language as a marker of a retained old identity vs. as a marker of a newly emerging identity
- the origins of different linguistic subsystems, in particular lexicon vs. grammatical structure
- the degree to which a mixed language has stabilized.

3 Amish Shwitzer

3.1 Roots of Amish Shwitzer

Amish Shwitzer is a language spoken in Adams County, Indiana (US), by a group of Old Order Amish, i.e. conservative horse-and-buggy-Amish who reject the use of any modern technologies. The Amish of Adams County are usually referred to as 'Swiss Amish', a handy but somewhat misleading term since many other Amish have their roots in Switzerland as well. The language spoken by the Swiss Amish today is referred to as 'Swiss', or 'Shwitzer' in their own language.[3] Amish Shwitzer has two parental languages: Pennsylvania Dutch and Bernese Swiss German.[4] With each of them, Amish Shwitzer shares a considerable part of its linguistic makeup.

Pennsylvania Dutch, on the one hand, emerged in the 18th century, as a language of immigrants (and their descendants) from southern parts of the German-speaking language area in Europe (Southern Germany, Alsace, Switzerland), whereby it is almost exclusively dialect features from Palatine German that became part of the emerging language, supplemented with innovations that are not found in other German varieties (cf. Louden 2016: Chapter 2). Anabaptist groups (Amish and Mennonites) were originally only a small fraction of the speaker population, yet these 'sectarian' groups are the ones who have maintained the language until the present day. Many Anabaptists have their roots in Switzerland, but they had to flee their homelands due to harsh prosecution. A considerable number of them found a safe haven in the Palatinate in Germany in the 17th century, from where they migrated to Pennsylvania in the 18th century, as a part of much larger migration waves to the United States.

Bernese Swiss German, on the other hand, subsumes a number of High and Highest Alemannic dialects spoken in the territory of today's Canton of Berne in Switzerland (cf. Marti 1985: 9–13). The Bernese Swiss German dialects that are involved in the emergence of Amish Shwitzer are predominantly the varieties spoken in the Emmental area (cf. Humpa 1996: 33).

The ancestors of the speakers of Amish Shwitzer migrated to the US in the mid-19th century. These Swiss Amish had lived in Franche-Comté in eastern France for a couple of decades before they migrated directly to Adams County in Indiana (cf. Hasse and Seiler *in press, a*: Section 1.1). We do not have any linguistic records of these early times of Amish Shwitzer. Yet it is very likely that the language was largely comparable to Bernese Swiss German. One piece of evidence comes from

---

3 There is yet another variety of Shwitzer spoken by the Mennonite neighbors of the Swiss Amish. Mennonite Shwitzer and Amish Shwitzer differ in a number of aspects. Mennonite Shwitzer resembles Bernese Swiss German as spoken in contemporary Switzerland to great extent. There are borrowings from English, but no borrowings from Pennsylvania Dutch. Mennonite Shwitzer is highly moribund, the youngest speakers we interviewed were born in 1953 (cf. Hasse 2022 for a detailed account of Mennonite Shwitzer).

4 Amish Shwitzer is a special case of a mixed language because its parents are closely related. Bakker (2003: 107–108) points out that in such cases it is "often not completely clear whether linguistic elements are genetically shared, or whether they are the result of contact". However, if the languages in contact – and preferably even previous stages of them – are well documented and/or described, a fine-grained analysis can ease this challenge. With regards of Amish Shwitzer, we have an ample foundation for such an analysis.

the comparison with the Swiss Mennonite neighbors of the Swiss Amish in contemporary Adams County, who also settled there in the mid-19th century. Their (nowadays highly moribund) variety resembles still very much the Bernese Swiss German dialect as we know it from the Swiss homeland (cf. Hasse 2022). In contrast to that, Amish Shwitzer displays a remarkable degree of linguistic development away from Bernese Swiss German.

As a result of the immigration history of the Swiss Amish – which is different from the one of the majority of other Old Order Amish – the settlement in Adams County has maintained some cultural and in particular linguistic distinctness, not only in relation to mainstream American society, but in particular also within the greater Old Order Amish community (cf. Meyers and Nolt 2005: Chapter 4).

3.2 Fieldwork on Amish Shwitzer in 2021 and 2022

Amish Shwitzer is a lesser-researched language. As such there is not much data available.[5] Additionally, Old Order Amish usually refuse to be recorded (cf. e.g. Johnson-Weiner 1998: 376). This makes every recording very valuable. As part of the project *Amish Shwitzer as a mixed language with closely related parents*[6] the authors did two fieldtrips to collect data among the (Swiss) Amish in Adams County, IN, and Allen County, IN, and the Swiss Mennonites in Adams County, IN, and Wayne County, OH.[7] During these two trips we conducted interviews with 15 speakers of Amish Shwitzer, four speakers of Pennsylvania Dutch,[8] and one speaker of Mennonite Shwitzer in Adams County, one speaker of Amish Alsatian in Allen County,[9] and eight speakers of Mennonite Shwitzer in Wayne County, OH. The interviews are based on a questionnaire with 76 translation tasks covering a range of grammatical phenomena with a special emphasis on morphological and (morpho-)syntactic features. Informants were asked to translate English sentences into Amish Shwitzer, which has not posed any problems to anyone. The task to translate Standard German sentences (cf. Section 3.3 on the use of Standard German among

---

5 For an overview of existing research and existing data sets of Amish Shwitzer cf. Hasse & Seiler (*in press, b*: Section 3).
6 Funded by the Swiss National Science Foundation, project number 189590.
7 Because of the COVID-19 pandemic, no fieldwork was possible in 2020, the first year of the project, and the first fieldtrip in 2021 was only possible thanks to a *National Interest Exception* issued by the US embassy in Switzerland.
8 There is a Pennsylvania Dutch-speaking minority in Adams County, among others Pennsylvania Dutch-speaking Amish who are married to Amish Shwitzer-speaking Amish.
9 The variety of Shwitzer from Allen County is regarded to be closer related to Alsatian German than to Bernese Swiss German (cf. Thompson 1994; Petrovich 2013).

the (Swiss) Amish) into Amish Shwitzer proved to be impossible for the informants though.

Since only some informants allowed it to be recorded, all interviews were transcribed in the field. In order to get the approval to record at least some speakers of Amish Shwitzer, we had to build a relationship of trust within the community first (cf. also Enninger 1988: 34). The informants who could be recorded were also asked to tell little stories so that we could document more spontaneous speech, too.

3.3 Modern (socio)linguistic situation of Amish Shwitzer

Humpa (1996: 27) estimates a population of approximately 4,400 Old Order Amish living in Adams County in 1992. Not all of them were speakers of Amish Shwitzer. We have to reckon with a certain, yet unknown number of speakers of Pennsylvania Dutch, the language spoken by the majority of Old Order Amish (cf. Louden 2016 with an extensive overview of Pennsylvania Dutch), and possibly some speakers of Amish Alsatian, a closely related variety spoken in neighboring Allen County (cf. Thompson 1994; Petrovich 2013). Twenty years later, Zook and Yoder (2017) estimate a population of already 8,600 Old Order Amish in Adams County, who live in 58 church districts. This means that (i) Adams County is one of the five largest Amish settlements overall, and (ii) the population of Old Order Amish in Adams County, and thereby the number of speakers of Amish Shwitzer, has doubled roughly within one generation.[10]

The Swiss Amish of Adams County tend to marry within their community, yet within as well as across church districts. Consequently, the Swiss Amish live rather isolated from other Amish, who speak Pennsylvania Dutch, and Non-Amish, who speak English, although some intermarriages with Pennsylvania Dutch-speaking Amish did and do occur (cf. Section 4). This is also reflected in onomastics. Smith (1968: 106) analyses 500 consecutive Amish marriages in Lancaster County, PA, from 1939 to 1954.[11] There they find "that the seven most common Amish names represented 76.9 per cent of all the names. These seven, in order of frequency, were Stoltzfus, King, Beiler, Fisher, Lapp, Zook, and Esh." Juberg et al. (1971: 481) list Miller, Yoder, and Bontrager as the three most common surnames in 30 Old Order Amish (Pennsylvania Dutch-speaking) church districts in Elkhart and LaGrange

---

[10] This is in line with a general trend of languages spoken by Old Orders, which tend to double every 20–25 years because of high birth and retention rates (cf. Louden 2020: 818). Yet, this makes Amish Shwitzer an exceptional case among the mixed languages, which else appear to be small, often with decreasing number of speakers.
[11] Lancaster County is a purely Pennsylvania Dutch-speaking Old Order Amish settlement.

Counties, IN. When comparing this settlement with the Swiss Amish settlement in Adams County, IN, they notice that "the eight most common surnames in Adams County do not appear among the eight most common surnames in any of the three others [= the three other Pennsylvania Dutch-speaking settlements included in their study]; the most common surname in Adams County, Schwartz, occurred in 50% of the population, but Swartz was 25th in Elkhart and Lagrange counties" Juberg et al. (1971: 482). Out of the ten names listed in Smith (1968), five are attested in Adams County (cf. Amish Directory 2013). The most frequent of them is Miller. In the Amish Directory of 2013, there are 20 entries of men named Miller as opposed to more than 580 entries of men named Schwar(t)z.[12]

In the context of these facts, it is remarkable how much Amish Shwitzer is linguistically influenced by Pennsylvania Dutch. Despite the relative separateness of the Swiss Amish population as it is reflected e.g. in surnames, the social contact with Pennsylvania Dutch-speaking Amish must have been intensive, which is reflected in the mixed Bernese Swiss German / Pennsylvania Dutch structure of today's Amish Shwitzer. We come back to the question of 'pennsylvanization' of Shwitzer in Section 3.5.

Amish Shwitzer is explicitly an in-group language. It is used only within the community and it is the only language used in the community. With outsiders, speakers of Amish Shwitzer use English, which they acquire as L2 at school. Most speakers have at least some passive knowledge of Pennsylvania Dutch, a much smaller number has some active knowledge of it. These speakers can use Pennsylvania Dutch when communicating with other Old Order Amish who are not Swiss. Otherwise, they use English as a *lingua franca* across Old Order Amish communities. Speakers of Amish Shwitzer comment regularly on Pennsylvania Dutch-speaking Amish that *mi chei si beser verschtee as si is* 'we can understand them better as they can understand us'. This is in line with findings made in perceptual dialectology. Speakers of Mid-Western Pennsylvania Dutch mark Adams and Allen County, IN, as very different from their own language in draw-a-map-tasks (cf. Keiser 2001: 234–237). Apart from English and Pennsylvania Dutch, at least to some extent, all speakers of Amish Shwitzer have knowledge of written German since German is the language of church and Bible study, and as such it is also taught at school once a week (cf. Louden 2016: 331–341).

Teenage and adult Swiss Amish are fully bilingual in Amish Shwitzer and English. Whereas Amish Shwitzer exists only as a medium of oral communication,

---

[12] Furthermore, there is one entry of Borntrager [sic], two of Byler and Zook, and nine of Yoder among the men, as well as one of Bontrager and Byler, six of Zook, 21 of Yoder, and 22 of Miller among the women.

English is used as an oral and written language, which makes English the only language that is used for writing. It is very natural for the Swiss Amish to use another language for writing than their L1 which exists only as a vernacular. This situation has some resemblance to diglossia in today's German-speaking Switzerland where the language for informal oral communication is the Swiss German dialect but another language, Standard German in this case, is used in writing.

The Amish Shwitzer language is a strong feature of the Swiss Amish identity. Shryock (2014: 34) states that "[t]he Swiss Amish value Swiss [= Amish Shwitzer] very highly, not only because it ties them to their cultural heritage, but it also acts as its own barrier to help separate them from the external society." Humpa (1996: 125) sees Amish Shwitzer "as a protection or buffer from the English speaking Non-Amish world." Yet, it serves not only the separation of the Non-Amish world, but also of the Non-Swiss Amish world, as will be shown in Section 4.1.

3.4 On the structure of Amish Shwitzer

The linguistic structure of Amish Shwitzer contains considerable parts from either of its parental languages, Bernese Swiss German and Pennsylvania Dutch. It must be noted that due to the close genetic relatedness of Bernese Swiss German and Pennsylvania Dutch a great proportion of grammatical but also lexical features is invariant across these two varieties. For example, basic clause structure is verb-second in main clauses and verb-final in subordinate clauses. Furthermore, Bernese Swiss German and Pennsylvania Dutch share a considerable amount of lexical items, e.g. *letz* (Pennsylvania Dutch), *lätz* (Bernese Swiss German; Amish Shwitzer) 'wrong' (but note the difference in vowel quality between Pennsylvania Dutch [ɛ] and Bernese Swiss German / Amish Shwitzer [æ]). In other words: The most revealing features are those where the parental languages Bernese Swiss German and Pennsylvania Dutch contrast with one another.

The close genetic affiliation of Amish Shwitzer with Bernese Swiss German is most obvious in vocabulary and phonology. As for vocabulary, we find many Amish Shwitzer lexical items that are inherited from Bernese Swiss German but unknown in Pennsylvania Dutch, e.g. *geng* 'always' (cf. Seiler 2017: 216), *lose* 'listen' (cf. Seiler 2017: 216), *luege* 'look' (cf. Bachmann-Geiser 1988: 42), *zmorge* 'breakfast' (cf. Fleischer and Louden 2010: 237), *znacht* 'dinner' (cf. MOE.212), *anke* 'butter' (cf. Humpa 1996: 89), *gig(g)el* 'rooster' (cf. MOE.212) etc. Note, however, that Amish Shwitzer borrowed some lexemes from Pennsylvania Dutch, e.g. *chrischdag* 'Christmas' (Pennsylvania Dutch *grischdag*, Bernese Swiss German *wienacht*) or *goul* 'horse' (Pennsylvania Dutch *gaul* or *gaal*, Bernese Swiss German *ross*; fieldnotes 2021). Moreover, the initial *ch-* (corresponding to /χ/) and the diphthong *ou* (corresponding to /oṷ/) in these examples demonstrate that the borrowed lexical items are phonologically integrated into the Amish Shwitzer sound pattern.

As for phonology in more general terms, Amish Shwitzer clearly reflects the Bernese Swiss German sound structure in both vowels and consonants. The Middle High German monophthongs /iː/, /uː/ /yː/ are still monophthongs in Bernese Swiss German and Amish Shwitzer, whereas they are diphthongized in Palatinate German and its daughter language Pennsylvania Dutch (cf. 'stay' and 'house' in Table 1). Both Bernese Swiss German and Amish Shwitzer retain the Middle High German falling diphthongs /iə/, /uə/ which are monophthongized in Pennsylvania Dutch (cf. 'good' in Table 1). The quality of Amish Shwitzer /æ/ and /ou/ is identical to Bernese Swiss German but different from Pennsylvania Dutch (/ɛ/ and /au, aː/) (cf. 'read' and 'tree' in Table 1). A typical feature of Swiss German (High Alemannic) consonant systems is the shift of word-initial k- > (k)χ-, again unknown in Pennsylvania Dutch, but found in Amish Shwitzer (cf. 'head' and 'kitchen' in Table 1).

Table 1: Phonological features of Amish Shwitzer in comparison with Bernese Swiss German and Pennsylvania Dutch.

Bernese Swiss German (cf. Idiotikon)	Amish Shwitzer (fieldnotes 2021, 2022)	Pennsylvania Dutch (cf. Stine 1996)	Translation
bliibe	*blibe*[13]	*blaibe*	'stay'
huus	*hus*	*haus, haas*	'house'
guet	*guet*	*gut*	'good'
läse	*läse*	*lese*	'read'
boum	*boum*	*baum, baam*	'tree'
chopf	*chopf*	*kopp*	'head'
chuchi	*chuchi*	*kich*	'kitchen'

The impression of a very strong Bernese Swiss German bias of Amish Shwitzer dramatically changes when we turn away from lexicon and phonology to morphosyntax. Within the verbal system, it is striking that only very few Bernese Swiss German features are retained (most of which must be categorized as lexical idiosyncrasy). Amish Shwitzer conserves the irregular morphology of so-called contracted verbs (German *Kurzverben*), viz. *tsea* 'see (INF)', *hoa* 'have (INF)', *mir hei* 'we have', *nea* 'take (INF)', *gnoa* 'taken'. Like Bernese Swiss German (cf. Lötscher

---

[13] The status of vowel quantity in Amish Shwitzer is yet unclear. Whereas Bernese Swiss German clearly distinguishes between short and long vowels, Amish Shwitzer vowels appear to be more variable in length. Our preliminary analysis is that vowel length occurs optionally and allophonically in stressed open syllables rather than as a lexical-phonemic contrast. Therefore, in transcriptions of Amish Shwitzer vowel length is not marked.

1993; Glaser and Frey 2011), Amish Shwitzer uses an infinitival particle *ge* that is inserted obligatorily before an infinitive governed by a *go*-verb, cf. (1a), whereby the *go*-verb itself can be omitted as a past participle in the periphrastic perfect, cf. (1b).[14]

(1) a. *ea   isch   gange   ge   eia   grige*
       he   be.PRS.3SG   go.PST.PTCP   PARTICLE   egg.PL   get.INF
       'He went to get eggs.' [f-vh-99]
   b. *e   sch   ge   eie   hole*
       he be.PRS.3SG   PARTICLE   egg.PL   get.INF
       'He went to get eggs.' [m-ms-64]

Another typical Bernese Swiss German (though not lexically-idiosyncratic) feature is the ascending (head-initial) ordering of elements in clause-final three verb clusters in (2) (cf. SADS, vol. 2: 115).[15]

(2) *säl   isch   dea   man   as   nit   hed   chenne   choa*
    that   be.PRS.3SG   the   man   REL   not   have.PRS.3SG   can.INF   come.INF
    geschta
    yesterday
    'That's the guy who wasn't able to come yesterday' [f-ie-56]

Otherwise the verbal system has completely converged with Pennsylvania Dutch, with regard to both inflectional morphology and the temporal-aspectual category system. Whereas Bernese Swiss German displays a stem vowel alternation in the present tense singular of strong verbs (*hälfe* 'help (INF)' – *er hilft* 'he helps', usually realized with *l*-vocalization, thus *er hiuft*, cf. SDS, vol. 1: 165), Amish Shwitzer has – exactly like Pennsylvania Dutch – levelled this alternation, thus *hälfe* 'help (INF)' – *er hälft* 'he helps'. Bernese Swiss German has no preterite (simple past) tense altogether, such that periphrastic perfect is used for any reference to past events. Pennsylvania Dutch generally uses the perfect, too, but with one notable exception, namely the copula verb, which is the only verb inflected for preterite tense (cf. Frey 1942: 55; Buffington and Barba 1965: 63). Amish Shwitzer shows precisely the same pattern: preterite *si ware* 'they were' but lack of any preterite forms for any other verb.

The following two, more complex examples demonstrate further examples of convergence of the Amish Shwitzer verbal system with Pennsylvania Dutch (while

---

14 English stimulus: *He went to get eggs.*
15 English stimulus: *That's the guy who wasn't able to come yesterday.*

lexical and phonological features are still highly reminiscent of the language's Bernese Swiss German ancestor): the obligatoriness of marking progressive aspect whenever progressive semantics is intended, a future auxiliary derived from 'count' (unique among the Germanic languages), and again the use of a synthetic preterite form of 'be'.

The first example is the translation of the English stimulus *But we will be painting the barn next week* by a male speaker (*1964) into Amish Shwitzer, cf. (3). (4) is the Bernese Swiss German equivalent to his translation.

(3) Amish Shwitzer:
abe   mi   tsele   di   schire a=m   ferbe[16] *si   negscht*
but   we   AUX.PRS.1PL   the barn   at=the paint.INF be.INF   next
wuch
week
'But we will be painting the barn next week' [m-ms-64]

(4) Bernese Swiss German:
aber mir schtriiche   nöchscht wuche d   schüüre
but   we   paint.PRS.1PL   next   week   the barn
'But we will be painting the barn next week' [f-dw-72]

There are remarkable grammatical differences between (3) and (4), namely the position of the adverbial, the use of future tense and the progressive aspect. In Amish Shwitzer, the adverbial *negscht wuch* cannot interfere the complex verbal phrase *tsele di schire am ferbe si*, cf. (3). In Bernese Swiss German, as in other varieties of German, the finite verb is at the second position of the sentence while the direct object appears at the right edge after the adverbial *nöchscht Wuche*, cf. (4). Furthermore, the English stimulus *will be painting* corresponds to synthetic present tense in Bernese Swiss German (*mir schtriiche*) (cf. Marti 1985: 131 on the absence of future tense in Bernese Swiss German). In Amish Shwitzer, however, future tense is expressed using the auxiliary *tsele* (lit. 'count') and a progressive construction *am ferbe si* is used in (3).

In terms of morphosyntactic structure, the Amish Shwitzer variant is identical to the Pennsylvania Dutch translation by a female speaker (*1967) who lives in Adams County, IN, cf. (5).

---

16 The semantics of *ferbe* 'to paint' is an innovation of Amish Shwitzer that is neither found in Pennsylvania Dutch (Mark Louden p.c.) nor Bernese Swiss German (cf. Idiotikon 1: 990).

(5) Pennsylvania Dutch:

ava	mi	tsele	di	schaia	a=m	painte	sai	negsch
but	we	AUX.PRS.1PL	the	barn	at=the	paint.INF	be.INF	next

wuch
week

'But we will be painting the barn next week' [f-ls-67]

Despite the great similarity between the Pennsylvania Dutch and the Amish Shwitzer translations (and despite the occurrence of the English borrowing *painte* in the Pennsylvania Dutch example), there are crucial differences in the phonological shape of words that make immediately clear that (5) is Pennsylvania Dutch. First, the medial bilabial consonant in the first word displays spirantization (*av̱a*) which is typical for Pennsylvania Dutch and its Palatinate German ancestor, whereas both Bernese Swiss German and Amish Shwitzer maintain the stop realization (*aḇe[r]*). Second, Bernese Swiss German and Amish Shwitzer both show the monophthongal realization of /y:/ in the word for English *barn* (Bernese Swiss German *schüür* > Amish Shwitzer *schiire*, with unrounding; the monophthongal realization is retained from Middle High German), while Pennsylvania Dutch shows the Palatinate German, i.e. diphthongized form (*scha̱ia*).

Another example is provided by translations of the English stimulus *A year ago the house was still being built*. A male speaker of Amish Shwitzer (*1942) uses a preterite passive progressive construction (*wa . . . am bout wiira*), cf. (6).

(6) Amish Shwitzer:

eis	joa	tsrig	wa	ds	huus	no	ging	a=m
a	year	back	be.PST.3SG	the	house	still	always	at=the

bout wiira
build.PST.PTCP become.INF

'A year ago the house was still being built.' [m-et-42]

In Bernese Swiss German, this stimulus can be translated with the progressive periphrases, too, but *not* under passivization. Instead, the stimulus is transformed into an active construction. Further note that there is no preterite tense of the auxiliary verb *be* in Bernese, so that present perfect is used, cf. (7):

(7) Bernese Swiss German:

Vor	emne	jaar	si	mer	no	a=m	boue	gsi
Before	a	year	be.PRS.3PL	we	still	at=the	build.INF	be.PST.PTCP

'A year ago the house was still being built.' [f-dw-72]

Again, Bernese Swiss German and Amish Shwitzer share the form *huus* 'house' with the retained Middle High German monophthong. Further, the lexeme *geng* 'always' occurs in both Amish Shwitzer and Bernese Swiss German (but not far beyond the Bern area in Switzerland, cf. Idiotikon 2: 356). This lexeme is completely unknown in Pennsylvania Dutch.

The structural resemblance of the Pennsylvania Dutch variant, cf. (8), (given by a female speaker) with Amish Shwitzer is striking:

(8) Pennsylvania Dutch:
en jaa   tsrig wa   s   haas noch an gmacht   were
a   year back   be.PST.3SG the house still at do.PST.PTCP become.INF
'A year ago the house was still being built.' [f-ls-67]

Despite the absence of the form *geng* 'always' (which would be *als* in Pennsylvania Dutch), we find another regular correspondent of the Middle High German monophthong /u:/, but this time a more innovative form as a result of diphthongization (*huus* > *haus*) in Palatinate German and subsequent monophthongization in varieties of Pennsylvania Dutch (*haus* > *haas*).

Turning now to the nominal system, Amish Shwitzer deviates from Bernese Swiss German and converges with Pennsylvania Dutch in similar ways. Like in sectarian Pennsylvania Dutch (and in English), Amish Shwitzer pronouns employ one oblique case form, thus do not inflectionally distinguish between what used to be accusative (*mi* 'me.ACC', cf. (9))[17] and dative (*mir* 'me.DAT', cf. (10))[18] in Bernese Swiss German.

(9) a. Bernese Swiss German:
       er hed   mi   gsee
       he have.PRS.3SG me.ACC see.PST.PTCP
       'He saw me.' [f-dw-72]
    b. Amish Shwitzer:
       er hed   mi   tsea
       he have.PRS.3SG me.OBL see.PST.PTCP
       'He saw me.' [f-ie-56]
    c. Pennsylvania Dutch:
       er had   mich   tsene
       he have.PRS.3SG me.OBL see.PST.PTCP
       'He saw me.' [f-rf-96].

---

17 English stimulus: *He saw me*.
18 English stimulus: *with me*.

(10) a. Bernese Swiss German:
   mit   mir
   with   me.DAT
   'with me' [f-dw-72]
   b. Amish Shwitzer:
   mit   mi
   with   me.OBL
   'with me' [f-ie-56]
   c. Pennsylvania Dutch:
   mid   mich
   with   me.OBL
   'with me' [f-rf-96]

Another example for the Pennsylvania Dutch influence on the nominal system is the Amish Shwitzer demonstrative pronoun *säl* (from Pennsylvania Dutch *sel*, cf. Frey 1942: 23; Buffington and Barba 1965: 31), which is unknown in Bernese Swiss German, cf. (2). Furthermore, in both Pennsylvania Dutch and Amish Shwitzer there is a habitual deverbal nominalizer *-es*, expressing 'the way X-ing is usually done', totally unknown in Bernese Swiss German and any other West-Germanic variety, viz. Amish Shwitzer *choches* 'the way cooking is usually done' (Pennsylvania Dutch *koches*; cf. Seiler 2017: 218, footnote 15).

As for subordination, we find the relative particle *as* (and less frequently *was*) in Amish Shwitzer, the same as in Pennsylvania Dutch (but unknown in Bernese Swiss German where relative clauses are introduced by *wo*), cf. (2). Infinitival purposive complements are not introduced by *für...z* 'for...to' like in Bernese, cf. (11a), but by *fe* (< *für* 'for') only, omitting the *z* particle, cf. (11b) for Amish Shwitzer, (11c) for Pennsylvania Dutch.[19]

(11) a. Bernese Swiss German:
   muescht   ds   licht   azünde   für   z   läse
   must.PRS.2SG the   lamp   light.INF for   to   read.INF
   'you have to light the lamp to read' [SADS, vol 1: 343]
   b. Amish Shwitzer:
   du   muesch   s   liecht   aschteke   fe   läse
   you   must.PRS.2SG the   lamp   light.INF for   read.INF
   'you have to light the lamp to read' [m-ms-64]

---

19 English stimulus: *You have to light the lamp to read.*

c. Pennsylvania Dutch:
du   musch   de   licht amache   fe   lese
you   must.PRS.2SG   the   lamp light.INF for   read.INF
'you have to light the lamp to read' [f-rf-96]

Overall, Amish Shwitzer contains many linguistic features that clearly reflect its Bernese Swiss German origin, and at the same time many features pointing into the direction of Pennsylvania Dutch. However, the distribution of Bernese Swiss German vs. Pennsylvania Dutch features is not entirely random. There is a very strong tendency that the morphosyntactic structure almost entirely converges with Pennsylvania Dutch, whereas Bernese Swiss German features are strikingly concentrated in lexicon and phonology. There are exceptions in both directions – lexical borrowings from Pennsylvania Dutch and a few morphosyntactic features that are Bernese Swiss German but unknown in Pennsylvania Dutch – but the split between Bernese Swiss German lexicon and Pennsylvania Dutch grammar is otherwise so sharp that it even goes through linguistic subsystems. This can be illustrated by the phonological system of Amish Shwitzer. Amish Shwitzer is Bernese Swiss German only insofar as the lexical phonology, i.e. the phonemic inventory and the distribution of phonemes over lexemes, is concerned. However, preliminary evidence suggests that the phonological grammar, i.e. the system of synchronically active phonological processes and constraints, is dissociated from Bernese Swiss German but associated with Pennsylvania Dutch. We have not yet found clear evidence for vocalization of /l/ in coda position in Amish Shwitzer (*milch* 'milk'), a process that is typical for Bernese Swiss German (*miuch*, cf. SDS, vol. 1: 165). On the other hand, Amish Shwitzer has place assimilation in onset clusters (*gsee > tsea*), and so does Pennsylvania Dutch (*gsehne > tsene*), but not Bernese Swiss German (*gsee*), cf. (9). For verbal morphology, we have noted earlier that the highly lexically-idiosyncratic inflection of contracted verbs is retained from Bernese Swiss German in Amish Shwitzer, while more rule-governed inflectional patterns (present tense singular of strong verbs) and the temporal-aspectual system as a whole are fully pennsylvanized. Finally, in the lexicon, we see that Amish Shwitzer contains a great proportion of clearly Bernese Swiss German content words (with some borrowings from Pennsylvania Dutch), but it is probably not by accident that function words like *säl* (demonstrative pronoun) or *as* (relative particle) are borrowed from Pennsylvania Dutch and replace their Bernese Swiss German functional equivalents.

We close this section by pointing out that not everything in Amish Shwitzer can be traced back to Bernese Swiss German or Pennsylvania Dutch. Amish Shwitzer as a vital, dynamic language contains also genuine linguistic innovations. In phonology, we find new falling diphthongs where Bernese Swiss German has long vowels, e.g. *choa* (<*choo*) 'come (INF)', *ghoa* (<*ghaa*) 'had (PST.PTCP)', *tsea* (<*gsee*) 'seen'. In morphology, there is analogical extension of the regular 3rd person singular suffix -*t* to modal verbs which are unsuffixed in Bernese Swiss German, viz. *er choat* 'he can' (Bernese Swiss German: *er cha*), *er muest* 'he must' (Bernese Swiss German: *er mues*). In the functional lexicon, there is variation between the relative particle *as* (from Pennsylvania Dutch) and *was* (unknown in this function in Pennsylvania Dutch or Bernese Swiss German). Finally, there are some genuinely Amish Shwitzer lexical innovations, e.g. *schaffgoul* 'draught horse' or *fari* 'driver'.

3.5 Amish Shwitzer as a mixed language

As illustrated in Section 3.4, Amish Shwitzer has a predominantly Bernese Swiss German lexicon, and a predominantly Pennsylvania Dutch grammatical system (cf. also Seiler 2017; Hasse and Seiler *in press a, b*), with a few exceptions in both directions (as is usually the case in mixed languages). In the framework of Bakker (2003), Amish Shwitzer is an intertwined language which – as in the case of Anglo-romani or Ma'a/Mbugu – can be allocated to both of the parental languages. Thus, Amish Shwitzer is a direct descendant of Bernese Swiss German and at the same time a direct descendant of Pennsylvania Dutch. Intertwined languages are typically spoken by mixed ethnic groups. In the case of Amish Shwitzer, we find a community which identifies itself explicitly as Swiss Amish. They are neither only Swiss, which would group them together for instance with the Swiss Mennonites in Adams County, nor are they only Old Order Amish, which would make them indistinguishable from other Old Order Amish. Within the group of intertwined languages, Amish Shwitzer belongs to the group of mixed languages with a grammar-lexicon split, the most common type among all the languages being classified as mixed languages.[20]

Even though speakers of Amish Shwitzer are multilingual, cf. Section 3.3, they acquire only Amish Shwitzer as L1, a situation comparable to the one we once found in Michif (cf. Bakker 1994: 14). However, Bakker (1994: 14) sets the age of the youngest L1 speakers of Michif at 60.

There is another similarity between Amish Shwitzer and Michif. Bakker (1994: 15) notes that "Michif is not a ritual language. The Métis are traditionally Roman Catholics, although there are some survivals of Indian religion as well. In many Métis communities, French seems to have been the language for (some) religious purposes. Songs on wedding ceremonies and other official gatherings were (are) traditionally in French". In Amish Shwitzer, Standard German is the language of

---

[20] Other examples include Anglo-Romani as well as other mixed languages with Romani as one of the parental languages, or Media Lengua (cf. Velupillai 2015: 71).

religion. The Bible is read in Standard German and church songs are sung in Standard German. The crucial difference between Michif and Amish Shwitzer, though, is that, in the case of Amish Shwitzer, the "ritual language" is not involved in the makeup of the mixed language.

The multilingual setting of Amish Shwitzer is even more complex. Not only do we find a diglossic situation of Standard German and Amish Shwitzer with regards to religious vs. everyday life, but also a medial diglossia of English and Amish Shwitzer. Amish Shwitzer is a purely spoken language. The written language – even within the community – is English. Again, English, like Standard German, is not one of the parental languages of the mixed language Amish Shwitzer. English contributes some lexical items, and there is some convergence with English regarding the grammatical structure such as e.g. the obligatoriness of progressive marking. Crucially, however, this influence is mediated by Pennsylvania Dutch: Amish Shwitzer copies the Pennsylvania Dutch way of overtly expressing abstract semantic-grammatical distinctions that are familiar from English.

Amish Shwitzer is a stable system. As far as we can tell, there are only minor linguistic differences within the speech community. These often concern single lexemes and not grammatical features.

To our knowledge, there are hardly any L2 speakers of Amish Shwitzer. There are a few examples of mixed families. Since Pennsylvania Dutch and Amish Shwitzer are closely related, both spouses in such mixed marriages acquire at least passive knowledge of the other language. The children often acquire both languages as separate linguistic systems.

Set within Bakker's (2015) dichotomy of mixed vs. blended languages, Amish Shwitzer belongs to the first type. In mixed languages we find relatively clear-cut compartmentalizations of larger linguistic subsystems (e.g. grammar vs. lexicon, nominal vs. verbal system) that are rooted in one or another parental language. In blended languages, we find abundant and quite unsystematic mixing *within* subsystems. Bakker (2015: 227) mentions Surzhyk/Surzyk (Ukrainian and Russian), Trasjanka (Belarusian and Russian), Fronteirizo (Spanish and Portuguese along Uruguayan-Brazilian border), Portunhol (at Portuguese-Spanish border), Ojicree (Ojibwe and Cree, Canada) as examples for blended languages. Other examples are Tojol-ab'al (Chuj and Tseltal; cf. Law 2017) or Reo Rapa (Rapa and Tahitian; cf. Walworth 2017). Bakker's (2015) typology of mixed languages suggests that compartmentalized mixed languages (i.e., with a systematic split between subsystems) stem from parental languages that are genetically unrelated whereas blended languages have parental languages that are genetically closely related to one another. Given this context, Amish Shwitzer seems to be the first described mixed language that shows compartmentalization although it stems from two closely related languages.

4 On the emergence of Amish Shwitzer

In Section 3.5, we have classified Amish Shwitzer as an intertwined language. Bakker (1994: 27–28) states that "[f]or language intertwining, it is also possible to retroactively draw conclusions about the social circumstances which lead to the intertwined language. If a certain language can be identified as an intertwined language, we expect it to be spoken either by descendants of a nomadic group who settled among speakers of other languages, or by a new group with a new identity, the result of the contact between two groups (although other possibilities cannot be excluded)". In the following, we will expand this approach of drawing retroactively conclusions on the setting in which Amish Shwitzer evolved.

4.1 The Swiss Amish identity – retained or new?

Mixed languages have been categorized as languages that either function as a marker of a retained identity or as a marker of a new identity, cf. Section 2.2. As presented in Section 3.3, Amish Shwitzer does not only fulfil communicative needs, but it is a strong marker of identity, yet the question is which type of identity the languages expresses and what this could tell us about the emergence of Amish Shwitzer.

In the first case – mixed language as a marker of a retained identity – one of the parental languages is dominating and creates some pressure on the speakers of the dominated language to shift towards the dominating one, such that resistance against a complete shift creates the mixed language. An example for this would be Ma'a/Mbugu, also a mixed language with a grammar-lexicon split with Bantu grammar and Cushitic lexicon: "The Mbugu were originally from the Cushitic area further north but had to resettle due to persecution. They have retained their Cushitic culture and economy, as well as their appearance. The mixed language forms part of this separate ethnic identity" (Velupillai 2015: 79). Applied to Amish Shwitzer, an analogous scenario would be: Speakers of Bernese Swiss German would have settled in a Pennsylvania Dutch-speaking environment in Adams County, accommodating linguistically to Pennsylvania Dutch (the dominating language in this scenario) while still retaining cultural practices along with their lexicon. This sounds plausible since the lexicon of Amish Shwitzer is indeed inherited from Bernese Swiss German. Besides, the Swiss Amish have pertained specific Swiss customs such as yodeling (cf. Nussbaumer 2022).

This scenario of a retained identity can be directly linked to Thomason's (2001) first setting, as mentioned in Section 2.1, in which the dominant language interferes increasingly with the receding group's language. The way for the speakers of the receding language to express their separate identity linguistically is by retaining their lexicon.

In the second scenario – mixed language as a marker of a new identity – "[the] mixed languages are spoken by people who form new ethnic groups in the societies they belong to. This not infrequently comes about due to mixed marriages, where the descendants form a new ethnic identity" (Velupillai 2015: 79). In the case of Amish Shwitzer, we would have to assume that through the contact between Bernese Swiss German- and Pennsylvania Dutch-speaking Amish, a new group emerged which identified themselves neither as being only Bernese Swiss German nor as being only Amish. Since the Amish perceive themselves predominantly as a group distinct from the Non-Amish world, it is questionable how plausible this scenario is. However, it becomes much more plausible, if we set this contact situation not only within the Amish, but within the wider Anabaptist world.

When the Swiss Amish migrated to the US in the 19th century, they did not come to Indiana via Pennsylvania, but rather migrated directly from Europe to Indiana (cf. Meyers and Nolt 2005: 30–31). In this respect, they clearly differ from other Amish, whose immigration to Pennsylvania dates back to the 18th century, from where they later settled in the Midwest (this includes other, i.e. Pennsylvania Dutch-speaking Amish settlements in Indiana, such as the Elkhart and La Grange settlements). In Indiana, the Swiss Amish settled in Adams County, where other Swiss Anabaptists, i.e. a group of Mennonites, already lived. The Swiss Mennonites shared their early ancestors with the Swiss Amish, along with their history of persecution, their culture and their language, Bernese Swiss German. These Swiss Mennonites came to Indiana in two migration waves. The first group had already been in the US (in Wayne County, OH, where they had founded the *Sonnenberg* community) before moving from Ohio westwards to Indiana in 1838 (cf. Wenger and Krabill 1987) joined by a second group of Bernese Mennonites immigrating directly from the Swiss Jura mountains in 1852–1854 (cf. Müller 1895: 371).[21] The Swiss Amish settlement in Adams County, on the other hand, was founded around 1840 (cf. Schelbert 1976: 236; Meyers and Nolt 2005: 167, endnote 7; Bachmann-Geiser 1988: 28 with different founding years). These Swiss Amish came to the US directly from Europe. This means that (i) the Swiss Amish were not part of the initial Pennsylvania Dutch-speaking melting pot in Pennsylvania and its Amish daughter settlements in other states, and (ii) the immediate neighbors of the Swiss Amish were not Pennsylvania Dutch-speaking Amish, but Bernese Swiss German-speaking Mennonites. As for (i), the Swiss Amish have maintained some ethnic and cultural dis-

---

21 Cf. Hasse (2022) for a detailed account of the migration of the Swiss Mennonites from Europe to the US.

tinctness and separation from their Non-Swiss Amish brethren in faith (cf. Meyers and Nolt 2005: 19). This is not only expressed linguistically, but also culturally. One example would be the use of exclusively open buggies as a means of transport (cf. Bachmann-Geiser 1988: 147). As for (ii), the Swiss Amish and the Swiss Mennonites shared a large number of cultural features, with one major exception that is crucial for their culture: their religious affiliation.[22] The newly emerging separate ethnic identity was Swiss Amish, placing the Swiss Amish of Adams County within the wider Old Order Amish world, and separating them from the Non-Amish Swiss Anabaptists of Adams County (i.e., the Mennonites). The new identity of the Swiss Amish is at the same time Amish, yet a special kind of Amish (namely *Swiss* Amish), and Swiss, yet a special kind of Swiss (namely Swiss *Amish*). Amish Shwitzer reflects this twofold distinct identity in its structure: It is a 'more Amish' way of speaking in comparison to the Bernese Swiss German spoken by the Swiss Mennonites who are the neighbors of the Swiss Amish, and a 'more Swiss' way in comparison to the Pennsylvania Dutch spoken by Amish from other settlements with a different migration history.

The potential role of the Mennonite neighbors in the 'pennsylvanization' of the original Bernese Swiss German dialect by the Swiss Amish (resulting in today's Amish Shwitzer) appears to be obscured by the fact that nowadays the Mennonites have almost completely shifted towards monolingual English (cf. Hasse 2022). Thus, from today's perspective the linguistic distance between Swiss Amish and Swiss Mennonites is warranted anyway: Shwitzer/English bilingualism on the Amish side, monolingualism in English on the Mennonite side. Yet this is an anachronistic perspective. Swiss Mennonites report that the shift away from Bernese Swiss German took place in the mid-20th century and the following decades, which means in turn: Until the mid-20th century, Bernese Swiss German was still widespread among the Swiss Mennonites and thereby among the immediate neighbors of the Swiss Amish.

Coming back to Velupillai's (2015) scenarios, a refinement seems to be necessary when applying them to the Amish Shwitzer situation. In Velupillai's (2015) approach, there are two linguistic and cultural groups that contribute to the linguistic as well as the cultural outcome of a scenario which could lead to the emergence of a mixed language.[23] If we assume that Amish Shwitzer is a marker of a retained identity – as discussed above – there are three groups involved. The Swiss Amish identity isolates the Swiss Amish from the Swiss Mennonites in Adams County. The Swiss Mennonites, however, do not contribute to the linguistic profile

---

22 The schism between Amish and Mennonites goes back to 1693 when the Swiss Anabaptist Jakob Amman split away from the other Anabaptists by forming a group with stricter church discipline rules, later known as the Amish (cf. Nolt 2003; Burridge 2007: 33).
23 This is not only true for Velupillai (2015), but for the majority of work on mixed languages.

4 Social factors in mixed language emergence: Solving the puzzle of Amish Shwitzer — **109**

of Amish Shwitzer. However, there is a different group contributing to the linguistic makeup of Amish Shwitzer, next to the formerly Bernese Swiss German-speaking Amish. These are the Pennsylvania Dutch-speaking Amish. Yet, how did Bernese Swiss German and Pennsylvania Dutch come into such an intense contact which would ultimately lead to the emergence of the mixed language Amish Shwitzer?

Going back to Bakker's (2003) two groups, cf. section 2.1, which can develop a mixed language (nomads vs. a newly emerged group), Amish Shwitzer can be grouped with other mixed languages spoken by groups that have newly emerged and have a specific group identity and an in-group language.

4.2 Bernese Swiss German or Pennsylvania Dutch – which is the heritage language?

As shown in Section 2.2, one typology of mixed languages is based on the classification of the languages involved in the emergence of a mixed language as heritage vs adoptive languages. This is another approach to hypothesize the scenario in which Amish Shwitzer arose. The question is what role the two languages, Bernese Swiss German and Pennsylvania Dutch, played within the community in the earliest days of the Adams County settlement. Which one of them was the heritage and which one the adoptive language?

From a modern point of view, we would tend to classify Bernese Swiss German as the heritage language, and Pennsylvania Dutch as the adoptive language because the Swiss Amish (with their language based on Bernese Swiss German) are a minority within the Pennsylvania Dutch-speaking Old Order Amish world, a minority that maintains linguistic traits (i.e., Bernese Swiss German features) that are absent in the majority's language (i.e., Pennsylvania Dutch). With regard to Croft's (2003) first two scenarios, as sketched in Section 2.2, this means that scenario I plausibly accounts for the linguistic outcome of the linguistic system found in Amish Shwitzer with its Bernese Swiss German lexicon and Pennsylvania Dutch grammar, cf. Table 2. In this scenario, the lexicon of the heritage language (Bernese Swiss German) is retained while the grammar has converged towards the grammar of the adoptive language (Pennsylvania Dutch).

Table 2: Croft's (2003) model with Bernese Swiss German as heritage language, and Pennsylvania Dutch as adoptive language.

	Lexicon	Grammar
Croft's (2003) Scenario I	Bernese Swiss German	Pennsylvania Dutch
Crofts's (2003) Scenario II	Pennsylvania Dutch	Bernese Swiss German

Such societies "are so focused that they defy cultural assimilation despite the extreme pressure of the adoptive society" (Croft 2003: 53). However, we have already stated that Pennsylvania Dutch-speaking Amish were not the culturally dominant group in the early days of the Swiss Amish settlement in the US. There is no reason to think that the Swiss Amish are exposed to "extreme pressure" in the direction of full adaptation to the Pennsylvania Dutch-speaking Amish. Anecdotal evidence suggests that the Swiss Amish' perception of Pennsylvania Dutch is highly variable. Whereas some say they feel it sounds nicer than Shwitzer, others even joke about the Pennsylvania Dutch-speaking Amish (*si wise nid wie rächt schwätze!* 'they don't know how to speak right!'). The Swiss Amish usually refer to Pennsylvania Dutch as *hochtitsch* 'High German' (cf. Seiler 2017: 227) but there is no evidence that this term is related to any sort of higher prestige of Pennsylvania Dutch. Instead Standard German, the language of religion, might have a higher prestige, but this language is usually referred to as *bibutitsch* 'Bible German'.

If the idea of "extreme pressure" towards Pennsylvania Dutch as a dominating language seems to be unapplicable to the situation of the Swiss Amish, such pressure might nevertheless have played a crucial role in the emergence of Amish Shwitzer – but in the inverse direction. Let us therefore have a second glance at the initial contact scenario and swap the roles of Pennsylvania Dutch and Bernese Swiss German. Let us assume that Pennsylvania Dutch was the heritage language and Bernese Swiss German the adoptive language, which will lead us back to scenario II in Croft (2003), cf. Table 3. "In this case, the speakers in a society appear to shift only part way to the adoptive society's language. The semi-shift may be due to lack of full access to the adoptive society's language, or may be a marker of a distinct social identity" (Croft 2003: 55). In this scenario, the mixed character of Amish Shwitzer would be the result of an incomplete shift from Pennsylvania Dutch towards Bernese Swiss German, whereby mainly Bernese Swiss German lexical items have been adopted but not grammatical structure, leading to a grammar-lexicon split. If Auer and Hakimov's (2021: 362) claim is right, namely that "even in radically fused languages, a structurally dominant (historical) source language can be identified which provides the basic grammatical patterns into which those of another (historical) source language were borrowed and integrated", the most natural assumption is that Amish Shwitzer is the result of heavy lexical borrowing into Pennsylvania Dutch which provided the basic grammatical patterns. This scenario, however, contradicts Bakker's (2003) typology according to which intertwined languages, such as Amish Shwitzer, draw their grammar from the surrounding language, cf. Section 2.1. This contradiction cannot be solved here. From a linguistic point of view, Amish Shwitzer is line with Bakker's (2003) type of intertwined languages, yet not from a sociolinguistic point of view. Amish Shwitzer might request a refinement of Bakker's (2003) typology.

Another example for this scenario is Media Lengua which emerged when monolingual Quechua-speaking men began to work in Spanish-speaking cities (cf. Muysken 1997: 374), leading to the adoption of Spanish lexical items but not grammatical structure. In the case of Amish Shwitzer it is very probable that it was women who sparked the linguistic change leading to the emergence of Amish Shwitzer, cf. Section 4.3.

Table 3: Croft's (2003) model with Pennsylvania Dutch as heritage language, and Bernese German as adoptive language.

	Lexicon	Grammar
Scenario I	Pennsylvania Dutch	Bernese German
Scenario II	Bernese German	Pennsylvania Dutch

The third scenario in Croft (2003) is dominated by a societal factor which is mentioned in various frameworks, typologies and approaches to mixed languages: mixed marriages. In Croft's classification, however, only those contact situations are classified as belonging to the third scenario which include a considerable number of such mixed marriages. So, our next question is to which extent mixed marriages between Bernese Swiss German-speaking and Pennsylvania Dutch-speaking Amish have existed.

4.3 The role of mixed marriages

The onomastic pattern of surnames found in Adams County, cf. Section 3.3, along with genetic evidence (cf. van der Walt et al. 2005: 120), indicates that there has never been a considerable number of mixed marriages between Swiss Amish from Adams County and Non-Swiss Amish from neighboring counties. At the same time, mixed marriages have occurred, not exactly as the dominating pattern, but they have not been totally uncommon. Most Swiss Amish report of one or two ancestors or relatives in their large families who married a *hochtitsch* person (i.e., Pennsylvania Dutch-speaking Amish). Also, there is evidence that intermarriages have occurred – even if in only relatively small numbers – from the early stages of Amish settlements on (Steven Nolt, p.c.). These intermarriages were typically between Swiss Amish men and Non-Swiss Amish women. This explains why the Swiss surnames are so stable in Adams County. Strikingly, it fits the findings by Bakker and Mous (1994: 8) that "mixed languages that arose out of mixed marriages take their grammar from the language of the mother."

The scenario we have to assume is thus: Amish yet Pennsylvania Dutch-speaking women from other settlements married into the Adams County settlement, i.e., into a society where Bernese Swiss German was the dominating language.[24] The fact that the Swiss Amish are quantitatively only a small minority in the total of the Old Order Amish world obscures the fact that *within* the Adams County settlement they have always clearly been the majority. Moreover, since a certain degree of cultural and linguistic separation from the rest of the Amish world is a central factor in the Swiss Amish identity, we may conclude that in the Adams County settlement there must have been considerable pressure to adopt to the dominating culture, or the community norm within this settlement, which includes linguistic adaptation towards Bernese Swiss German. Incoming Pennsylvania Dutch-speaking women therefore acquired Bernese Swiss German, but as native speakers of Pennsylvania Dutch (and as adults, acquiring Bernese Swiss German as an L2) they acquired it incompletely. While they acquired the more salient component of language, i.e. the Bernese Swiss German lexicon, they retained their Pennsylvania Dutch grammar. Mixed speech by these women did not have any particular pragmatic function (contra Auer 2014, Matras 2021) other than accommodating to the community norm. These women gave birth to children who were exposed to this mixed speech as their primary linguistic input, and ultimately acquired it as their L1.[25]

Going back to Thomason (2001), Amish Shwitzer resembles rather her second scenario of an abrupt creation of a mixed language than a scenario of gradually increasing interferences between two languages. This abrupt change from Bernese Swiss German or Pennsylvania Dutch, respectively, happened in the course of L1 acquisition by children in various mixed families. Language mixing as such was caused by the Pennsylvania Dutch-speaking women, but this mix got a chance to stabilize in the linguistic system of their children. This again fits the observation by Thomason (2001: 205–206) that the emergence of such a mixed language requires very close contact between two speech communities.

An interesting partial parallel case is the emergence of Light Warlpiri, a mixed language stemming from Warlpiri and Aboriginal English/Kriol (cf. O'Shannessy 2012).[26] O'Shannessy claims that Light Warlpiri emerged in two steps: first, "adults

---

24 A similar situation is found in Michif where French-speaking fur traders and Amerindian wives married, only that in this case the outcome was an intertwined language with verbs predominantly from Cree, and (pro)nouns from French. Bakker (1994: 21) notes "[l]anguages like these are often spoken by people of dual ancestry, where all fathers spoke the same language, which differed from the one language spoken by all the mothers. Their bilingual children must be responsible for the creation of the mixed language."
25 Many thanks to Marit Westergaard for pointing this out.
26 Cf. also Matras (2021) for mixing of various input languages by children.

directed codeswitched Warlpiri-A[boriginal]E[nglish]/Kriol speech to children as part of a baby talk register" (O'Shannessy 2012: 306), which the children then conventionalized so that that speech lost its specific communicative function as codeswitching and became just the target language of the acquisition process. The parallel between Light Warlpiri and (potentially) Amish Shwitzer lies in the central role of nativization of mixed input by the next generation of acquirers/speakers. Unlike in Light Warlpiri, the mixed input is not due to parents' deliberate codeswitching but rather due to incomplete acquisition of Bernese Swiss German as an L2 by L1 speakers of Pennsylvania Dutch. This means that in our proposal acquirers play the crucial part in the emergence of Amish Shwitzer even twice: first as adult L2 learners, then as young L1 learners.

Yet, if Pennsylvania Dutch-speaking women marrying into the Adams County settlement and their children were the agents of the emergence of Amish Shwitzer as a mixed language, we are faced with another issue. Given that intermarriages were only a minority of all marriages in the Adams County settlement, we still need to answer the question as to how the "mixture" between Pennsylvania Dutch and Bernese Swiss German, the later Amish Shwitzer, could have spread across the Swiss Amish community as a whole. This leads us back to the role of Amish Shwitzer as an identity marker.

4.4 What is the story behind it?

If the number of mixed marriages between Swiss and Non-Swiss Amish was never particularly high, we have to answer the question as to why and how Amish Shwitzer had a chance to spread from those few families to the whole Amish settlement of Adams County and ultimately became the community norm there. This question leads us back to the role of identity. The newly emerging language Amish Shwitzer still allowed the Swiss Amish to retain a clear linguistic difference from other Amish and thus helped them to retain their specific identity within the broader Old Order Amish society. It must be noted that the Old Order Amish are not one homogenous group. It is rather a "patchwork" (Meyers and Nolt 2005) of communities which all share crucial properties of their culture and more importantly their faith. However, there is a considerable degree of variation. Every church district has its own *Ordnung* regulating many aspects of life. They have different demographic profiles and different occupations from one community to the next (cf. Cross 2018; Donnermeyer *in press*). Within this world, the Swiss Amish have a further feature distinguishing them from other Old Order Amish communities: their language. By retaining their lexicon, the early speakers of Amish Shwitzer could continue to give expression to their own, specific community not only in their customs, but also in their language.

Yet, why did the early speakers of Amish Shwitzer not just maintain the Bernese Swiss German dialect which they spoke when they settled in Adams County? While the mixed variety first emerged in mixed families certainly not for purpose (but rather because incoming Pennsylvania Dutch-speaking women just incompletely acquired Bernese Swiss German as an L2, which naturally became nativized by their children), this newly emerging variety must have been attractive for all other Swiss Amish in such a way that it was ultimately adopted by the whole community. Theoretically, strictly endogamous Swiss Amish families could have continued speaking Bernese Swiss German, but this is not what happened.

Remember that the Swiss Amish are not the only community living in Adams County with a Swiss (Bernese) background. Bernese Swiss German was not only the language of the Swiss Amish, but also of the Swiss Mennonites until the mid-20th century. From an Amish perspective on the Amish schism of 1693 the Mennonites are 'fallen'. As long as both communities speak Bernese Swiss German, the Swiss Amish share one common language with their closely related but 'fallen' immediate neighbors. Now, when a new 'accent' emerges in families with Swiss and Non-Swiss Amish members (i.e., the mixed variety which became Amish Shwitzer), a variety comes into play that is different from the languages spoken by Non-Swiss Amish *and* by Swiss Mennonites. The newly emerging mixed variety must have been an attractive vehicle for the Swiss Amish to express their two-sided separation from both the Non-Swiss Amish and the Swiss Mennonites. At the same time, Amish Shwitzer guarantees a strong connection to 'Swissness' (via the Bernese Swiss German vocabulary) as well as 'Amishness' (via the Pennsylvania Dutch overall structure of grammar). Speakers of this language were clearly not perceived as Non-Swiss Amish because their lexicon was mostly Swiss, nor were they perceived as Swiss Mennonites because their grammar was mostly Pennsylvania Dutch. The adoption of Pennsylvania Dutch features gave the (formerly Bernese Swiss German-speaking) Swiss Amish the opportunity to speak in a 'more Amish way'. Nowadays, there are only very few Mennonite speakers in the US left who still speak Bernese Swiss German (cf. Hasse 2022). One of the last speakers in Adams County refers to the Amish Shwitzer language simply as "Amish".

Since we do not have direct historical evidence of the earliest time of the Swiss Amish, we do not know when Amish Shwitzer emerged. Indirect evidence consists of older recordings, present-day apparent-time comparisons, and individual speaker biographies. The oldest recordings of Amish Shwitzer are from the 1980s when researchers recorded Old Order Amish across the US for an atlas of Pennsylvania Dutch, (cf. Moelleken 1988). Five of these recordings were made in Adams and Allen Counties. The oldest speaker, a male speaker from Allen County, was born in 1905, and he already shows the grammatical features of Pennsylvania Dutch as we know them from today's Amish Shwitzer. Furthermore, data from contemporary Amish Shwitzer collected in 2021 and 2022 suggest that the linguistic features with a Pennsylvania Dutch origin in Amish Shwitzer have been in place (and stable) for a relatively long time since no intergenerational differences have been detected with regard to those features. Another piece of evidence are individual speaker biographies. One Swiss Mennonite speaker uses suspiciously many expressions reminiscent of Amish Shwitzer and Pennsylvania Dutch origin. The speaker is born in the 1930s, to parents who grew up Amish but had left the Amish before they gave birth to their son. Thus, the speaker has never been Amish throughout his lifetime, but he acquired Amish Shwitzer, with all the Pennsylvania Dutch features, in the 1930s already. Putting all those little pieces of evidence together, we might tentatively conclude that Amish Shwitzer has existed at least since the early 20th century.[27] It dates back to a time when the Bernese Swiss German dialect was still widespread among the Mennonite community, which makes it plausible that Amish Shwitzer was so successful because it was a strategy to speak in a 'more Amish way' than the Mennonite neighbors.

There is a more general lesson to learn from our scenario of the emergence of Amish Shwitzer. We have seen that the question of how this mixed variety emerged must be broken down into two questions: (i) how the specific mixed structure of the language evolved, and (ii) how the newly emerging variety got the momentum to spread across the whole community. As for (i), we argued that incomplete L2 acquisition of Bernese Swiss German by Pennsylvania Dutch-speaking incomers (and subsequent nativization by their children) must have played a crucial part. As for (ii), the new variety became an attractive vehicle for the Swiss Amish community to express themselves as being Swiss (but not the same kind of Swiss as their Mennonite neighbors) and Amish (but not the same kind of Amish as the Non-Swiss Amish). In other words: Mixed language emergence is a two-step process.

There is a well-established conceptual distinction in historical linguistics and sociolinguistics, the distinction between actuation vs. diffusion of a linguistic innovation (cf. Weinreich, Labov and Herzog 1968; De Vogelaer 2006; De Vogelaer and Seiler 2012). Actuation refers to Weinreich, Labov and Herzog's (1968) question on how it is possible that a change in linguistic structure comes into play at all. Diffusion refers to Weinreich, Labov and Herzog's (1968) transition problem: Once a new linguistic variant is in play, how is it possible that it may spread from speaker to speaker, possibly across a whole community? As far as we can tell, the actuation vs. diffusion distinction has only been applied to changes of individual linguistic

---

27 Therefore, we have to reject Humpa's (1996: 35) hypothesis that the mixed structure of Amish Shwitzer is due to an increase of intermarriages with Non-Swiss Amish only since the 1960s (as a reaction to a rise of hereditary diseases).

features. However, we believe that it can (and must) be applied for whole varieties, too. It is one question to ask how a newly emerging variety gets its specific linguistic structure, and it is another, equally relevant question to ask how this variety reaches other speakers, perhaps a whole community.

5 Conclusion

Amish Shwitzer is an intertwined, stabilized mixed language with a predominantly Bernese Swiss German lexicon and predominantly Pennsylvania Dutch grammatical structure. It does not only fulfil needs of communication, but also of identity. It is the exclusive in-group language of the Swiss Amish of Adams County, IN, separating them linguistically from the (Pennsylvania Dutch-speaking) Non-Swiss Amish and (English-speaking) Non-Amish outsiders, including their Mennonite neighbors who used to speak Bernese Swiss German but without the Pennsylvania Dutch component which creates the specific structure of Amish Shwitzer. After reviewing several existing proposals on the relevance of social factors in mixed language emergence, we arrived to the question as to which one of Amish Shwitzer's parental languages, Pennsylvania Dutch or Bernese Swiss German, played the part of the heritage language and which one was the adoptive language in the emergence process. We concluded that the most plausible scenario is one where Amish Shwitzer is not regarded as pennsylvanized Swiss German, but rather as swissified Pennsylvania Dutch. Non-Swiss, Pennsylvania Dutch-speaking Amish married into the Adams County settlement and accommodated linguistically to the local community norm (i.e., Bernese Swiss German) as far as they were able to. As adult L2 learners, they successfully adopted the Bernese Swiss German lexicon while they maintained Pennsylvania Dutch morphosyntactic structure. Their children were exposed to that mixed input and nativized it. This newly emerging mixed variety became very successful in the community as a whole because its Swiss component expresses separation from the Non-Swiss Amish and its Pennsylvania Dutch component expresses separation from the local Swiss Mennonites.

We would like to close with two general theoretical points. First, L1 acquisition can be a relevant locus for the stabilization and nativization of mixed input available to children (cf. already O'Shannessy 2012), but furthermore (incomplete) L2 acquisition by the earlier generation may even be the relevant locus for the emergence of that mixed input at all. Second, mixed language emergence is, like all language change, a two-step process of actuation and diffusion. We argued that not only the emergence of an individual linguistic innovation, but even the emergence of a whole variety must be explained on grounds of those two dimensions. On the one hand, we have to explain how the innovative structure comes into being at all, and on the other, we have to answer the question how it is possible that this structure can successfully spread across a community of speakers.

References

Amish Directory 2013 = *Amish directory: Adams and Jay Counties and vicinity 2013*. Volume Eight. Monroe: Hilty Home Sales.
Auer, Peter. 1999. From codeswitching via language mixing to fused lects: Toward a dynamic typology of bilingual speech. *International Journal of Bilingualism* 3(4). 309–332.
Auer, Peter. 2014. Language mixing and language fusion: When bilingual talk becomes monolingual. In Juliane Besters-Dilger, Cynthia Dermarkar, Stefan Pfänder & Achim Rabus (eds.), *Congruence in contact-induced language change. Language families, typological resemblance, and perceived similarity*, 294–333. (Linguae & Litterae 27). Berlin & Boston: de Gruyter.
Auer, Peter & Nikolay Hakimov. 2021. From language mixing to fused lects: The process and its outcomes. *International Journal of Bilingualism* 25(2). 361–368.
Bachmann-Geiser, Brigitte & Eugen Bachmann-Geiser. 1988. *Amische. Die Lebensweise der Amischen in Berne, Indiana*. Bern: Benteli.
Bakker, Peter. 1994. Michif, the Cree-French mixed language of the Métis buffalo hunters in Canada. In Peter Bakker & Maarten Mous (eds.), *Mixed languages. 15 case studies in language intertwining*, 13–33. Amsterdam: Uitgave IFOTT.
Bakker, Peter. 1997. *A language of our own. The genesis of Michif, the mixed Cree-French language of the Canadian Métis*. New York: Oxford University Press.
Bakker, Peter. 2003. Mixed languages as autonomous systems. In Yaron Matras & Peter Bakker (eds.), *The mixed language debate. Theoretical and empirical advances*, 107–150. Berlin & Boston: de Gruyter.
Bakker, Peter. 2015. Typology of mixed languages. In Aleksandra Y. Aikhenvald & Robert M. W. Dixon (eds.), *The Cambridge handbook of linguistic typology*, 217–253. Cambridge: Cambridge University Press.
Bakker, Peter & Maarten Mous. 1994. Introduction. In Peter Bakker & Maarten Mous (eds.), *Mixed languages. 15 case studies in language intertwining*, 1–11. Amsterdam: Uitgave IFOTT.
Buffington, Albert F. & Preston A. Barba. 1965. *A Pennsylvania German grammar*. Revised Edition. Allentown: Schlechter's.
Burridge, Kate. 2007. A separate and peculiar people. Fieldwork and the Pennsylvania Ger-mans. *Language Typology and Universals* 60(1). 32–41.
Croft, William. 2000. *Explaining language change: An evolutionary approach*. Harlow, Essex: Longman.
Croft, William. 2003. Mixed languages and acts of identity: An evolutionary approach. In Yaron Matras & Peter Bakker (eds.), *The mixed language debate. Theoretical and empirical advances*, 41–72. Berlin/New York: de Gruyter.
Cross, John. 2018. Occupation patterns of Amish settlements in Wisconsin. *Journal of Amish and Plain Anabaptist Studies* 6(2). 192–212.
Donnermeyer, Joseph. in press. A population profile of the Amish in Michigan. *The Journal of Plain Anabaptist Communities*.

Enninger, Werner. 1988. Zur Erhaltung deutscher Sprachvarietäten unter den Altamischen. *International Journal of the Sociology of Language* 69. 33–57.

Frey, John William. 1942. *A simple grammar of Pennsylvania Dutch*. Clinton, S.C.: John William Frey.

Gillon, Carrie & Nicole Rosen. 2018. *Nominal contact in Michif*. Oxford: Oxford University Press.

Glaser, Elvira & Natascha Frey. 2011. Vorwort/Editorial. In Elvira Glaser & Natascha Frey (eds.), *Empirical studies on verb doubling in Swiss German dialects / Empirische Studien zur Verbverdoppelung in schweizerdeutschen Dialekten*, 3–7. https://bop.unibe.ch/linguistik-online/article/view/384/598 (accessed 27 February 2023).

Hasse, Anja. 2022. Die berndeutschsprachigen Mennoniten im Jura, in Wayne County, OH, und in Adams County, IN. Spracherhalt, Sprachwandel, Sprachwechsel, Spracherosion. *Mennonitica Helvetica* 45. 6–34.

Hasse, Anja & Guido Seiler. in press, a. Amisches und mennonitisches Shwitzer im Vergleich: Ergebnisse einer Pilotstudie. *Zeitschrift für Dialektologie und Linguistik*.

Hasse, Anja & Guido Seiler. in press, b. Amish Shwitzer – an Old Order contact language. *Journal of Amish and Plain Anabaptist Studies*.

Humpa, Gregory J. 1996. *Retention and loss of Bernese Alemannic traits in an Indiana Amish dialect. A comparative-historical study*. West Lafayette, IN: Purdue University dissertation.

Keiser, Steven Hartman. 2001. *Language change across speech islands. The emergence of a midwestern dialect of Pennsylvania German*. Columbus: Ohio State University dissertation.

Idiotikon = *Schweizerisches Idiotikon. Wörterbuch der schweizerdeutschen Sprache*. Begonnen von Friedrich Staub und Ludwig Tobler und fortgesetzt von Albert Bachmann, Otto Gröger, Hans Wanner, Peter Dalcher, Peter Ott und Hans-Peter Schifferle. Frauenfeld: Huber (Volumes 1–16, 1881–2012) / Basel: Schwabe (Volume 17, 2013–).

Johnson-Weiner, Karen M. 1998. Community identity and language change in North American Anabaptist communities. *Journal of Sociolinguistics* 3(2). 375–394.

Juberg, Richard C., William J. Schull, Henry Gershowitz & Louise M. Davis. 1971. Blood group gene frequencies in an Amish deme of Northern Indiana. Comparison with other Amish demes. *Human Biology* 43(4). 477–485.

Law, Danny. 2017. Language mixing and genetic similarity. The case of Tojol-ab'al. *Diachronica* 34. 40–78.

Lötscher, Andreas. 1993. Zur Genese der Verbverdoppiung bei gaa, choo, laa, aafaa ("gehen", "kommen", "lassen", "anfangen") im Schweizerdeutschen. In Werner Abraham & Josef Bayer (eds.), *Dialektsyntax*, 180–200. (Linguistische Berichte Sonderheft 5). Opladen: Westdeutscher Verlag.

Louden, Mark. 2016. *Pennsylvania Dutch: The story of an American language*. Baltimore: John Hopkins University Press.

Louden, Mark. 2020. Minority Germanic languages. In Michael T. Putnam & B. Richard Page (eds.), *The Cambridge handbook of Germanic linguistics*, 807–832. Cambridge: Cambridge University Press.

Matras, Yaron. 2000. Mixed languages: A functional-communicative approach. *Bilingualism: Language and Cognition* 3. 79–99.

Matras, Yaron. 2021. Repertoire management and the performative origin of mixed languages. In Maria Mazzoli & Eeva Sippola (eds.), *New perspectives on mixed languages. From core to fringe*, 362–403. Berlin/New York: de Gruyter.

Meakins, Felicity. 2011. *Case marking in contact: The development and function of case morphology in Gurindji Kriol*. Amsterdam/Philadelphia: John Benjamins.

Meyers, Thomas J. & Steven M. Nolt. 2005. *An Amish patchwork. Indiana's Old Orders in the modern world*. Bloomington: Indiana University Press.

MOE = Recordings from 1986 by Wolfgang Moelleken for a linguistic atlas of Pennsylvania German, archived at Max Kade Institute for German-American Studies, Madison, Wisconsin.
Moelleken, Wolfgang W. 1988. A new linguistic atlas of Pennsylvania German. *Monatshefte* 80(1). 105–114.
Müller, Ernst. 1895. *Geschichte der Bernischen Täufer. Nach den Urkunden dargestellt.* Frauenfeld: Huber.
Muysken, Pieter. 1997. Media Lengua. In Sarah G. Thomason (ed.), *Contact languages. A wider perspective*, 365–426. Amsterdam/Philadelphia: John Benjamins.
Nussbaumer, Thomas. 2002. Jodler und Jodlerlieder der 'Swiss Amish' – aufgenommen in Kalona, Iowa. In Thomas Nussbaumer & Raymond Ammann (eds.), *Alpenstimmen. Beiträge zum Jodeln und mehrstimmigen Singen*, 329–361. Innsbruck: Universitätsverlag Wagner.
O'Shannessy, Carmel. 2012. The role of codeswitched input to children in the origin of a new mixed language. *Linguistics* 50(2). 305–340.
Petrovich, Christopher. 2013. Realignment and division in the Amish Community of Allen County. *Journal of Amish and Plain Anabaptist Studies* 1(1). 167–196.
SADS = Glaser, Elvira (ed.), *Syntaktischer Atlas der Deutschen Schweiz.* Vol. 1: Einleitung und Kommentare. Bearbeitet von Elvira Glaser und Gabriela Bart, sowie Claudia Bucheli Berger, Guido Seiler, Sandro Bachmann und Anja Hasse, unter Mitarbeit von Matthias Friedli und Janine Richner-Steiner. Vol. 2: Karten. Bearbeitet von Sandro Bachmann, Gabriela Bart und Elvira Glaser, sowie Claudia Bucheli Berger und Guido Seiler. Tübingen: Narr.
Schelbert, Leo. 1976. *Einführung in die schweizerische Auswanderungsgeschichte der Neuzeit.* Zürich: Verlag Stäubli.
SDS = Baumgartner, Heinrich & Rudolf Hotzenköcherle (eds.), *Sprachatlas der deutschen Schweiz.* Frauenfeld: Huber.
Seiler, Guido. 2017. Wenn Dialekte Sprachen sind, dann ist Dialektkontakt Sprachkontakt. Zum «Shwitzer» der Amischen in Adams County (Indiana, USA). *Zeitschrift für Dialektologie und Linguistik* 84 (2/3). 202–231.
Shryock, Kylie. 2014. *Social structures and language maintenance of the Old Order Amish in Adams County, IN.* Chapel Hill, NC: University of North Carolina BA Thesis.
Smith, Elmar L. 1968. Amish Names. *Names. A Journal of Onomastics* 16(2). 105–110.
Stine, Eugene S. 1996. *Pennsylvania German dictionary: Pennsylvania German-English, English-Pennsylvania German.* Ephrata, PA: The Pennsylvania German Society.
Thomason, Sarah. 2001. *Language contact. An introduction.* Edinburgh: Edinburgh University Press.
Thomason, Sarah. 2003. Social factors and linguistic processes in the emergence of stable mixed languages. In Yaron Matras & Peter Bakker (eds.), *The mixed language debate. Theoretical and empirical advances*, 21–39. Berlin/New York: de Gruyter.
Thompson, Chad L. 1994. The languages of the Amish of Allen County, Indiana. Multilingualism and convergence. *Anthropological Linguistics* 36(1). 69–91.
Velupillai, Viveka. 2015. *Pidgins, creoles and mixed languages. An introduction.* Amsterdam/Philadephia: John Benjamins.
Vogelaer, Gunther de. 2006. Actuation, diffusion, and universals: Change in the pronominal system in Dutch dialects. *Zeitschrift für Dialektologie und Linguistik* 73. 259–274.
Vogelaer, Gunther de & Guido Seiler. 2012. The dialect laboratory. Introductory remarks. In Gunther de Vogelaer & Guido Seiler (eds.), *The dialect laboratory. Dialects as a testing ground for theories of language change*, 1–31. Amsterdam/Philadelphia: John Benjamins.
Walt, Joelle van der, William K. Scott, Susan Slifer, P. C. Gaskell, Eden R. Martin, Kathleen Welsh-Bohmer, Marilyn Creason, Amy Crunk, Denise Fuzzell, Lynne McFarland, Charles C. Kroner, C. E. Jackson,

Jonathan L. Haines & Margaret A. Pericak-Vance. 2005. Maternal lineages and Alzheimer disease risk in the Old Order Amish. *Human Genetics* 118. 115–122.

Walworth, Mary. 2017. Reo Rapa: A Polynesian contact language. *Journal of Language Contact* 10. 98–141.

Weinreich, Uriel, William Labov & Marvin I. Herzog. 1968. Empirical foundations for a theory of language change. In Winfred P. Lehmann & Yakov Malkiel (eds.), *Directions for historical linguistics: A symposium*, 97–195. Austin: University of Texas Press.

Wenger, John C. & Russell R. Krabill. 1987. Indiana (USA). *Global Anabaptist Mennonite Encyclopedia Online*. https://gameo.org/index.php?title=Indiana_(USA)&oldid=147969 (accessed 30 August 2022).

Zook, Noah & Samuel Y. Yoder. 2017. Berne Old Order Amish settlement (Berne, Indiana, USA). *Global Anabaptist Mennonite Encyclopedia*. https://gameo.org/index.php?title=Berne_Old_Order_Amish_Settlement_(Adams_County,_Indiana,_USA) (accessed 30 August 2022).

Laura Becker, Matías Guzmán Naranjo and Samira Ochs
5 Socio-linguistic effects on conditional constructions: A quantitative typological study

Abstract: Recent typological studies have shown that socio-linguistic factors have a substantial effect on at least certain structures of language. However, we are still far from understanding how such factors should be operationalized and how they interact with other factors in shaping grammar. To address both questions, this study examines the influence of socio-linguistic factors on the number of dedicated conditional constructions in a sample of 374 languages. We test the number of speakers, the degree of multilingualism, the availability of a literature tradition, the use of writing, and the use of the language in the education system. At the same time, we control for genealogical, contact, and bibliographical biases. Our results suggest that the number of speakers is the most informative predictor. However, we find that the association between the number of speakers and the number of dedicated conditional constructions is much weaker than assumed, once genealogical and contact biases are controlled for.

Acknowledgments: We wish to thank the discussants from the 2021 SLE workshop "Integrating socio-linguistic and typological perspectives on language variation: methods and concepts", the participants of the Freiburg Linguistics reading group, Marvin Martiny, Uta Reinöhl and Maria Vollmer as well as two anonymous reviewers for their valuable comments on earlier versions of this study. Furthermore, this paper was supported by a Junior Fellowship from the Freiburg Institute for Advanced Studies (FRIAS), University of Freiburg (Germany), by the European Research Council (ERC) under the European Union's Horizon 2020 research and innovation programme (Grant agreement 834050), and the Emmy Noether project 'Bayesian modelling of spatial typology' (project number 504155622).

Laura Becker, University of Freiburg, Belfortstraße 18, 79098 Freiburg im Breisgau,
e-mail: laura.becker@linguistik.uni-freiburg.de
Matías Guzmán Naranjo, University of Freiburg, Belfortstraße 18, 79098 Freiburg im Breisgau,
e-mail: matias.guzman.naranjo@linguistik.uni-freiburg.de
Samira Ochs, Leibniz-Institut für Deutsche Sprache (IDS), R5, 6-13, 68161 Mannheim,
e-mail: ochs@ids-mannheim.de

1 Introduction

Following the spirit of socio-typology of Trudgill (2008), a number of recent quantitative typological and crosslinguistic studies have shown that socio-linguistic factors such as the number of speakers or the proportion of L2-speakers have a substantial effect on at least certain structures of language (Bentz & Winter 2013; De Busser & LaPolla 2015; Karlsson, Miestamo & Sinnemäki 2008; Ladd, Roberts & Dediu 2015; Lupyan & Dale 2016; Sinnemäki 2020; Sinnemäki & Di Garbo 2018; Trudgill 2008, 2011b). The idea is that the structure of a linguistic community can have an effect on the grammatical properties that the language of that community may develop. The prime example of this is the claim that larger communities with many adult L2-speakers will tend to develop simpler morphology as adults have more difficulties with learning complex morphology (Trudgill 2011b). On the other hand, smaller communities with a high number of bilingual children can develop more complex morphological systems due to transfer (Trudgill 2010: 301–306).

While the question of how socio-linguistic factors can shape grammar is a promising research area, we are still far from having a solid understanding of which factors play a role in shaping grammar, how the different factors interact, or how they should be operationalised. So far, most large scale studies in socio-linguistic typology have focused on only one or two factors, namely population size and L2-speaker proportion. Besides these factors, the use of the language in writing and its literature tradition may also impact its grammatical properties over the course of time. Additionally, while most work on socio-linguistic typology has tried to control for genetic bias, there are other sources of bias that we need to consider as well: areal effects due to contact and diffusion, as well as cultural or socio-linguistic, typological and bibliographical biases. Despite the areal bias being well known, it is also harder to control or to account for, which explains that it has not received sufficient attention in typological studies in the past.

The linguistic phenomenon that we will examine in this study is the expression of conditionals. Conditional constructions lend themselves as a testing ground for the impact of socio-linguistic factors on language structure for two reasons. First, all languages have some way of expressing conditions (cf. Wierzbicka 1996: 68–70) and, second, conditional constructions show a large degree of crosslinguistic variation that we can make use of to determine the impact of socio-linguistic variables. In addition, previous work suggests that the degree of lexicalization, grammaticalization and explicitness of conditional constructions and markers is prone to be influenced by socio-linguistic factors (Martowicz 2011). Building on this, we compiled a sample of 374 languages and annotated for the number of dedicated conditional constructions in each language. We use this linguistic phenomenon to examine the influence that genealogical, contact and socio-linguistic factors have on language once we consider their interaction.

This chapter is structured as follows: Section 2 provides a brief overview of conditional constructions and Section 3 introduces the known socio-linguistic factors that impact language structure. In Section 4, we present our case study, describing the sample and the annotation. Section 5 presents and analyzes our results, which are further discussed in Section 6. Section 7 concludes.

2 Conditional constructions: Preliminary remarks

Conditional expressions relate two events, a main event and a condition of that event. Formally, the condition can be expressed through an adverbial clause, which is also referred to as the protasis. The main event, often formally expressed in a main clause, is called the apodosis. Semantically, we can distinguish between three broad types of conditional expressions: real, hypothetical, and counterfactual conditionals (e.g. Hetterle 2015: 48–50, Kortmann 1997: 85, Thompson, Longacre & Hwang 2007: 255–256). Real conditionals refer to real present, past, future or general events. While the condition of the main event does not necessarily have to occur, once the condition occurs, the main event does so as well. Two examples of real conditionals from English are given in (1) and (2). Example (1) refers to a specific situation, and (2) contains a generic conditional, expressing a general truth.[1]

(1) *[If it's raining on my way home]$_{PRO}$, [I will get wet]$_{APO}$.*

(2) *[If you do not get enough sleep]$_{PRO}$, [you will be tired]$_{APO}$.*

In hypothetical conditionals, both the conditional and the main event are more imaginative and less likely to happen compared to real conditionals; they express what might be. In the case of example (3), the speaker expresses that the condition (meeting her friend), is unlikely in the first place, making the main event (that she does not recognise her) unlikely as well.

(3) *[If I met my friend from kindergarden]$_{PRO}$, [I would not recognise her]$_{APO}$.*

The third main type of conditional expressions is the counterfactual conditional. Counterfactuals express events that did not happen. In this case, it is presupposed

---

[1] The protasis is marked by PRO and the apodosis by APO here and in the following examples.

that the condition was not met. An example of a counterfactual conditional is given in (4).

(4) *[If you had been in class today]$_{PRO}$, [you would have seen the new teacher]$_{APO}$.*

For the purposes of the present study, we include conditional constructions of all three types, i.e. real, hypothetical and counterfactual conditionals without further distinctions between the three types. We include all types because the distinction of different types is irrelevant for our research question, as we compare the effect of socio-linguistic factors on the overall number of dedicated conditional constructions in a given language.

We know about a few typologically common and less common properties of conditional constructions from the literature concerned with either adverbial clauses in general (Diessel & Gast 2012; Hetterle 2015; Kortmann 1997) or conditional expressions and constructions more specifically (Athanasiadou & Dirven 1997; Khrakovskij 2005; Podlesskaya 2001; Thompson, Longacre & Hwang 2007; Traugott et al. 1986). For instance, the statement containing the condition (protasis) usually precedes the statement of the main event (apodosis), as could be seen in examples (1) to (4). This order is also the default order across languages, although it can be reversed in certain cases depending on context and language-specific conditions.[2] For the purposes of the present study, the order of protasis and apodosis does not play a role in that we count pairs such as *if it rains, I will get wet* and *I will get wet if it rains* as a single construction.[3]

Another property concerns the type of conditional marker. Thompson, Longacre & Hwang (2007) note that an equivalent of the English *if* marker is typologically quite common, i.e. many languages use a subordinator of some sort in the protasis to express conditionality. Example (5) shows this for Goemai (Chadic, Nigeria). Goemai uses the marker *là* in the protasis to signal conditionality similarly to the use of *if* in English.

(5) *[Là   góe=p'ét]$_{PRO}$ [t'òng   góe=múút]$_{APO}$.*
    COND   2SG.M.S=exit.SG   IRR   2SG.M.S=die. SG
    'If you go out, you will die.'
    Goemai (Hellwig 2011: 457)

---

[2] Already Greenberg (1963: 66) proposes the order of protasis preceding the apodosis as being universally preferred. It is also this default order of the protasis preceding the apodosis that inspired analyses of conditional statements as topics (e.g. Haiman 1978; Podlesskaya 2001).
[3] This is mainly a practical decision because most descriptions do not provide explicit information on the (preferred) order of the protasis and the apodosis outside of the examples shown.

Comrie (1986), Podlesskaya (2001) and Thompson, Longacre & Hwang (2007) observe that it is very common to mark the protasis as in English or Goemai, and that most languages do not use any obligatory marker in the apodosis. The constructions in our sample show the same trend. Some languages or single constructions in a given language may use a marker in the apodosis, but it is often used emphatically in addition to another marker in the protasis.[4] For instance, in their description of Yanyuwa (Pama-Nyungan, Australia), Kirton & Charlie (1996: 190–191) write: "[t]he apodosis is usually unmarked, but if the speaker wishes to emphasise the sureness of the consequence, then the apodosis is introduced by one of the following: *kulu* 'and, then', *mardalmarda barra* 'and, also' or *barra* 'then'." This is shown in (6) and (7) below. In (6), we see a conditional construction marked by *namba* in the protasis, and in (7), *barra* is used in addition to *namba* in the apodosis of the conditional expression. In such cases, we do however treat the expressions shown in (6) and (7) as two variants of a single construction, i.e. they are counted in as one. Languages almost always allow the (spontaneous) use of an additional marker equivalent to English *then* in the apodosis, but this is not always made explicit in the descriptions. This makes the consistent distinction of such variants very difficult crosslinguistically, and we therefore do not count them in as separate constructions.

(6) [***Namba*** *kurdardi buyuka-wu*]$_{PRO}$ *yijini-nja-rra,   wurnda ma-nja-rra*
    if   not   fire-DAT   kindle-PTCP-PRS WOOD   break-PTCP-PRS
    yijini-nja-rra-i,   baki wakara, buyuka, ji-walanyma-nji]$_{APO}$.
    kindle- PTCP-PRS-on.and.on and success fire   it-emerge-PRS
    "If (there is) no fire, (then there is) making fire (by twrling one firestick into another), breaking wood making fire on and on, and it's there! - fire! - it is coming."
    Yanyuwa (Kirton & Charlie 1996: 176)

(7) [***Namba*** *kari-wayka wabuda   ki-walanyma-njima*]$_{PRO}$,
    if   from-down   water   it-emerge-POT
    [***barra*** *manthalmanthal nawu awara,   wararr barra*]$_{APO}$.
    then   soft   now   ground   mud   now
    'If the water should come up from down there, then the ground is soft, there is mud.'
    Yanyuwa (Kirton & Charlie 1996: 191)

---

4 Out of 1142 conditional constructions in our dataset, 871 only use a marker in the protasis, 107 constructions have a marker in both clauses, 87 use no overt marker, 36 have an optional marker in the apodosis in addition to the one in the protasis, 13 feature a marker in the apodosis with an optional additional marker in the protasis, 23 only have a marker in the apodosis, and 5 constructions use the same marker either in the apodosis or in the protasis.

In addition, Thompson, Longacre & Hwang (2007: 256–257) mention that it is common to use a dedicated marker or construction in hypothetical and counterfactual conditionals, and less so in real conditionals, which are often expressed as temporal clauses. This is also what we find in our dataset; usually, if conditionality is expressed by juxtaposition only, we are dealing with a real conditional, in which case the main event can still occur. Hypothetical or counterfactual conditionals, on the other hand, are usually formally marked in some way. Examples (8) and (9) show this for Bengali (Indo-European, Bangladesh). Bengali has a conditional marker, *yôdi*, which is systematically used to mark counterfactual conditionals. This is shown in (8). Example (9) then shows that real conditional statements can be expressed by the juxtaposition of protasis and apodosis without the use of *yôdi*.[5] Because we will analyze the number of dedicated conditional constructions, expressions involving no dedicated marker such as the juxtapposition of two clauses in (9) will not count towards the number of constructions. In other words, a language that only marks conditional relations using the juxtapposition of clauses will be treated to have a count of 0 dedicated conditional constructions.

(8) [*yôdi ami susthô thaktam*]$_{PRO}$ [*tahôle côle yetam*
    if   I   well be.PST.HAB.1   then   move.PTCP go.PST.HAB.1
kothao]$_{APO}$.
somewhere
'If I were well, I would go away somewhere.'
Bengali (Thompson 2012: 243)

(9) [*bhorbæla sarţer gɔlaŷ ţai thake na*]$_{PRO}$, [*kæmôn*
    dawn.hour shirt.GEN throat.LOC tie stay.PRS.3 not   how
yænô khali ga mône hɔŷ tãr]$_{APO}$.
as.if empty body mind.LOC be.PRS.3 he.HON.GEN
'If he does not have a tie round his neck by dawn, he feels somehow naked.'
Bengali (Thompson 2012: 246)

Although it is common to have a syntactic marker such as the subordinator *if* in English to signal the conditionality in the protasis, previous work has revealed much variation in how conditionals can be expressed (e.g. Khrakovskij 2005; Podlesskaya 2001; Thompson, Longacre & Hwang 2007). In our dataset, we find

---

5 It is likely that intonation and prosody play a role in those cases in which conditionals are expressed only by juxtapposition of two clauses, but a systematic analysis thereof, also for other languages, is not available yet.

various formal strategies as well. In a number of languages, conditionality is expressed morphologically by a verbal marker. This is shown for Oko (Benue-Congo, Nigeria) in (10). Other languages make use of nominal or nominalization strategies. For instance, in Kwini (Worroran, Australia) conditionals can be expressed through the use of the nominalizer *-ngay* which attaches to the verb in the protasis. As can be seen in (11), the nominalizer is the only formal marker of conditionality. Other languages use topic markers to express conditionals. One such example is shown in (12) from Shiwiar (Chicham, Ecuador). Here the topic marker =*ka* is used in the protasis to encode conditionality. Yet another strategy is shown in example (13) for Bilinarra (Pama-Nyungan, Australia), which expresses conditionals by the relativization of the protasis.

(10) *[wà-á -gám-yà]$_{PRO}$ [e-èké-gúnówó]$_{APO}$*
 s:2SG-COND-greet-O:3SG   s:3SG-NEG.FUT-answer
 'If you greet X, X will not respond.'
 Oko (Atoyebi 2010: 94)

(11) *[ajalwarra   darrug   arrunje-ngay]$_{PRO}$ [barramara]$_{APO}$*
 rain   falls   it.does-NMLZ   you.tell.me
 'If it rains, tell me.'
 Kwini (McGregor 1993: 55)

(12) *[páki   má^N-rmɨ=ka]$_{PRO}$;   [ini-t-r-i-t^{j}aram]$_{APO}$.*
 peccary   kill-2PL.SS=TOP   bring-APPL-1SG.O-PFV-2PL.S:IMP
 'If you kill a peccary, bring it to me.'
 Shiwiar (Kohlberger 2020: 195)

(13) *[Nyila=ma=rna=nga   warlagu=ma   ba-rru   guliyan=ma]$_{APO}$*
 that=TOP=1MIN.S=DUB   dog=TOP   hit-POT   dangerous=TOP
 [nyamu=yi=nga   baya-wu]$_{PRO}$.
 REL=1MIN.O=DUB   bite-POT
 'I'll hit the agressive dog, if it bites me.'
 Bilinarra (Meakins & Nordlinger 2013: 307)

For the analysis presented in Section 5, verbal conditional markers such as *-a-* in Oko shown in (10) count as dedicated conditional constructions, since their primary function is the expression of conditionality. The marking strategies shown in (11), (12) and (13), on the other hand, have other primary functions (i.e. nominalizing, topicalizing and relativizing an event, respectively). Therefore, they do not count towards the number of dedicated conditional constructions for our analysis in Section 5.

Another common expression used especially for real and predictive conditionals is a temporal clause. According to Thompson, Longacre & Hwang (2007), this is often found in Austronesian languages and in the macro area of Papunesia in general. Also Martowicz. (2011: 278) shows that languages in that area, i.e. in New Guinea and Australia tend to show a lower degree of expliciteness for conditional expressions than in other areas of the world. To give an example, we can see that the temporal subordinator *xən* in Oksapmin (Nuclear Trans New Guinea, Papua New Guinea) can be used to express both a temporal (14) and a conditional context (15).

(14)   was   n-x-ti-pel=**xən**   nox   skul   xəm
       wash   1/2.O-make-PFV-FUT.PL=**SBRD**   1SG   school   down
       əp-di-p
       come-PFV-EVID.PST.SG
       'After they washed me, I came down to school.'
       Oksapmin (Loughnane 2009: 442)

(15)   [dit   blel   mox   o=m-de-m   s-ja=**xən**]$_{PRO}$
       1DU.INCL child   ANAPH   leave=PROX.O-make-SEQ   go-PRS.PL=**SBRD**
       [ixil   i=n-x-ti-pli=xən=o]$_{APO}$
       3PL   angry=1/2.O-make-PFV-FUT.PL=IRR=QUOT
       'If we leave the child behind and go, they might be angry with us.'
       Oksapmin (Loughnane 2009: 433)

The functional extension of temporal markers or constructions to conditionality has also been noted from a grammaticalization perspective; durative or non-punctual temporal expressions are one of the most common sources for conditional markers identified in Traugott (1985). Conditional expressions that originate from temporal expressions such as the one shown in (15) do not count towards the number of dedicated conditional constructions either, their main function being the expression of temporal relations.

3 Socio-linguistic factors shaping language structure

3.1 Effects of population size and structure

There is ample evidence for the impact of various extra-linguistic factors on language structure and grammar. An early typological study of the role of socio-linguistic factors on grammatical structures was done by Perkins (1992), who found an effect of cultural properties on the systems of deictic expressions. Smaller, more intimate societies with stronger social ties between members were shown to have more complex deictic systems, as they rely on more knowledge shared between the members of the speech community. Larger societies were shown to have less complex deictic systems, which was explained in terms of loser ties between members and thus less shared knowledge between any two speakers of the community. This general observation that "societies of intimates" and "societies of strangers" develop languages with systematic differences due to differences in their social structures has been discussed in many other typologically-oriented studies (e.g. De Busser & LaPolla 2015; Sampson, Gil & Trudgill 2009; Trudgill 2011b; Wray & Grace 2007).

In addition, there is a substantial body of quantitative work that investigates the influence of social structures on grammar. Most studies, especially earlier ones, used population sizes as a proxy for the structures of the speech communities. The choice of using population sizes is probably a practical one; even though obtaining accurate numbers for the size of various speech communities comes with many difficulties as well, it is still one of the easiest variable related to social complexity to quantify at a large scale.

More recent studies, however, have started to move away from this overly simplistic representation and have tried to include information on especially L2-speaker proportions. While this may still not be sufficient to accurately capture social structures based on what we know from the theoretical literature, L2-speaker proportions seem to be an equally or even more relevant socio-linguistic predictor of language structure than population sizes. For instance, Bentz & Winter (2013) find that the L2-speaker proportion is a better predictor of the size of nominal case systems than the number of speakers. However, Sinnemäki & Di Garbo (2018) find that combining the information of population size and the proportion of L2-speakers leads to better predictions of verbal inflectional synthesis. The study by Sinnemäki (2020) is remarkable in that it analyzes the interaction of phylogenetic, areal, socio-linguistic (language-external) and language-internal factors (word order) in their influence on the development of complex case systems. Indeed, he finds complex interactions between these different factors, which, together with other more recent findings, also serve as a motivation for the present study.

Other important case studies besides the ones mentioned above are Lupyan & Dale (2010) and Sinnemäki (2009), who have used typological datasets to show that larger population sizes tend to be associated with less complex inflectional morphology. Dale & Lupyan (2012) and Nettle (2012) find similar effects of population size based on computer simulations. There are also a number of smaller case studies focusing on selected languages or language families reporting similar tendencies. For instance, DeLancey (2014) suggests that socio-linguistic factors can account for the development of analytical vs. synthetic structures in different Tibeto-Burman languages. Kusters (2003), focusing on Arabic, Scandinavian, Quechua and Swahili, also shows that the number of L2-speakers, the social tightness of the speech community and the prestige of a language can shape the linguistic complexity of verbal inflection morphology.

Besides population sizes, Sinnemäki & Di Garbo (2018) show that L2-speaker proportions are an important additional predictor of verbal morphological complexity and grammatical gender. Looking at the number of nominal cases, Bentz & Winter (2013) find that the proportion of L2-speakers is a better socio-linguistic predictor compared to the population size; the higher the L2-proportion, the fewer case distinctions languages tend to have.[6]

Apart from work on structural complexity, previous studies have also found that vocabulary size is affected by socio-linguistic factors. Larger speech communities, which tend to have less complex structures, were shown to have larger vocabulary sizes than smaller speech communities (e.g. Reali, Chater & Christiansen 2018).

3.2 Modality effects: Written and spoken language

There is also a long tradition of investigating the impact of the modality, e.g. written vs. spoken language, on grammar. Modality effects are relevant on the synchronic as well as on the diachronic level. On the one hand, different modalities of the same language can show different preferences for certain linguistic structures. For instance, the preference against complex syntactic structures in spoken as opposed

---

[6] Also phonological complexity in the form of phoneme inventory sizes has been suggested to correlate with social complexity. For instance, Trudgill (2004) argued that population size, the degree of linguistic contact, the tightness of social networks and the degree of social stability can influence the size of phoneme inventories. See Donohue & Nichols (e.g. 2011); Moran, McCloy & Wright (2012); Pericliev (2004); Wichmann, Rama & Holman (2011) for quantitative crosslinguistic studies of the association between phoneme inventory size and population size.

to written varieties of English was already shown by various authors early on (e.g. Halliday 1994; Miller & Weinert 1998; Pawley & Syder 1983; Redeker 1984; Tannen 1982). Especially the works by Biber, analyzing data from mainly English, but also Somali, Tuvaluan and Korean, revealed a more complex interaction between modalities and registers, leading to systematic structural differences between varieties of the same language (Biber 1995, 2006; 2009).[7]

The written modality can also shape language structure in its long-term availability or in the form of a literature tradition.[8] Here, the availability and use of clause-combining devices is especially relevant for conditional constructions. In his seminal work, Ong (1982) discusses the following structural properties that languages with a primarily oral tradition have: (i) additive rather than subordinative syntactic structures, (ii) aggregative expressions, i.e. the use of epiteths or parallel structures and (iii) redundancy and repetition in order to ensure that both the speaker and the hearer keep track with the discourse.[9] He thus already notes that the use of complex syntactic structures with dependent clauses is favoured by written uses of languages, whereas chained clauses with no syntactic dependencies and repetitions are a typical property of spoken language. Over the course of time, then, the use of such structures is conventionalised. This in turn is argued to lead to systematic syntactic differences between languages with an orality tradition vs. languages with a literature tradition.

Related to that, Mithun (1984) discusses corpus data from Guwinggu (Gunwinyguan, Australia), Mohawk (Iroquoian, Canada & USA) and Kathlamet (Chinookan, USA), showing that these languages use deictic markers and independent clauses for what is usually expressed by complex clauses (matrix clauses with relative, complement or adverbial clauses) in English. She argues that this difference in the use and availability of syntactic subordination can, at least in part, be accounted for by the development of a literature tradition in languages like English. This then leads to the observable pattern that languages with a literature tradition tend to make use of more subordination than languages with a primarily oral tradition.

Furthermore, Biber (2006), Chafe (1982), Mithun (1984) and Ong (1982) argue that these modality differences can lead to systematic typological differences across

---

[7] See Dąbrowska (2020) for a recent overview of such synchronic, individual effects of writing on language.
[8] We follow Ong (1982: 1–3) and use the notion of "literacy" and "literature tradition" to refer to a written tradition only, which is opposed to a culture of oral traditions, which we will refer to as "orality" or "oralility tradition".
[9] Ong (1982) discusses many other typical properties of languages with oral traditions, which are however less relevant for the purposes of the present paper.

languages. From the speaker's perspective, written language can be planned ahead more carefully than spoken language, and written language can also be adjusted, which is not possible in the spoken modality. Spoken language is thus typically more spontaneous and less planned. From the addressee's perspective, reading is usually much faster than listening to spoken language. Requiring less time makes it cognitively easier for the reader to keep all the parts of a complex sentence in their working memory, which may be more difficult with slower, spoken language.

In addition, subordination could also be required in written texts, for which much less context is provided by the information contained in discourse context of spoken language. The link between utterances can often successfully be conveyed by the use of prosodic devices in spoken language, as both the speaker and the hearer share much more information from the discourse situation itself. This is not necessarily the case for written texts, which may need to compensate for the lack of context and be much more explicit in how certain ideas, expressed as different clauses, are related to each other. Furthermore, Deutscher (2000: 182) points out that writing allows for the expression of more complex concepts and can ultimately lead to more complex communicative patterns that can influence language structures independently of the modality of use over the course of time.

Similarly, in his analysis of adverbial constructions in European languages, Kortmann (1997) finds systematic correspondences between the most elaborate systems of adverbial subordinators and the literature tradition of the languages. Languages with fewer adverbial subordinators are also the languages with relatively young or no literature traditions, namely Romani, Talysh, Karaim, Sardinian, Manx, Gagauz, Ossetic, Udmurt, Komi, Nenets (Kortmann 1997: 254–255). He also points to the distance between the writer and the reader in written communication and the lack of extra-linguistic clues. Kortmann argues that those characteristics lead to a higher degree of syntactic explicitness being necessary for successful communication.

Another piece of evidence pointing in the same direction is that subordinators are sometimes borrowed from national languages with a writing tradition into other, local languages as a consequence of language contact. To give one example, Bakker & Hekking (2012) show how Otomi (Otomanguean, Mexico) borrowed a number of conjunctions and subjunctions from Spanish. Otomi is a predominantly oral language, having been in contact with Spanish for about 500 years. However, until recently, the Otomi communities could stay fairly monolingual due to their remote locations, and widespread bilingualism with Spanish in the Otomi communities only started around 1950. Bakker & Hekking (2012) show that the combination of clauses in Otomi can be left implicit in many cases and that existing conjunctions and subjunctions have rather broad semantic functions. Due to contact with Spanish, however, various explicit markers to combine clauses have been borrowed from Spanish, and the existing Otomi markers have also become semantically more restrictive and specialised over time.

3.3 Implications for the number of conditional constructions

The effects that especially population size and L2-speaker proportions appear to have on the structural complexity of languages suggest that we may also find effects on the types of conditional constructions, which in turn could influence the number of dedicated constructions. Given that we see effects of population size on the morphosyntactic complexity of languages, we may expect languages with smaller speech communities to be more likely to make use of verbal inflection to encode conditionality, while languages with larger speech communities may tend to use syntactic markers. Once a system already has a morphological marker as a part of the verbal paradigm, its availability may in turn lead to fewer additional syntactic constructions. In languages with no morphological means to express conditionality, the development of syntactic conditional constructions may be favoured.

Similarly to the situation of Otomi mentioned in the previous section, we expect borrowing of conditional constructions and markers to take place in settings where most speakers of the community are bilingual. Only a general dominance of both languages in the community will allow for code-switching and language mixing, which is how a syntactic marker or construction could be borrowed from one language into another. We thus expect a higher number of conditional constructions in languages with smaller population sizes in those cases in which its speakers are multilingual and use another language with a more official status and a writing tradition.

Besides the effects of writing mentioned in Section 3.2, there is also evidence that the expression of conditionality, together with anteriority, is prone to be influenced by the written use of a language. In her 2011 study, Martowicz examined the properties of the expression of anteriority, causality, purpose and conditionality in a sample of 84 languages. She found an association between the grammaticalization, lexicalization and explicitness of conditional markers and various sociolinguistic factors: "By contrast, the evidence gathered for anteriority and conditionality suggest [sic.] that encoding of these two relations is very prone to the influence of socio-cultural factors" (Martowicz 2011: 310). Especially the level of written form development, the presence of radio and TV broadcasts, the number of speakers and the type of society (predominantly non-urban, mixed, predominantly urban) were found to be associated with the degree of explicitness of conditional constructions (Martowicz 2011: 312). This result also suggests that we should find a higher number of dedicated (i.e. explicit) conditional constructions in languages that are used in writing and formal ways of communication, which is typical for languages with larger population sizes. At the same time, we may also expect that the absence of dedicated conditional constructions is more likely in oral languages of small communities which do not have a writing tradition.

4 Sample and annotation

Our dataset consists of 374 languages from 118 top-level families across the six macro-areas of Africa, Australia, Eurasia, North America, Papunesia and South America as used in Glottolog (Hammarström et al. 2021).[10] We included 50 languages for each macro-area.[11] Because of more data being available, including the results from Khrakovskij (2005), we have data from 127 languages for Eurasia (cf. Section 5.2 for how we control for a potential phylogenetic and contact bias). The relevant information was taken from reference grammars and language descriptions. If possible, both the grammatical and the socio-linguistic information was extracted from the language descriptions. For some languages, appropriate online databases were consulted for the sociological and demographic details.[12]

Figure 1 gives an overview of the distribution of the languages in the sample. The languages are coloured according to the number of dedicated conditional constructions they have, ranging from 0 constructions (dark) to 15 (light). The map already shows that most of the world's languages have a small number of constructions, higher numbers appear to be especially common in Europe and to a lesser extent in Asia and Africa. Due to the complexity of uses and variation in the descriptions, we did not exclude or distinguish conditional constructions according to their type (real, hypothetical and counterfactual). However, we only counted in

---

10 All data, sources and the code are provided in the online supplementary materials: https://gitlab.com/mguzmann89/conditionals-paper-lb-mgn-so.
11 The macro areas used in WALS and Glottolog are designed in a way that they are maximally independent of each other and comparable in terms of their genetic and typological diversity (Hammarström & Donohue 2014: 169).
12 For instance, we consulted the AustLang resource for Australian languages (https://collection.aiatsis.gov.au/austlang/search), the Endangered Languages Project (https://www.endangeredlanguages.com/), as well as census data, e.g. the "Report on the Status of B.C. First Nations Languages" (https://fpcc.ca/wp-content/uploads/2020/07/FPCC-LanguageReport-180716-WEB.pdf), the Mexican "Censo de Población y Vivienda 2020" (https://cuentame.inegi.org.mx/hipertexto/todas_lenguas.htm), and the "Philippine Statistics Authority 2014" (https://psa.gov.ph/sites/default/files/2014%20PIF_0.pdf).

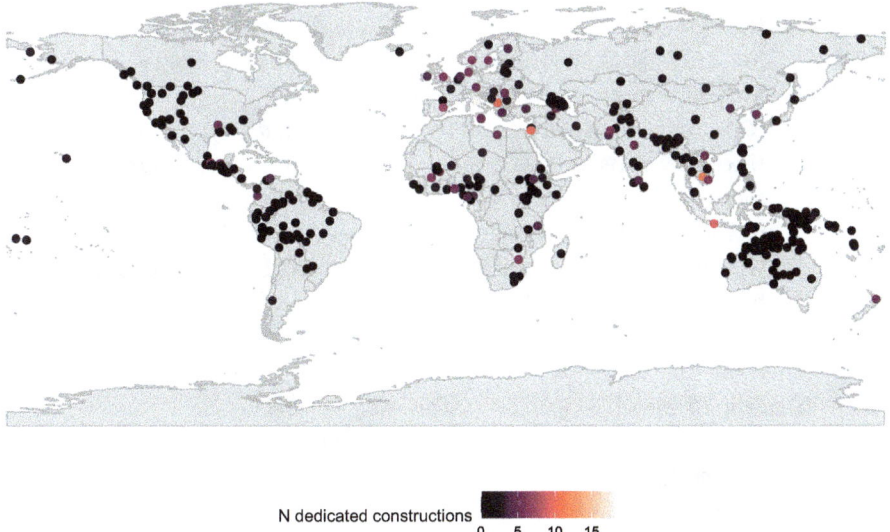

Figure 1: Map of the sample.

overtly marked, dedicated conditional constructions. In other words, constructions corresponding to juxtaposed clauses which are not formally marked (cf. example (9)) are not treated as a dedicated conditional construction. Neither are formally marked constructions counted in if they are used in other contexts, e.g. as a temporal or relative construction (cf. examples (11)-(15) from Section 2). This led to some languages of the dataset having 0 dedicated conditional constructions.

To give an example of how we counted dedicated conditional constructions, we can consider Bariai (Austronesian, Papua New Guinea). Gallagher & Baehr (2005: 161) discuss two conditional markers, *oangga* 'if/when' and *padam* 'only if'. Both markers occur in the protasis and they can additionally be accompanied by *eine* 'then' or *tota* 'therefore' in the apodosis. Example (16a) shows the use of *oannga* 'if/when' on its own, and (16b) together with *tota* 'therefore' in the apodosis. In (17), we see the use of *padam* in the protasis together with *eine* 'then' in the apodosis. Because the markers *eine* and *tota* are described as being optionally used in addition to one of the two conditional markers in the protasis, we treat cases such as (16a) and (16b) as two variants of a single construction. However, since *oannga* is used to express both temporal and conditional relations without necessarily disambiguating the two interpretations in a given context, we do not treat the construction containing *oannga* as a dedicated conditional construction. Thus, only the construction with *padam*, shown in (17) counts towards the number of dedicated constructions in Bariai.

(16) a. *[Ei ga i-pul ei mulian]*_{APO} *[oannga i-gera go.]*_{PRO}
3SG FUT S.3SG-turn 3SG back **if/when** S.3SG-see O.2SG
'He will turn back when he sees you.'

b. *[Oangga a-ean-ean annga toaiua dadanga-i,]*_{PRO}
if/when S.1PL.EXCL-RED-eat food that garden-LOC
*[oangga kus, tota amai annga eta mao.]*_{APO}
if/when be.done therefore POSS.1PL.EXCL food one.IRR not
'When we are eating that food in the garden, if it's gone, then we don't have any (more) food.'
Bariai (Gallagher & Baehr 2005: 161)

(17) *[***Padam** *le-da eau i-eno-no,]*_{PRO} *[eina*
if.only POSS-1PL.INCL water S.3SG-lay-RED then.there.2
*ta-kona-ona.]*_{APO}
S.1PL.INCL-hook-red
'If only some of our fuel was left, then we (could) hook-fish.'
Bariai (Gallagher & Baehr 2005: 161)

The socio-linguistic and extra-linguistic factors that we annotated for each language can be seen in Table 1.

Table 1: Socio-linguistic and extra-linguistic variables annotated.

variable	values
N speakers	(log) number of speakers
N L2-speakers	number of L2-speakers
multilinguals	no < some < many < most < all
literature	no literature, literature
writing	no < little < yes
education	no < language classes < little < yes
phylo	phylogenetic tree (taken from Glottolog)
latitude	latitude of the language's location (taken from Glottolog)
longitude	longitude of the language's location (taken from Glottolog)
biblio	grammar length measured in number of pages

Besides the number of speakers, there is evidence pointing towards the importance of L2-speaker proportions when examining the effects of socio-linguistic factors on grammar (cf. Section 3.1). However, similarly to previous studies, we had difficulties gathering sufficient information on the number of L2-speakers of all languages in the sample. We could only find reliable numbers for 43 out of 374 languages.

Some grammars describe the language as a lingua franca of the region, but they do not necessarily give any numbers of L2-speakers.[13]

Because exact numbers of L2-speakers were difficult to come by for most languages of the sample, we included a less exact measure of the proportion of multilinguals in the speech community, distinguishing between 5 ordinal values of no < some < many < most < all speakers being multilingual. We could annotate this information for most of the languages, as most grammars provide a rough estimate of the proportion of multilingual speakers. Only for 9 languages of the sample, we could not determine the proportion of multilingual speakers from the sources; we annotated their level as "unknown". We are aware that such an ordinal representation of the proportion of multilingual speakers does not correspond to the proportions of L2-speakers in the strict sense, but we included this variable for practical and exploratory reasons. Still, we hypothesize that a high degree of multilingualism could reflect a high degree of language contact, which could result in more constructions due to borrowing and calquing.

In addition to the information on speaker numbers, we annotated the following three socio-linguistic variables: the availability of a literature tradition, the use of the language in writing and in the educational system. Ideally, we would have used a much more fine-grained distinction, including for instance the presence of the language in TV, in radio, in newspapers, the use of the language in legal circumstances, etc., similarly to the variables used by Martowicz (2011). Unfortunately, including this information for a large crosslinguistic sample is hardly possible at the moment–this kind of information is only available for a few languages from the sample. For the purposes of the present study, we prioritized sample size over a rich and detailed socio-linguistic annotation as a first approach that can be supplemented by a smaller but more detailed follow-up study.

For the availability of a literature tradition, we simply made a binary distinction between the presence vs. the absence thereof. Whenever only a bible translation (or an equivalent translation of a religious text) was available, the language was annotated as having no literature tradition. Only if the community was described as producing written literature of their own accord, the language was annotated as having a literature tradition.

In addition to the availability of a literature tradition, we also annotated the extent to which a language is currently used in writing. Most language descriptions note in detail whether an orthography exists and whether it is used productively by the community. If the language had an alphabet but the community scarcely

---

[13] This is not to criticize the authors of the grammar; rather, it shows how difficult it is to quantify the number of L2-speakers even for experts on a given language.

used it, we marked its use in writing as 'little'. The same holds if there were only translated texts such as the bible. If the orthography was solely used for scientific purposes or no orthography existed, the language was annotated as not being used in writing. Only if the orthography was accepted and used by the community to produce a variety of written texts, the language was considered to be fully used in writing.

For the use in education, we distinguished between four values. If the language was used as the medium of instructions in schooling and/or in higher education, we annotated it as used in education. If the use of the language as the medium of instruction only had a very limited range, e.g. only in the first classes of elementary school, its use in education was annotated as 'little'. If only language classes (for children and/or adults) but no other education in the language was available, we annotated it as having language classes. If there was neither formal instruction in a language nor language classes, we marked it as not being used in education.

As mentioned in Section 3.3, we hypothesize that both the availability of a literature tradition and its use in writing makes a higher number of conditional constructions more likely. The use of the language in the educational system is very likely correlated with the other two variables; we included it because we did not know a priori which variable proved to be the most informative predictor (and because we had sufficient information about this variable for the languages in the sample). As was mentioned in Section 3.2, we know that this modality effect holds for adverbial markers in general; we can assume that it is the written modality that requires conditionals to be made more explicit as opposed to the spoken modality, where conditionals can be left morpho-syntactically unmarked and where the discourse context and prosody play a more important role.

We know that the degree to which languages are fully described varies drastically across areas and families and individual languages, and it is very likely that we miss linguistic details on conditional constructions in a given language simply because there is only a single description which has to focus on many different aspects of the language. In order to account for such a potential bibliographical bias (cf. Bakker 2010), we also annotated the length of the grammars used. The length was measured in number of pages.[14] In case more than one source per language was consulted, we used the longest description.

Finally, we included two other extra-linguistic variables from Glottolog, namely the phylogenetic information and the coordinates of the languages. We used these

---

[14] Alternatively, one could have coded the length of the sections or chapters on conditional constructions. While more precise in theory, we did not opt for this solution because conditional constructions were often treated in more than one section in the descriptions.

two variables to account for phylogenetic and contact biases in our model, which will be explained in more detail in Section 5.2.

5 Results

5.1 Overall distributions

In this section, we will give an overview of the raw distributions, showing the relevant patterns to examine the association between the number of conditional constructions and various socio-linguistic factors. Figure 2 shows how the number of conditional constructions is associated with the log number of speakers (left) and the degree of multilingualism (right).

As we can see in the left plot of Figure 2, the number of speakers appears to be weakly associated with the number of conditional constructions in that all languages in the dataset with a high number of constructions (>10) also have larger population sizes. Indeed, the two measures have a moderate positive correlation of 0.46. However, fewer conditional constructions are found independently of the number of speakers.

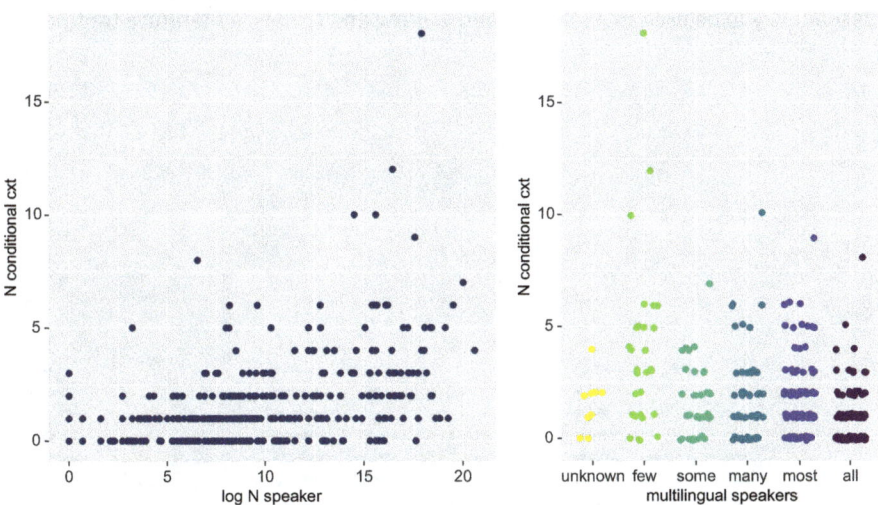

Figure 2: The number of conditional constructions by log N speaker (left) & multilinguals (right).

Regarding the degree of multilingualism or rather the importance and use of other languages, the right plot in Figure 2 does not show any clear trends. If at all, it appears that languages with fewer multilingual speakers may have slightly more conditional constructions. This may be due to the fact that the languages with few multilingual speakers usually correspond to national languages with larger population sizes, and the languages with many multilingual speakers are often those that have only a small number of speakers.

Figure 3 shows the associations between the number of conditional constructions and three socio-linguistic variables: the use of the language in education (left), in writing (center) and the availability of a literature tradition (right). For all three of those variables, we see a very weak association with the number of conditional constructions. Again, the association rather concerns high numbers of constructions; they only occur in those languages that are fully used in the educational system and in writing and that have a literature tradition. At the same time, lower numbers of conditional constructions are found across all categories of the three socio-linguistic variables.

One of the issues with the associations seen in Figures 2 and 3 above is that the socio-linguistic values that we want to examine as predictors of linguistic properties are correlated with each other. To show a few examples, Figure 4 plots log N speakers against education, writing and literature. We see a very clear association with the number of speakers of a language; the more speakers a language has, the higher its tendency to be used in education and writing and to have a literature tradition.

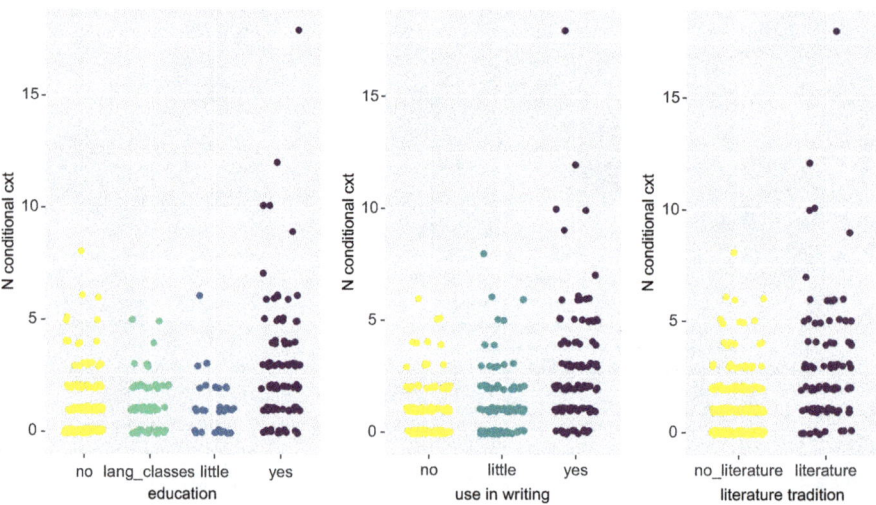

Figure 3: The number of conditional constructions by education (left) & writing (center) & literature (right).

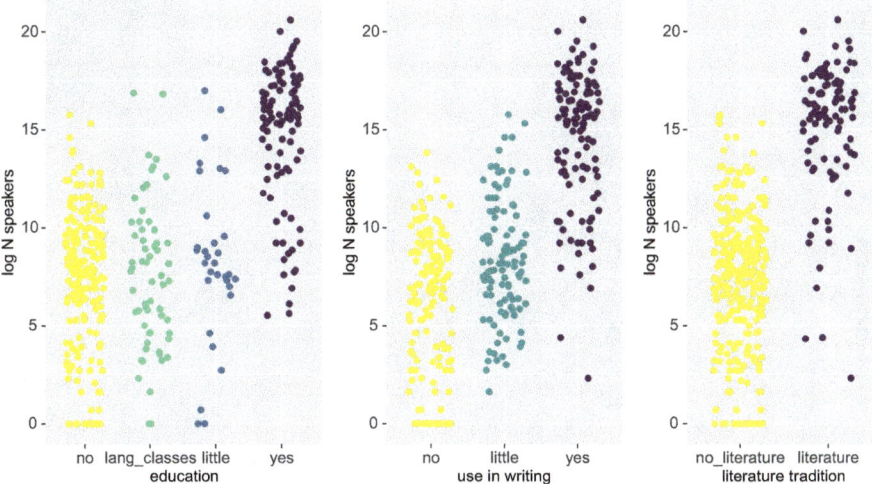

Figure 4: Log N speakers by education (left) & writing (center) & literature (right).

Another bias to consider is the bibliographical bias. To ensure that we do not find a higher number of constructions simply because of an overall more thorough language description, we checked for the association between the number of conditional constructions and the length of grammars measured in number of pages. The association between the two variables can be seen in Figure 5.

The distribution in Figure 5 shows that there does not seem to be any clear correlation between those two variables. Indeed, their correlation is 0.005, which points to virtually no association between the two variables.

5.2 Modelling the number of conditional constructions

The aim of this section is to analyze the effect of various socio-linguistic variables on the number of conditional constructions, taking into account phylogenetic, contact and bibliographical effects. As was mentioned in the previous section, we used grammar length as an approximation of the bibliographical control. For phylogenetic and contact controls, we followed the method described in Guzmán Naranjo & Becker (2021). In order to control for contact effects, we used a two-dimensional Gaussian Process with the coordinates of the languages. The basic idea behind the Gaussian Process term is that languages that are spoken in closer proximity are more likely to influence each other than languages that are spoken with larger distances between them. While this still is a very crude approximation, the Gaussian Process has the advantage that we do not have to assume a constant effect of dis-

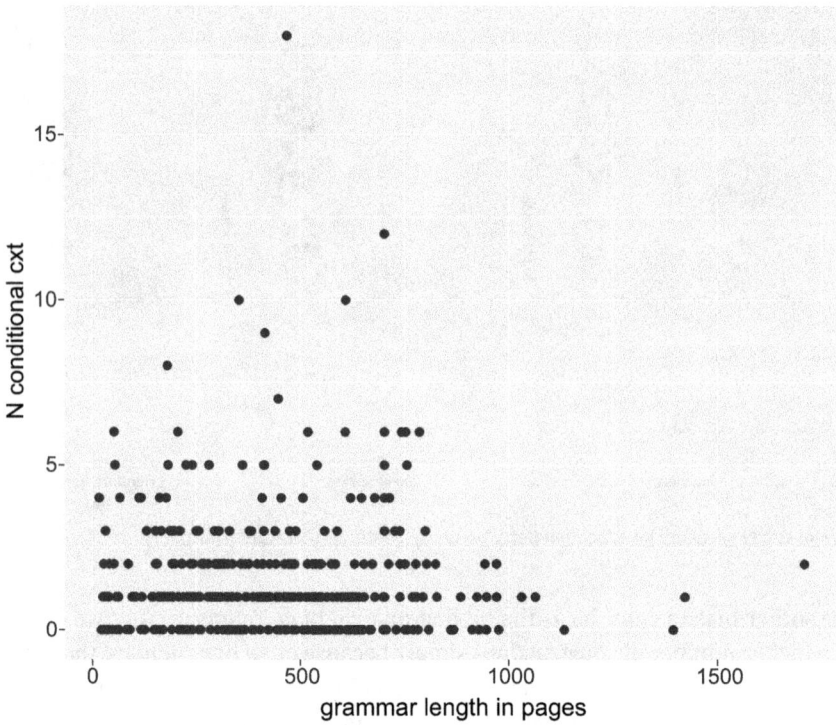

Figure 5: The number of conditional constructions by grammar length.

tance between two languages. In other words, based on the data itself, the model is able to find the distances relevant for contact between languages in a non-linear way.[15] The other additional control consists of a phylogenetic regression term, using the information of the entire phylogenetic trees of the languages to model phylogenetic effects. This method allows us to represent phylogenetic relations in a gradient way instead of grouping languages together at an arbitrarily chosen family level. The model thus forces the estimates of closely related languages to be more similar than those of less closely related languages.

As was shown in the preceding section, our socio-linguistic variables (N speakers, education, writing, literature, multilinguals) are heavily correlated. Because of that, including all relevant variables as predictors can lead to biased estimates in a model, and a more complex procedure of model selection is necessary.

---

[15] This is important, since we know that the distance between two languages in contact depends on e.g. the linguistic density of the area; it differs substantially across different areas of the world.

5 Socio-linguistic effects on conditional constructions: A quantitative typological study — 143

Since we are dealing with count data, we used a Poisson distribution. We fitted two types of regression models with the controls described above.[16] The first model ("controls+5" model) includes all five socio-linguistic predictors as well as the phylogenetic, contact and bibliographical controls. The second type of models each includes one single predictor in addition to the three controls ("controls+1" models). By fitting these two types of models, we can compare the effects of the predictors in the presence of the other predictors (controls+5 model) to their effects in isolation (controls+1 models). This ensures that we do not miss an effect that the predictors could have in the presence of the other predictors and the controls.

Figures 6 to 10 show the conditional effects for the five predictors. Conditional effects correspond to the estimated effects drawn from the model predictions.[17] The red dots or lines represent the mean values of the posterior distribution of the number of conditional constructions, and the error bars or bands show the 95% uncertainty intervals. The uncertainty intervals correspond to the intervals that 95% of the posterior distribution falls into. This means that given the data and the model, we can be 95% certain that the number of conditional markers will fall in that interval. In each of the figures, the left plot shows the conditional effects of the predictor in the controls+5 model, i.e. the one including all five predictors. The right plots all show the conditional effects of the predictor in the controls+1 model, where no additional socio-linguistic predictor is used. As expected, across all five predictors, the controls+1 model with only one of the predictors (right) shows

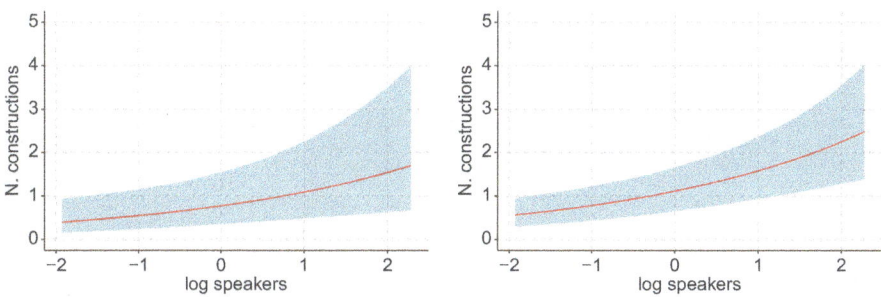

Figure 6: Conditional effects for N_speaker: controls+5 model (left) and controls+1 model (right).

---

16 The models were fitted using Bayesian methods with Stan (Carpenter et al. 2017) and the *brms package* Bürkner 2017) in R (R Core Team 2021). See the supplementary materials for the code.
17 Note that we centered and scaled both the log value of the number of speakers and the grammar length, which is why there are negative values for number of speakers in the conditional effects plot.

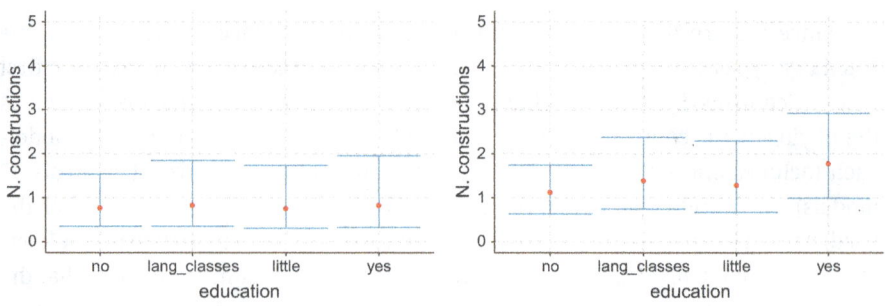

Figure 7: Conditional effects for education: controls+5 model (left) and controls+1 model (right).

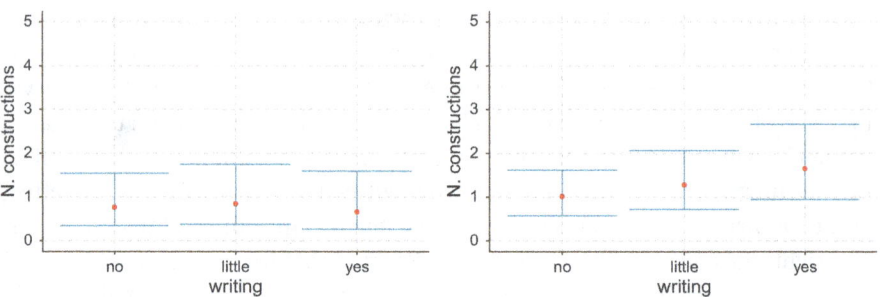

Figure 8: Conditional effects for writing: controls+5 model (left) and controls+1 model (right).

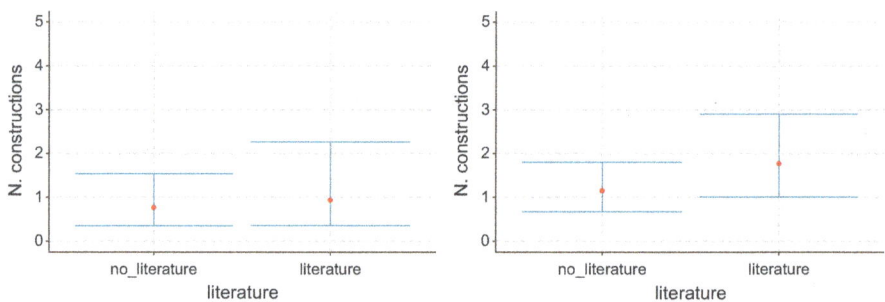

Figure 9: Conditional effects for literature: controls+5 model (left) and controls+1 model (right).

larger effect sizes than the controls+5 model (left) which includes all five socio-linguistic predictors. The important point here is that even though effect sizes are larger, the uncertainty intervals are so large that the models suggest a non-effect. The only predictor which has a weak effect in the presence of the controls is the number of speakers shown in Figure 6. For the other predictors, the uncertainty intervals strongly suggest that there is in fact no effect. We can thus say that, based

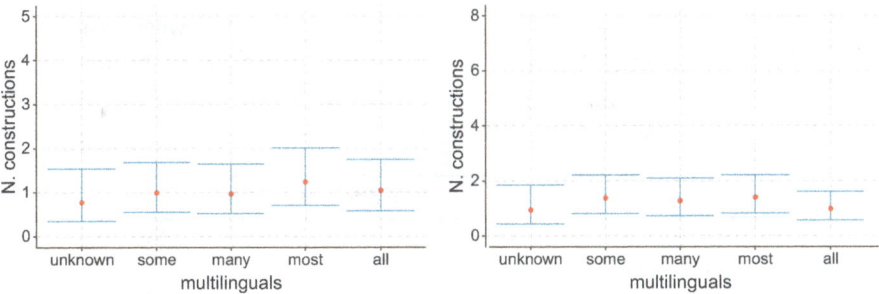

Figure 10: Conditional effects for multilinguals: controls+5 model (left) and controls+1 model (right).

on the conditional effects of the models discussed so far, only the number of speakers appears to have a weak influence on the number of conditional constructions if phylogenetic, contact and bibliographical biases are controlled for. All other socio-linguistic predictors, i.e. the use in education, in writing, the availability of a literature tradition and the proportion of multilingual speakers do not appear to be informative for the number of conditional constructions.

In addition to analyzing the effect sizes of the predictors, we can also assess and compare the predictive power of the models in order to select a final model that is the best one to generalize to new data from our sample. To do so, we compared model performance using 10-fold cross-validation following Vehtari, Gelman & Gabry (2017). 10-fold cross-validation re-fits a model leaving out 10% of the data at a time and then predicts those data points. This allows to evaluate the overall model performance against data which has not been used to train the model. To compare models we use the ELPD value (theoretical expected log pointwise predictive density), which measures how well a model is expected to predict a new dataset. The absolute value itself is not relevant here; it is rather the relative difference of ELPD values that can be used to compare models in terms of their predictive power.

Table 2 shows the comparison of a number of models with different combinations of predictors. The model with neither predictors nor controls (10) serves as a no-information-baseline, showing the predictive power of a model that does not have any information other than the overall distribution of the number of conditional constructions to predict from. The 10 models are ranked from highest (top, 1) to lowest (bottom, 10) predictive power. They are listed with their relative ELPD difference to the best performing model and with the standard error for that difference. The standard error helps to assess the ELPD difference between two models; only a difference larger than twice its standard error is likely to be meaningful.[18]

Table 2: Model comparison (10-fold cross-validation).

		ELPD difference	SE difference
1	phylo + contact + biblio + log N speaker	0.0	0.0
2	phylo + contact + biblio + literature	−4.2	4.1
3	phylo + contact + biblio + education	−4.3	3.9
4	contact	−7.7	8.5
5	phylo + contact + biblio	−9.8	5.3
6	all predictors	−12.7	3.5
7	phylo + contact + biblio + multilinguals	−17.7	4.5
8	phylo + contact + biblio + writing	−18.2	5.6
9	phylo	−53.7	8.8
10	no controls / predictors	−121.5	29.6

The model with the best performance in terms of predictive power is the model with all three controls and only log N speakers as a predictor (1). Adding any other predictor (and combinations thereof) does not seem to improve the model. While adding literature (2) or education (3) leads to better models than the one with controls only (5), the difference is too small for us to conclude that it is not due to random variation. Adding multilinguals (7) or writing (10) results in worse models in terms of performance. As for the socio-linguistic predictors, we can thus conclude that the best predictor is the number of speakers. It is also likely that education and literature only improve the model by virtue of being correlated proxies of the number of speakers.

An interesting point is that the model including the three controls (5) has almost as much predictive power as the model including only contact (4). This strongly points towards the possibility that the main driving force behind the distribution of our data is contact, more so than genetic effects or socio-linguistic factors.

---

[18] A more conservative estimate is that the ELPD difference should be at least four times larger than its standard error because standard error estimates can be biased (cf. Vehtari, Gelman & Gabry 2017).

6 Discussion

As for the relation between the socio-linguistic variables, we showed that the number of speakers, the use of the language in education and in writing as well as the availability of a literature tradition are highly correlated with each other. This made it difficult to determine which variable was the best predictor of the number of conditional constructions in a given language. Our model comparisons in Section 5.2 showed that in our case, the most informative socio-linguistic predictor was the number of speakers. The best-performing model predicted more conditional constructions for languages with higher numbers of speakers, and less constructions for languages with smaller population sizes. Although the effect of the number of speakers was rather weak, the results of this study are somewhat in line with the results from earlier studies, reporting on associations between socio-linguistic factors and the availability of (a high number of) explicit adverbial subordinators (Kortmann 1997: 254–255) and the degree of lexicalization, grammaticalization and explicitness of conditionals (Martowicz 2011: 310). Yet, as the effect was shown to be very weak, we should probably be careful in assuming a strong and direct effect of socio-linguistics factors such as the written use of a language on complex syntax. There may be many single cases to evidence such effects, and we may find a crosslinguistic association in larger samples. Including controls for other biases, however, showed that the effects of socio-linguistic factors on complex (morpho-) syntax such as conditional constructions are probably much less direct and less strong than previously assumed.

One potential issue that is very hard to resolve in practice concerns the time depth of our information. All our variables represent the current situation of the language, and we would have to assume that we can generalize from that to the point in time in which the conditional constructions formed. It is possible that some of the uses of the language (e.g. in the educational system) are too recent in order to lead to changes in the language, and numbers of speakers may have drastically varied for other points in time. Related to that, we do not necessarily know when the constructions in question developed; conditional constructions (and probably also other complex constructions) may also have developed at different points in time in a given language. These issues likely also contribute to the rather weak association that we found, as it is not feasible to obtain accurate historic information on these variables for such a large dataset. A future small-scale study with a subset of the languages of the current sample where more historical data is available may be useful to verify whether or not we can work with such approximations.

Also, finding the strongest effects for number of speakers may be somewhat surprising, given the trend in quantitative socio-typology to move away from population sizes and to focus on the proportions of L2-speakers (Bentz & Winter 2013;

Sinnemäki 2020; Sinnemäki & Di Garbo 2018). This was one of our motivations to include the additional socio-linguistic variables in the first place. Although our data suggests that the number of speakers has a stronger effect on the number of conditional constructions in a language compared to the other variables, we cannot fully discard the latter. Since it was difficult to gather accurate and detailed information on the use of the language and its domains, it could also be the case that our additional socio-linguistic variables proved to be less informative due to the lack of consistent crosslinguistic documentation. It could well be that with more detailed data being available, variables such as the use in writing and the availability of a literature tradition could be included in a more fine-grained manner, which could in turn make it a more important predictor of the linguistic property analyzed. As we used those predictors in the present study, only the number of speakers was a numeric variable, whereas the other four socio-linguistic variables were ordinal or binary, i.e. of a different data type with inherently less information.

The danger of reducing complex socio-linguistic realities to population sizes was also expressed by Trudgill (2011a: 156) in the debate about a relation between population sizes and phoneme inventory sizes:

> My suggestion was very much that the five social factors could be expected, in combination, to have various kinds of influence on phoneme inventory size; it will never, I suggest, be sufficient to look at population figures alone. It is of course not surprising that Pericliev and other statistically-minded linguists have neglected this point and focussed on population size to the exclusion of the other factors, because the other factors are much less readily susceptible to quantification than community population size. But from my perspective this is actually a mistaken exercise – I see no socio-linguistic reason to suppose that population size alone will have any straightforward consequences for phoneme inventory size.

In the present study, we attempted to do justice to this very relevant objection. However, as long as the information on other socio-linguistic variables is not systematically included in language descriptions or linguistic databases such as Glottolog, it may well be that the number of speakers remains the most reliable socio-linguistic variable available on a large scale. Also, including information on the number of speakers is not necessarily a bad practice. In the light of more and more studies that uncover effects of socio-linguistic variables on grammatical structures, quantitative typological studies should include (at the very least) the number of speakers as a control, similarly to how macro areas or language families are generally controlled for in the modelling of typological data.

Besides analyzing the effect of socio-linguistic variables on the number of conditional constructions, we also included statistical controls for potential phylogenetic, contact and bibliographical biases. Our results showed that those control variables are equally important as the socio-linguistic ones. It is also important to note that the contact control seemed to lead to a higher predictive power than the phylogenetic control. In other words, only controlling for language families is not enough – large-scale typological studies should always control for potential contact biases as well. We also saw in Section 5.2 that the effects of the socio-linguistic predictors were stronger in the absence of the controls. This means that part of the information of the socio-linguistic variables is already included in the controls; therefore, it is crucial for socio-typological studies to properly control for such additional effects. Finally, we also included a bibliographical bias control in our models. As far as we are aware, this is not yet a standard in quantitative typology, even though it is very easy to implement. Including such information in future studies can help to better understand the complex interactions of the different extra-linguistic variables.

7 Conclusion

In this paper, we analyzed the effects of several socio-linguistic variables on the number of conditional constructions while controlling for phylogenetic, contact and bibliographical biases. In order to allow for a more variegated picture than "simply" using population size, we included the following additional variables: the use of the language in education and in writing, and the availability of a literature tradition. Our objective was to be able to better explore the effect of written language and a tradition of literature on complex expressions such as conditionals. We chose conditionals as a testing ground because results from previous studies pointed towards an association between the use and availability of written language and number of explicit conditional constructions. Our results, however, suggested only a very weak association with the number of speakers when controlling for phylogenetic, contact and bibliographical biases. We showed that it is important to properly control for phylogenetic and contact relations, as they are at least as important (if not more important) predictors to determine the number of conditional constructions in a given language. We did not find any strong bibliographical bias in our data, but we believe that it is an important and easy-to-implement variable in any quantitative typological study. The other socio-linguistic predictors did not show any effects. We argued that this does not necessarily reflect the inherent nature of the associations; instead, it could well be due to the lack of detailed and consistent information on various socio-linguistic factors on a typological scale. Therefore, closing this information gap should be one of the priorities of of language description and typology.

GLOSSES

1	first person
2	second person
3	third person
ANAPH	anaphoric
APPL	applicative
COND	conditional
DAT	dative
DU	dual
DUB	dubitative
EVID	evidential
EXCL	exclusive
FUT	future
GEN	genitive
HAB	habitual
HON	honorific
IMP	imperative
INCL	inclusive
IRR	irrealis
LOC	locative
M	masculine
MIN	minimal
NEG	negative
NMLZ	nominalizer
O	object
PFV	perfective
PL	plural
POSS	possessive
POT	potential
PROX	proximate
PRS	present
PST	past
PTCP	participle
QUOT	quotative
REL	relativizer
RED	reduplication
S	subject
SBRD	subordinator
SEQ	sequential
SG	singular
SS	same subject
TOP	topic

References

Athanasiadou, Angeliki & René Dirven (eds.). 1997. *On conditionals again*. Amsterdam: Benjamins.
Atoyebi, Joseph Dele. 2010. *A reference grammar of Oko*. Köln: Köppe.
Bakker, Dik. 2010. Language sampling. In Jae Jung Song (ed.), *The Oxford handbook of linguistic typology*, 100–127. Oxford: Oxford University Press.
Bakker, Dik & Ewald Hekking. 2012. Clause combining in Otomi before and after contact with Spanish. *Linguistic Discovery* 10(1). 42–61.
Bentz, Christian & Bodo Winter. 2013. Languages with more second language learners tend to lose nominal case. *Language Dynamics and Change* 3. 1–27.
Biber, Douglas. 1995. *Dimensions of register variation*. Cambridge: Cambridge University Press.
Biber, Douglas. 2006. *University language: a corpus-based study of spoken and written registers*. Amsterdam: Benjamins.
Biber, Douglas. 2009. Are there linguistic consequences of literacy? comparing the potentials of language use in speech and writing. In *The Cambridge Handbook of Literacy*. Cambridge: Cambridge University Press.
Bürkner, Paul-Christian. 2017. Brms: an r package for bayesian multilevel models using stan. *Journal of Statistical Software* 80(1). 1–28.
Carpenter, Bob, Andrew Gelman, Matthew Hoffman, Daniel Lee, Ben Goodrich, Michael Betancourt, Marcus Brubaker, Jiqiang Guo, Peter Li & Allen Riddell. 2017. Stan: A probabilistic programming language. *Journal of Statistical Software* 76(1). 1–32.
Chafe, Wallace. 1982. Integration and involvement in speaking, writing, and oral literature. In Deborah Tannen (ed.), *Spoken and written language: Exploring orality and literacy*, 35–53. Norwood, NJ: Ablex.
Comrie, Bernard. 1986. Conditionals: A typology. In Elizabeth Closs Traugott, Alice Ter Meulen, Judy Snitzer Reilly & Charles A. Ferguson (eds.), *On conditionals*, 77–99. Cambridge: Cambridge University Press.
Dąbrowska, Ewa. 2020. How writing changes language. In Anna Mauranen & Svetlana Vetchinnikova (eds.), *Language Change: The Impact of English as a Lingua Franca*, 75–94. Cambridge: Cambridge University Press.
Dale, Rick & Gary Lupyan. 2012. Understanding the origins of morphological diversity: The linguistic niche hypothesis. *Advances in Complex Systems* 15(3/4). 1150017.
De Busser, Rik & Randy LaPolla (eds.). 2015. *Language structure and environment: Social, cultural, and natural factors*. Amsterdam: Benjamins.
DeLancey, Scott. 2014. Sociolinguistic typology in North East India: A tale of two branches. *Journal of South Asian Languages and Linguistics* 1(1). 59–82.
Deutscher, Guy. 2000. *Syntactic change in Akkadian: The evolution of sentential complementation*. Oxford: Oxford University Press.
Diessel, Holger & Volker Gast. 2012. *Clause linkage in cross-linguistic perspective: data-driven approaches to cross-clausal syntax*. Berlin: De Gruyter Mouton.
Donohue, Mark & Johanna Nichols. 2011. Does phoneme inventory size correlate with population size? *Linguistic Typology* 15(2). 161–170.
Gallagher, Steve & Peirce Baehr. 2005. *Bariai grammar sketch*. Ukarumpa, Papua New Guinea: SIL.
Greenberg, Joseph. 1963. Some universals of grammar with particular reference to the order of meaningful elements. In Joseph Greenberg (ed.), *Universals of language*, 73–113. Cambridge, MA: MIT Press.

Guzmán Naranjo, Matías & Laura Becker. 2021. Statistical bias control in typology. *Linguistic Typology* 26(3). 605–670.
Haiman, John. 1978. Conditionals are topics. *Language* 54(3). 564–589.
Halliday, Michael. 1994. *Spoken and written language*. Oxford: Oxford University Press.
Hammarström, Harald & Mark Donohue. 2014. Some principles on the use of macro-areas in typological comparison. *Language Dynamics and Change* 4(1). 167–187.
Hammarström, Harald, Robert Forkel, Martin Haspelmath & Sebastian Bank. 2021. *Glottolog 4.4*. Leipzig: Max Planck Institute for the Science of Human History.
Hellwig, Birgit. 2011. *A grammar of Goemai*. Berlin: De Gruyter Mouton.
Hetterle, Katja. 2015. *Adverbial clauses in cross-linguistic perspective*. Berlin: De Gruyter Mouton.
Karlsson, Fred, Matti Miestamo & Kaius Sinnemäki. 2008. *Linguistic complexity. Typology, contact, change*. Amsterdam: Benjamins.
Khrakovskij, Viktor S. (ed.). 2005. *Typology of conditional constructions*. München: Lincom Europa.
Kirton, Jean F. & Bella Charlie. 1996. *Further aspects of the grammar of Yanyuwa, Northern Australia*. Canberra: Pacific Linguistics.
Kohlberger, Martin. 2020. *A grammatical description of Shiwiar*. Amsterdam: LOT.
Kortmann, Bernd (ed.). 1997. *Adverbial subordination: A typology and history of adverbial subordinators based on European languages*. Berlin: De Gruyter Mouton.
Kusters, Wouter. 2003. *Linguistic complexity: The influence of social change on verbal inflection*. Utrecht: LOT.
Ladd, D Robert, Seán G Roberts & Dan Dediu. 2015. Correlational studies in typological and historical linguistics. *Annual Review of Linguistics* 1. 221–241.
Loughnane, Robyn. 2009. *A grammar of Oksapmin*. Melbourne: University of Melbourne dissertation.
Lupyan, Gary & Rick Dale. 2010. Language structure is partly determined by social structure. *PLoS ONE* 5(1). e8559.
Lupyan, Gary & Rick Dale. 2016. Why are there different languages? The role of adaptation in linguistic diversity. *Trends in Cognitive Sciences* 20(9). 649–660.
Martowicz, Anna. 2011. *The origin and functioning of circumstantial clause linkers: A crosslinguistic study*. Edinburgh: University of Edinburgh dissertation.
McGregor, William. 1993. *Gunin / Kwini*. München: Lincom Europa.
Meakins, Felicity & Rachel Nordlinger. 2013. *A grammar of Bilinarra, an Australian Aboriginal language of the Northern Territory*. Berlin: De Gruyter Mouton.
Miller, Jim & Regina Weinert. 1998. *Spontaneous spoken language: syntax and discourse*. Oxford: Clarendon.
Mithun, Marianne. 1984. How to avoid subordination. *Annual Meeting of the Berkeley Linguistics Society* 10(0). 493–509.
Moran, Steven, Daniel McCloy & Richard Wright. 2012. Revisiting population size vs. phoneme inventory size. *Language* 88(4). 877–893.
Nettle, Daniel. 2012. Social scale and structural complexity in human languages. *Philosophical Transactions of the Royal Society B: Biological Sciences* 367(1597). 1829–1836.
Ong, Walter. 1982. *Orality and literacy: The technologizing of the word*. New York: Methuen.
Pawley, Andrew & Frances Hodgetts Syder. 1983. Natural selection in syntax: Notes on adaptive variation and change in vernacular and literary grammar. *Journal of Pragmatics* 7(5). 551–579.
Pericliev, Vladimir. 2004. There is no correlation between the size of a community speaking a language and the size of the phonological inventory of that language. *Linguistic Typology* 8(3). 376–383.
Perkins, Revere. 1992. *Deixis, grammar and culture*. Amsterdam: Benjamins.

Podlesskaya, Vera. 2001. Conditional constructions. In Martin Haspelmath, Ekkehard König, Wulf Oesterreicher & Wolfgang Raible (eds.), *Language typology and language universals. An international handbook*, vol. 2, 998–1010. Berlin: De Gruyter Mouton.

R Core Team. 2021. *R: A Language and Environment for Statistical Computing*. Manual. R Foundation for Statistical Computing. Vienna, Austria.

Reali, Florencia, Nick Chater & Morten Christiansen. 2018. Simpler grammar, larger vocabulary: How population size affects language. *Proceedings of the Royal Society B: Biological Sciences* 285(1871). 20172586.

Redeker, Gisela. 1984. On differences between spoken and written language. *Discourse Processes* 7. 43–55.

Sampson, Geoffrey, David Gil & Peter Trudgill (eds.). 2009. *Language complexity as an evolving variable*. Oxford: Oxford University Press.

Sinnemäki, Kaius. 2009. Complexity in core argument marking and population size. In Geoffrey Sampson, David Gil & Peter Trudgill (eds.), *Language complexity as an evolving variable*, 125–140. Oxford: Oxford University Press.

Sinnemäki, Kaius. 2020. Linguistic system and sociolinguistic environment as competing factors in linguistic variation: A typological approach. *Journal of Historical Sociolinguistics* 6(2). 20191010.

Sinnemäki, Kaius & Francesca Di Garbo. 2018. Language structures may adapt to the sociolinguistic environment, but it matters what and how you count: A typological study of verbal and nominal complexity. *Frontiers in Psychology* 9. 1141.

Tannen, Deborah. 1982. Oral and literate strategies in spoken and written narratives. *Language* 58(1). 1–21.

Thompson, Hanne-Ruth. 2012. *Bengali*. Amsterdam: Benjamins.

Thompson, Sandra A., Robert E. Longacre & Shin Ja J. Hwang. 2007. Adverbial clauses. In Timothy Shopen (ed.), *Language typology and syntactic description*, vol. 2, 237–300. Cambridge: Cambridge University Press.

Traugott, Elizabeth Closs. 1985. Conditional markers. In John Haiman (ed.), *Iconicity in syntax*, 289–307. Amsterdam: Benjamins.

Traugott, Elizabeth Closs, Alice Ter Meulen, Judy Snitzer Reilly & Charles A. Ferguson. 1986. *On conditionals*. Cambridge: Cambridge University Press.

Trudgill, Peter. 2004. Linguistic and social typology: The Austronesian migrations and phoneme inventories. *Linguistic Typology* 8(3). 305–320.

Trudgill, Peter. 2008. Linguistic and social typology. In J. K. Chambers, Peter Trudgill & Natalie Schilling-Estes (eds.), *The handbook of language variation and change*, 707–728. London: Wiley.

Trudgill, Peter. 2010. Contact and sociolinguistic typology. In Raymond Hickey (ed.), *The handbook of language contact*, 299–319. New York: Wiley Online Library.

Trudgill, Peter. 2011a. Social structure and phoneme inventories. *Linguistic Typology* 15(2). 155–160.

Trudgill, Peter. 2011b. *Sociolinguistic typology: Social determinants of linguistic complexity*. Oxford: Oxford University Press.

Vehtari, Aki, Andrew Gelman & Jonah Gabry. 2017. Practical Bayesian model evaluation using leave-one-out cross-validation and WAIC. *Statistics and Computing* 27(5). 1413–1432.

Wichmann, Søren, Taraka Rama & Eric W. Holman. 2011. Phonological diversity, word length, and population sizes across languages: The ASJP evidence. *Linguistic Typology* 15(2). 177–197.

Wierzbicka, Anna. 1996. *Semantics: Primes and universals*. Oxford: Oxford University Press.

Wray, Alison & George W. Grace. 2007. The consequences of talking to strangers: Evolutionary corollaries of socio-cultural influences on linguistic form. *Lingua* 117(3). 543–578.

Caterina Mauri, Alessandra Barotto and Simone Mattiola
6 Counterfactual conditionals: Linguistic variation in Italian and beyond

Abstract: The aim of this paper is to integrate the analysis of the intra-linguistic variation attested in the coding of counterfactual conditionals in spoken Italian with a larger cross-linguistic perspective. We start by providing a sociolinguistically-informed discussion of the counterfactual conditional strategies attested in spoken Italian, through a corpus-based analysis. After describing the corpus and the parameters of analysis, we provide a typology of the attested constructions, based on the verbal forms employed for protasis and apodosis, showing that the observed variation goes beyond the representations available in the literature. In particular, we describe the spread of counterfactual imperfective past indicative forms, which are especially frequent in symmetrical constructions and are argued to be associated to lower educational achievements and, to a lesser extent, to informal contexts. We then consider the picture of Italian counterfactual conditionals within a wider perspective, to verify whether the patterns described for Italian follow more general tendencies. After addressing some crucial methodological issues, concerning the problems raised by the integration of a sociolinguistic and a cross-linguistic approach, we argue that Italian data are probably to be analyzed as manifestations of a widespread trend towards the use of symmetrical countefactual constructions on the one hand and the use of past habituals for functions connected to the irrealis domain on the other hand.

1 Introduction

1.1 Counterfactual conditionals: Defining the object of analysis

In the literature, different types of conditional constructions are usually identified on the basis of their factuality status (cf. Zaefferer 1991; Sweetser 1990; Taylor 1997; Thompson et al. 2007), even though the number of types and the terminology tend to vary. Thompson et al. (2007), following Schachter (1971), propose a two-way clas-

---

Caterina Mauri, University of Bologna, e-mail: caterina.mauri@unibo.it
Alessandra Barotto, University of Insubria, e-mail: alessandra.barotto@uninsubria.it
Simone Mattiola, University of Bologna, e-mail: simone.mattiola@unibo.it

sification, distinguishing between *reality* conditionals and *unreality* conditionals. Reality conditionals refer to 'real' present, 'habitual/generic', or past situations, whereas unreality conditionals refer to situations in which we imagine what might be or what might have been (*imaginative* conditionals) or situations in which we predict what will be (*predictive* conditionals). Imaginative conditionals are further subdivided into *hypothetical* (what might be) and *counterfactual* (what might have been) conditionals.

In this paper, we will focus on the latter, thus considering constructions conveying a conditional relation between two events that the speaker acknowledges as not realized.[1] If on the one hand counterfactual conditionals are associated to the domain of so-called irrealis (cf. Elliot 2000; Mauri and Sansò 2012), on the other hand within conditional types they happen to be the most connected to an epistemic condition of certainty, given the fact that both protasis and apodosis are known to have *not* occurred. In all the other types, indeed, the occurrence of the conditional relation is a possibility, though with different probability expectations, and the speaker is necessarily in an epistemic state of uncertainty.

Taylor (1997: 301–302) opposes *counterfactual* conditionals to *factual* conditionals on the one hand and to *hypothetical* conditionals on the other hand (emphasis and italics added):

> In a **factual** conditional, the content of the if-clause is *presumed* to be the case, whilst in a **counterfactual** the content of the if-clause is *taken to be* contrary to fact. Between these categories stand the **hypothetical** conditionals, in which the content of the if-clause is entertained as a *possibility*, neither in accordance with reality, nor necessarily inconsistent with it.

Taylor (1997: 302) notes that is possible to propose a "gradience of epistemic likelihood of the protasis", ranging from factual conditionals, in which the content of the *if*-clause is presumed to be the case at some point as in (1a), to hypothetical conditionals, in which the content of the *if*-clause is entertained as a possibility as shown in (1b), to counterfactuals, in which the content of the *if*-clause is taken to be contrary to fact as shows in (1c).

(1) a. *If he said that (and we heard him), he's a liar.* (factual)
 b. *If he said that (and we don't know if he did), he'd be a liar.* (hypothetical)
 c. *If he had said that (and we know that he didn't), he would be a liar.* (counterfactual)

---

[1] This paper is the result of a continuous collaboration between the authors, who jointly wrote §1. Caterina Mauri is responsible for §2, Alessandra Barotto is responsible for §3.2 and §3.3, Simone Mattiola is responsible for §3.1 and §4.

This notion of "gradience of epistemic likelihood" can be found also in Comrie (1986), who in turn proposes a different approach that rejects classifications based on discrete categories. Comrie suggests that conditional types fall along a continuum of hypotheticality, with reality conditionals at the higher end and counterfactual conditionals at the extreme lower end. This continuum can thus be segmented differently by natural languages, which can express linguistically different distinctions.

Despite the differences that can be found in the literature, counterfactual conditionals are generally considered the type with the lower degree of factuality or likelihood of actualization. Indeed, by definition, counterfactual conditionals represent an interesting conundrum for philosophy and logic, since they "hypothetically present[s] as having happened an event which did not happen" (Lazard 2006: 61).

Interesting tendencies have been identified with regard to counterfactual conditionals in sociolinguistic and typological approaches. For instance, Singaporean English has been observed to have variable marking for counterfactuality (cf. Crewe 1984). Ziegeler (1994) notes that in Singaporean English counterfactual ideas and concepts are encoded through different means (e.g., *wish, suppose/supposing*) and "are not systematically similar to the means of expressing distinctions of temporality and modality in standard varieties" (Ziegeler 1994: 46). Haiman and Kuteva (2002) identify a cross-linguistic tendency for the use of symmetric counterfactual constructions (i.e. having the same verbal forms in protasis and apodosis), especially in nonstandard varieties: according to them, in counterfactuals it is frequent that "the protasis and the apodosis clauses, irrespective of their particular morphological form, have parallel structures" (Haiman and Kuteva 2002:102). They provide examples of nonstandard English, French, Spanish, Bulgarian, Welsh and propose an explanation in terms of iconicity. A recent study dedicated to counterfactuals from a typological perspective is the one by Olguín Martínez and Lester (2021): based on a 106-language sample, they conclude that the symmetry of counterfactuals is dependent on the irrealis *vs.* realis (or unmarked) coding of the protasis. They argue that "symmetrical systems tend to be those that treat the entire counterfactual conditional construction as ungrounded or hypothetical. Asymmetrical systems tend to be those which afford special status (either grounded or unmarked) to the protasis while leaving the apodosis non-actualized" (Olguín Martínez and Lester 2021: 175).

The case of Italian is challenging with respect to the existing literature. In standard Italian, counterfactual conditionals are asymmetric and require the use of a subjunctive form in the protasis and conditional form in the apodosis ((2a), cf. Wiberg 2010). However, as shown in example (2b), another construction is well attested especially in spoken language, in which the past imperfective indicative form is used both in the protasis and in the apodosis. This strategy has been classified as substandard in the literature (see Berruto 1983: 59; Bertinetto 1986; Berretta 1993; Mazzoleni 2013) and appears to be attested mainly for counterfactuals but marginally also for hypothetical conditionals.

(2) Italian
    a. *Se lo avessi spedito stamattina, sarebbe*
        if   it   AUX:SUBJ.PAST:1SG send:PAST.PTCP this.morning AUX:COND:3SG
        arrivato domani.
        arrive:PAST.PTCP:M tomorrow
        'If you had shipped it this morning, it would have arrived tomorrow.'
        (standard Italian)
    b. *Se lo spedivi stamattina arrivava*
        if   it   send:IND.IMPF.PAST:2SG this.morning arrive:IND.IMPF.PAST:3SG
        domani
        tomorrow
        'If you had shipped it this morning, it would have arrived tomorrow.'
        (Mazzoleni 2013: 5)

Apparently, then, Italian shows a standard asymmetric construction (2a) and a nonstandard symmetric construction (2b), in line with Haiman and Kuteva's (2002) observations, but in the latter it involves the use of past imperfective indicative forms, which would be classified by Olguín Martínez and Lester as actualized, thus going against their prediction.

1.2 Aims and overview

The aim of this paper is to provide a corpus-based, sociolinguistically-informed analysis of the intra-linguistic variation attested in the coding of counterfactual conditionals in spoken Italian, focusing on the construction symmetry and the verbal forms employed in protasis and apodosis (§2). The results will be then compared to the wider picture of cross-linguistic variation, in order to understand and explain the features observed in Italian also in the light of typological patterns (§3).

After describing the corpus and the parameters based on which Italian data have been examined (§2.1), in §2.2 we provide a typology of the attested constructions, based on the verbal forms employed for protasis and apodosis, showing that the observed variation goes beyond the binary representations available in the literature (cf. (2)). In particular, we will focus on the spread of counterfactual imperfective past indicative forms, which are especially frequent in symmetrical constructions (as exemplified in (2b)) and will be argued to be associated to lower educational achievements and to informal contexts (§2.3).

In §3 we aim to analyze the rise and spread of symmetric counterfactual constructions in the light of the attested cross-linguistic variation. In §3.1 we address some crucial methodological issues, concerning some problems raised by the integration of the intra-linguistic and inter-linguistic perspectives. A preliminary typological analysis is then described in §3.2, showing that the attested cross-linguistic variation confirms both the widespread use of symmetrical counterfactual constructions, if compared to other types of coniditonals, and the crucial role played by past forms. A focus on the relation between past habituals and irrealis is finally presented in §3.3, with the aim to explain why the symmetric construction of Italian shows an allegedly actualized form, such as the indicative past imperfective, going against Olguín Martínez and Lester's (2021) predictions. Finally, some conclusive remarks will be presented in §4.

2 Counterfactual conditionals: A sociolinguistic approach to spoken Italian

When it comes to counterfactual conditional constructions in spoken Italian, two main strategies have been acknowledged in the literature (Berruto 1983; Bertinetto 1986; Berretta 1993): the strategy that is ascribed to the standard variety includes the use of a past subjunctive form in the protasis and a past conditional in the apodosis (as exemplified in (2a) and (3), henceforth SUB-COND strategy), while the strategy that is ascribed to the nonstandard varieties (substandard, according to Berruto 1983) includes the use of a past imperfective indicative form both in the protasis and in the apodosis (as exemplified in (4) and (5), henceforth DOUBLE-IND strategy).

(3) ParlaTO, PTA18
01   TOI031 *ovviamente se   poi   avesse   partorito*
             obviously   if   then AUX:SUBJ.PAST:3SG   give.birth:PAST.PTCP
             'obviously if then she had'
02   *ci   saremmo   dovuti   fermare in*
             REFL.1PL   AUX:COND:1PL   must:PAST.PTCP:M.PL stop:INF in
             ambulanza
             ambulance
             'we should have stopped in an ambulance'

(4) KIP, TOA3001
01 TO029 *immaginate   così x una   scena del   genere*
         imagine:IMP.2PL so   INDEF scene of.DEF genre
         'Imagine this, a scene like this'
02 TO033 *certo sì che non hai   neanche tempo x x*
         sure yes that NEG have:IND.PRES.2SG   even   time   X X
         cioè   hai capito
         I.mean you know
         'sure yes, that you don't even have time, I mean, you know'
03 TO029 *ah la   rossi ci   **faceva il culo**   soltanto se lo*
         ah DEF Rossi 1PL.DAT scold:IND.IMPF.PAST:3SG   only   if it
         pensavamo   *di fare   una   roba del   genere*
         think:IND.IMPF.PAST:3SG   of do:INF INDEF thing of:DEF genre
         'ah, the Rossi would have scolded us if we had even thought about doing such a thing'

(5) ParlaTO, PTD006
    *se non **trovavo**   niente   m'   **attaccavo***
    if NEG find:IND.IMPF.PAST:1SG   nothing 1SG.ACC   hang:IND.IMPF.PAST:1SG
    al   tram
    to:DEF tram
    'if I had not found anything I could have sung for it'

Both in the SUB-COND and in the DOUBLE-IND construction the verb forms are in the past, but what crucially differentiates the two strategies is the mood. While conditional and subjunctive are typically associated to irrealis and potential states of affairs (cf. Mauri and Sansò 2016), indicative is the mood for realis and actualized events. Furthermore, whereas in the Italian subjunctive and conditional paradigms there is no alternative between perfective and imperfective past forms,[2] in the indicative mood speakers may choose between two perfective past forms, namely simple past (*passato prossimo*) and perfective remote past (*passato remoto*), and one imperfective past form (*imperfetto*),[3] depending on aspectual features and on

---

[2] In the subjunctive paradigm, the choice between so-called 'past subjunctive' (*che abbia partorito*), 'imperfect subjunctive' (*che partorisse*) and 'pluperfect subjunctive' (*che avesse partorito*) in subordinate clauses is governed by the tense selected in the main clause (cf. Bertinetto 1986).

[3] There are also two additional past forms, the first composed by the auxiliary inflected for the remote past followed by a past participle (*trapassato remoto*) and the second composed by the auxiliary inflected for the imperfective past followed by a past participle (*trapassato prossimo*). They are used to refer to some anteriority relation with respect to a past event.

how recent is the past event they are referring to. The indicative forms attested in counterfactual strategies show a specific type of past, namely imperfective.

Indicative imperfective past (henceforth PastImpf indicative) is employed in spoken Italian mainly for descriptions in the past, to refer to states of affairs taking place at the same (past) time, and to denote habitual states or events in the past. In addition to these three uses, it is the only indicative past form that also shows functions related to the domain of imagination, possibility or courtesy, where subjunctive or conditional would be required. We find it for example in fictitious contexts, as in (6) where it is introduced by *come se* 'as if', or in children's fantasy games.

(6) ParlaTO, PTB007
01 TOI021 *no perché tanto s(e) andavi a*
 no because anyway if go:IND.IMPF.PAST:2SG to
 chiederglieli
 ask:3SG.DAT:3PL.OBJ.M.PL
 'no, because anyway if you went to ask them [the money] to them'
02 *è è è* **come se tu dovevi**
 it.is it.is it.is as if you must:IND.IMPF.PAST:2SG
 'it's as if you had to'
03 *dare tu dei soldi a loro e non che lo(ro)*
 give you INDEF.PL money to them and NEG that they
 'it was you who had to give money to them and not them who'
04 **dovevano** *darli a te*
 must:IND.IMPF.PAST:3PL give:3PL.OBJ.M to you
 'had to give money to you'

PastImpf indicative is also widespread in polite requests, instead of the conditional: in (7) we note, at the beginning of an interview, the expression *volevo sapere* 'I wanted to know', which clearly does not refer to an earlier stage, but replaces the conditional *vorrei sapere* 'I would like to know'. These uses derive from an anaphoric reference to some previous context motivating the speech act, which thus appears to be justified.

(7) KIP, BOD2016
01 BO119 *okay*
 okay
 'okay'
02 *ci siamo*
 LOC be:IND.PRES.1PL
 'we're here'

03   *allora ciao*
                 then   hello
                 'hello then'

04   BO120   *ciao*
                 hello
                 'hello'

05   BO119   *tu   ti   chiami*
                 you   REFL.2SG   call:IND.PRES.2SG
                 'your name is'

06   BO120   *francesco*
                 Francesco
                 'Francesco'

07   BO119   *okay franci   allora   ehm*
                 okay Franci   so   ehm
                 'okay Franci, so ehm'

08   **volevo**   **sapere** eh   *tu*   *vivi*   *qua*
                 want:IND.IMPF.PAST:3PL   know   eh   you   live:IND.PRES.2SG   here
                 a   bologna
                 in   Bologna
                 'I wanted to know eh you live here in Bologna'

09   BO120   *sì*
                 yes
                 'yes'

The use of PastImpf indicative in counterfactual conditionals (as in (4) and (5)) has been analyzed as a typical feature of nonstandard varieties, not only for Italian (Berruto 1983; Bertinetto 1986; Berretta 1993), but also for other languages (cf. Ziegeler 1994 for Singapore English). However, little if any corpus evidence has been provided in the literature.

In order to fill this gap, in this section we will provide a systematic analysis of how counterfactual conditionals are conveyed in spoken Italian, based on the KIParla corpus (Mauri et al. 2019). Since this resource allows to access metadata regarding both speakers and conversations, we will connect the variation observed in the data with two main sociolinguistic variables, namely (i) conversation formality on the one hand, and (ii) speakers' educational achievement on the other hand. We aim to understand whether the strategies attested in spoken Italian to express counterfactual conditionals have a non-random distribution across the diaphasic and diastratic axes, thus showing preferential associations with specific registers and/or speakers with particular educational achievements.

2.1 Data and parameters of analysis

The KIParla corpus of spoken Italian (Mauri et al. 2019) is a resource characterized by a modular and incremental structure. At present (July 2022), it consists of two modules, which together amount to 1.125.996 words (ca. 110 hours of recording).[4] For both modules, it is possible to search transcriptions aligned with the audio files, accessing the metadata regarding both speakers and conversations.

The KIP module consists of 70 hours of recorded speech collected in Turin and Bologna between 2016 and 2019. It has relatively few internal diastratic variation, if we consider the educational degree, because it only comprises conversations by speakers with higher educational achievement (university students and professors). On the contrary, it shows a good range of diaphasic variation, including both informal interaction (free conversation, semi-structured interviews) and formal interaction (lessons, exams, office hours). The ParlaTO module consists of 40 hours of recorded speech collected in Turin between 2018 and 2019. It has no internal diaphasic variation because it includes only informal interaction (semi-structured interviews). It shows instead a good degree of diastratic variation, including speakers with varying levels of educational achievement and varying employment. The joint analysis of the modules allows to integrate both diastratic and diaphasic variation in the study.

For the aim of this research, we extracted and annotated all the conditional constructions introduced by *se* 'if' attested in the KIP and in ParlaTO modules (tot. 1856 occurrences), out of which we identified 104 occurrences of counterfactual conditional constructions that constitute our dataset. We considered both linguistic and extra-linguistic parameters, which will be employed as predictors in §2.3. The list of parameters is summarized in Table 1:

Table 1: Linguistic and extra-linguistic parameters.

Linguistic parameters		Extra-linguistic parameters	
(i)	Verb form for protasis and apodosis	(v)	Formality of the interaction
(ii)	Symmetry of the construction	(vi)	Speakers' educational achievement
(iii)	Order of protasis and apodosis	(vii)	Speakers' age
(iv)	Subject agreement on the verbs	(viii)	Speakers' origin

As far as the linguistic predictors are concerned, we annotated the (i) verb form used for protasis and apodosis (past conditional, past subjunctive or PastImpf indicative),

---

4 The KIParla Corpus is freely available at www.kiparla.it

(ii) the symmetry *vs.* asymmetry of the construction (same verbal form or different verb form for protasis and apodosis), (iii) the respective order of protasis and apodosis (preposed *vs.* post-posed protasis) and (iv) the subject agreement of the two verb forms (1s/p, 2s/p, 3s/p, impersonal, for both verbs in protasis and apodosis).

As for the extra-linguistic predictors, we considered the (v) formality of the interaction (formal *vs.* informal), (vi) the educational achievement of the speaker (higher *vs.* lower), (vii) age, (viii) origin. Formality and educational achievement have been considered as binary parameters (Table 2).

Table 2: Interaction types and formality; degree type and educational achievement.

FORMALITY OF THE INTERACTION	
Formal interaction	**Informal interaction**
– lessons – exams – office hours	– free conversations – semi-structured interviews
LEVEL OF EDUCATIONAL ACHIEVEMENT	
Lower educational achievement	**Higher educational achievement**
– elementary degree – middle school degree – secondary school degree and working	– secondary school degree and attending university – university degree – phd

Lectures, exams and office hours were classified as formal interactions, while free conversation and semi-structured interviews were classified as informal interactions. Speakers who studied until elementary or middle school were grouped with working graduates, while university students were assimilated to graduates and PhDs.

2.2 Counterfactual constructions in Spoken Italian

If we consider the 104 occurrences of counterfactual constructions attested in ca. 110 hours of spontaneous speech, we first of all observe a greater variation of constructions than the SUB-COND *vs.* DOUBLE-IMPF opposition, exemplified in (3) and (4)-(5), respectively. As shown by Figure 1, the category OTHER indeed corresponds to roughly one fourth of the total (23%) and in the ParlaTO module it reaches the 27% of occurrences, exceeding the percentage of SUB-COND strategies (see Figure 3). Let us first of all see what types of strategies fall within the label OTHER.

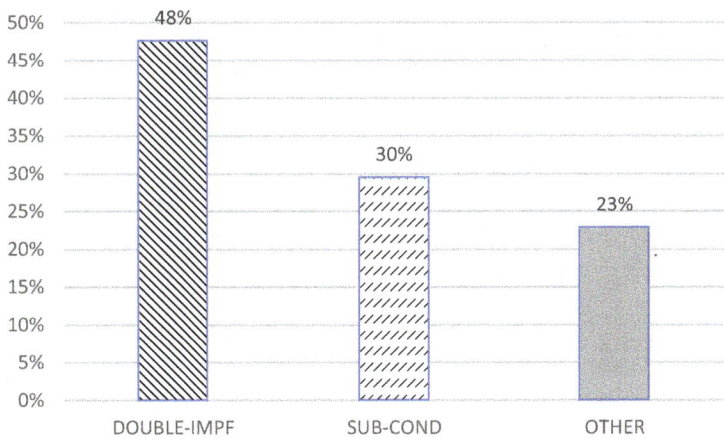

Figure 1: Counterfactual strategies in the KIParla Corpus.

Under the label OTHER we find several combinations of verbal forms, each of which has a low occurrence rate. Yet, the relatively high ratio of strategies deviating from what is expected is revealing of the high degree of fluctuation attested in the expression of counterfactual conditionals, which are rare enough to leave room for a certain indecision by speakers, who frequently find themselves self-repairing in the search for the 'correct' verb form to use. We can observe an example of self-repair in (9) (line 03): the speaker starts to utter the standard conditional form in the apodosis (*ci sar. . .*) but then stops and self-repairs (*cioè* 'I mean') by choosing the PastImpf indicative *potevo*. In this case, the speaker is uncertain in using the standard strategy and decides to recur the indicative.

Under OTHER we find the following combinations (a-c):[5]

a) <u>PastImpf indicative</u> in the protasis + <u>past conditional</u> in the apodosis, exemplified in (8):

(8) ParlaTO, PTA001
01 TOI001 *eh beh tutto è nato da bambino quando mia madre mi disse un giorno che*
'everything started when I was a child, when my mother once told me that'

---

5 In these examples, glosses are provided only for the relevant verb forms.

02   **se   tifavo**   juve   mio   padre   non
     if   support:IND.IMPF.PAST:1SG   Juventus my   father NEG
     sarebbe
     AUX:COND.3SG
     'if I had supported Juventus, my father would'
03   **tornato**   più   a   casa
     come.back.PAST.PTCP:M.SG   anymore   to   home
     'never have returned home'

b) <u>Past subjunctive</u> in the protasis + <u>PastImpf indicative</u> in the apodosis, exemplified in (9):

(9) KIP, BOD2008
01 BO053 [...] magari   se   qualcuno   m'   **avesse**   un
               maybe   if   someone   1SG.ACC   AUX:SUBJ.PAST:3SG   a
         minimo   spinto
         bit   push:PAST.PTCP
         '[...] maybe if someone had pushed me a bit'
02   e   m'   **avesse**   **detto**   dai   oh
         and   1SG.ACC   AUX:SUBJ.PAST:3SG   say:PAST.PTCP   come.on   oh
         andiamo
         let's.go
         'and had told me *come on oh let's go*'
03   probabilmente   ci   sar   cioè   **potevo**
         probably   LOC   AUX:COND.1SG   I.mean   can:IND.IMPF.PAST:1SG
         anche   andarci
         also   go.there
         'probably I would... I mean I could have gone'

c) <u>Indicative present or simple past</u> in the protasis + <u>PastImpf indicative</u> in the apodosis, exemplified in (10):

(10) ParlaTO, PTB014
     Se   **vado**   dritto   **andavo**   a   san peyre
     if   go:IND.PRES:1SG   straight   go IND.IMPF.PAST:1SG   to   San Peyre
     'if I had gone straight I would have arrived to San Payre'

The only symmetric strategy attested in the KIParla is the DOUBLE-IMPF construction exemplified in (4) and (5), while SUB-COND and OTHER strategies are all asymmetric, since they show different verbal forms for protasis and apodosis. Furthermore, the great majority (87%) of the counterfactual constructions attested in our dataset show the protasis preceding the apodosis. If we consider the relative frequencies of person agreements on the two verb forms (Figure 2), we see that 3rd person singular is the most frequent one in both protasis and apodosis, immediately followed by 1st person singular and 3rd person plural. The use of impersonal forms is more frequent in the apodosis, while 2nd person singular is easier to find in the protasis (in some cases, it is a generic 2nd person, not referring to the actual interlocutor).

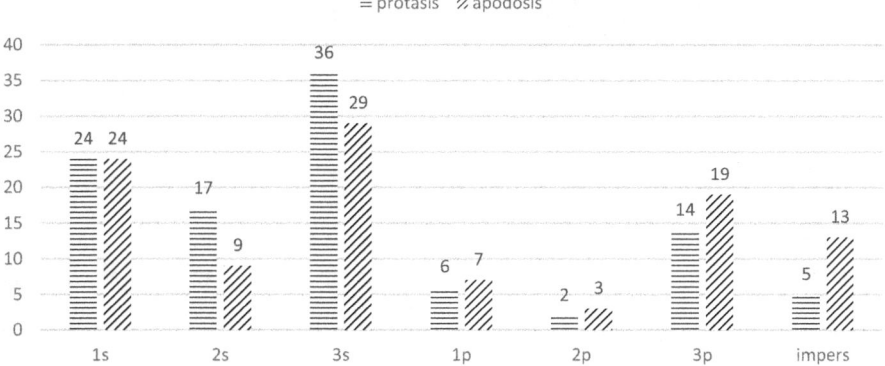

Figure 2: Subject agreement on verb forms in protasis and apodosis (in this chart, the absolute numbers are provided).

Going back to the general picture represented in Figure 1, we can see that the DOUBLE-IMPF strategy is by far the most frequently attested in the KIParla corpus, covering almost half of the total occurrences, while the SUB-COND strategy covers one third of the total. Given the different socio-demographic composition of the two KIParla modules, it is worth considering the distribution of the attested counterfactual constructions separately in the KIP and ParlaTO corpora.

Figure 3 indeed shows that there is a significant difference between the two corpora, especially concerning the respective ratio of the SUB-COND and DOUBLE-IMPF strategies: in the KIP module the SUB-COND construction is the most frequently used one (47%), immediately followed by the DOUBLE-IMPF one (40%), while in the ParlaTO module we observe a much higher percentage for the DOUBLE-IMPF strategy, attested in the 57% of the cases, and an extremely lower percentage for the SUB-COND strategy, which is attested only the 16% of the occurrences, and is exceeded by OTHER strategies, characterized by the use of PastImpf indicative in just one of the linked clauses (cf. (8)-(10)).

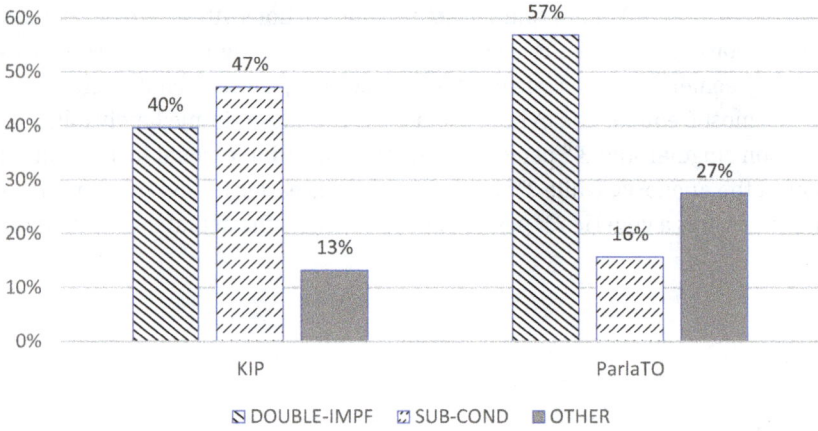

Figure 3: Counterfactual strategies in the KIP and ParlaTO modules.[6]

Since the use of PastImpf indicative characterizes both DOUBLE-IMPF and OTHER strategies, we can oppose the use of the SUB-COND strategy to all the strategies including at least one PastImpf indicative form (in the protasis, in the apodosis, in both – henceforth IND-IMPF), as shown in Figure 4:

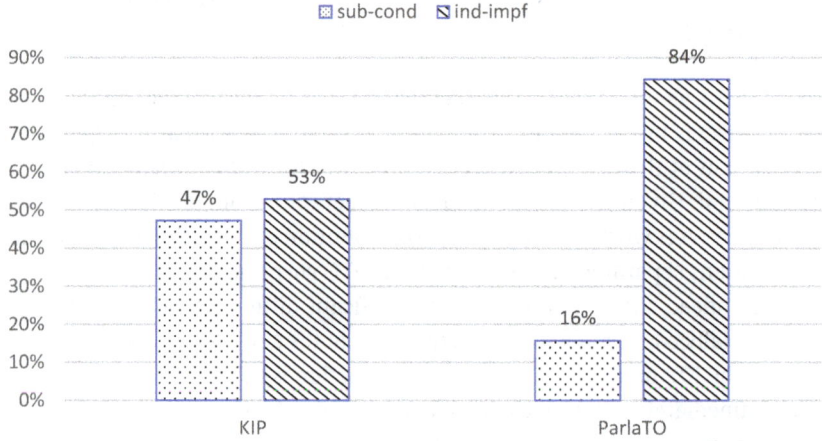

Figure 4: Distribution of SUB-COND and IND-IMPF strategies in KIP and ParlaTO.[7]

---

[6] According to the Chi-Square Test, the result is significant at $p < .01^{**}$, with $p =< 0.002094$, N=104.
[7] According to the Fisher exact test, the result is significant at $p < .001^{***}$, with $p =< 0.0007$, N=104.

As Figure 4 shows, the frequency of IND-IMPF counterfactual strategies, that is, strategies including one or two PastImpf indicative forms, is significantly higher in the ParlaTO corpus (84%), where the use of the SUB-COND strategy does not reach the 20% of the cases. Conversely, in the KIP corpus the distribution of SUB-COND strategies and IND-IMPF strategies is roughly even. How can we explain these data?

Given the socio-demographic differences between the two corpora (cf. §2.1), we can hypothesize that the most frequent use of the SUB-COND strategy in KIP is due to the higher ratio of educated speakers in that module and that, on the other hand, the greater frequency of the IND-IMPF strategy in the ParlaTO is due to the presence of a grater variation on the diastratic dimension, which would favor traits of popular and substandard Italian (Berruto 2012: 129; cf. Berruto 2014; Cerruti 2018). However, the difference between the two modules lies also on the diaphasic axis, so we cannot exclude that the differences are due to the presence of formal interactions in the KIP, which are instead completely absent in the ParlaTO, that is, to a difference of register. In the next section, we will answer this question, analyzing the distribution of the different constructions according to the parameters adopted in this study, focusing on the formality of the interaction (diaphasic indicator) and the educational qualification (diastratic indicator).

2.3 Diaphasic and diastratic variation

To test the statistical significance of our data, we employed the Random Forest method. The Random Forest method is useful in studies where the dataset is small, but the number of predictors is large. It is made up of several inference trees, therefore it has better predictive accuracy than a single tree, allowing to rank the predictors (Tagliamonte and Baayen 2012; Levshina 2015).

Let us first consider the distribution of SUB-COND vs. IND-IMPF constructions. As Figure 5 shows, the use of SUB-COND strategy reveals a significant relation with both the level of formality and the degree of the speakers' educational achievement, i.e. the two dots located in the right-hand part of the plot.

If we employ the Fisher Exact Test to verify the respective significance of these two predictors, we observe that the factor having the highest predictive value ($p < .001^{***}$) is the degree of educational achievement. In other words, speakers with higher educational achievement (i.e. higher on the diastratic axis) are more likely to convey counterfactual conditionals by means of past subjunctive followed by past conditional, than speakers with lower educational achievement (Figure 6). The latter tend to use instead counterfactual strategies including an ImpfPast indicative form (i.e. IND-IMPF strategy).

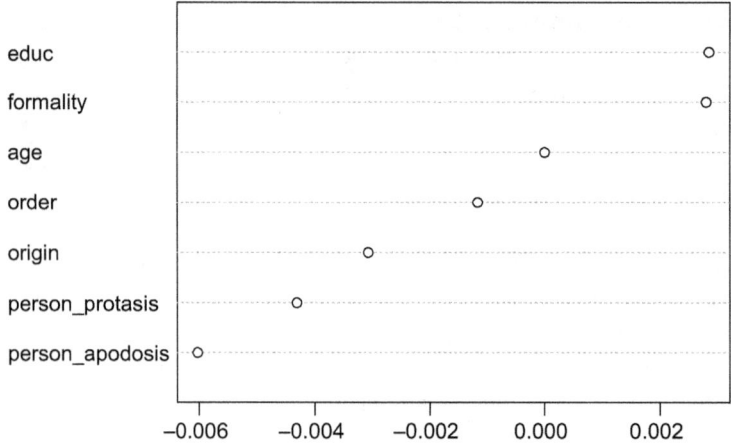

Figure 5: Plot ranking linguistic and extra-linguistic predictors for the occurrence of SUB-COND counterfactual strategies.[8]

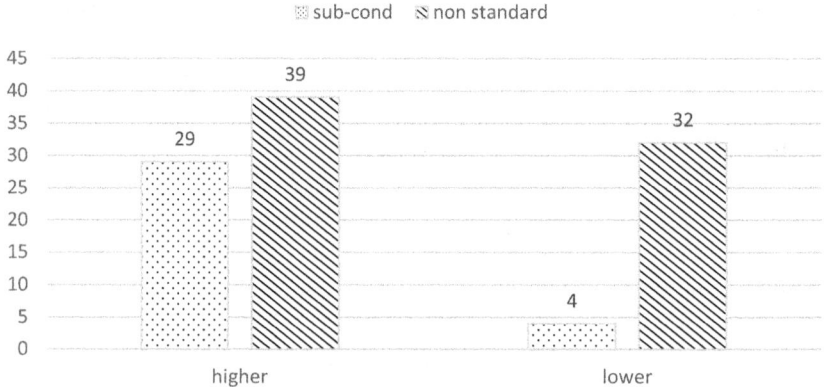

Figure 6: Use of SUB-COND and IND-IMPF strategies by higher educated and lower educated speakers (in this chart, the absolute numbers are provided).[9]

The formality of the interaction has a lower predictive value (p<.01**), but still significantly correlates with the type of counterfactual construction being used. As shown by Figure 7, in informal contexts, speakers are more likely to employ IND-IMPF strategies, thus recurring to counterfactual indicative forms, than in formal contexts, where the SUB-COND strategy prevails.

---

8 The model validity is excellent (Goodness of fit): C= 0.8014385.
9 According to the Fisher exact test, the result is significant at p < .001***, with p=< 0.0009, N=104.

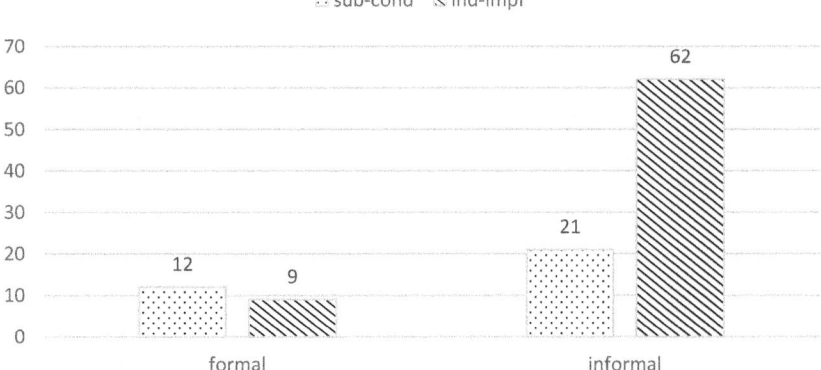

Figure 7: Use of SUB-COND and IND-IMPF strategies in formal and informal interactions speakers (in this chart, the absolute numbers are provided).[10]

Up to now, we opposed the SUB-COND strategy to the IND-IMPF strategy, which includes all the constructions in which a counterfactual PastImpf indicative occurs, either in isolation, followed or preceded by a subjunctive or a conditional, or in combination with another PastImpf indicative form. If we focus on the latter case, namely on the symmetric DOUBLE-IND strategy, we note that it does not show a significant correlation with formality, but only with the degree of educational achievement, which is the only predictor having statistical significance (Figure 8).

However, even for the degree of educational achievement, the Fisher Exact Test provides a low value of significance (p < .05*), correlating the use of the double PastImpf indicative to speakers with lower educational achievements, as shown in Figure 9. In the light of what we have seen in this section, we can confirm that the distribution of the different counterfactual strategies attested in Spoken Italian is mainly affected by the diastratic variation, in particular it can be linked to the level of educational achievement: a lower level of educational achievement strongly correlates with the use of counterfactual indicative forms (ImpfPast indicative), both in symmetric and asymmetric constructions, whereas a higher level of educational achievement correlates with the use of the asymmetric SUB-COND strategy, with past subjunctive in the protasis and past conditional in the apodosis. The use of counterfactual indicative also correlates, though with a weaker significance, to informal interactions, in which also educated speakers tend to recur to IND-IMPF strategies. We could not find such strong correlations explaining the distribution of symmetric constructions with double ImpfPast indicative (DOUBLE-IND), which appear to be

---

10 According to the Fisher exact test, the result is significant at p < .01**, with p=< 0.0082, N=104.

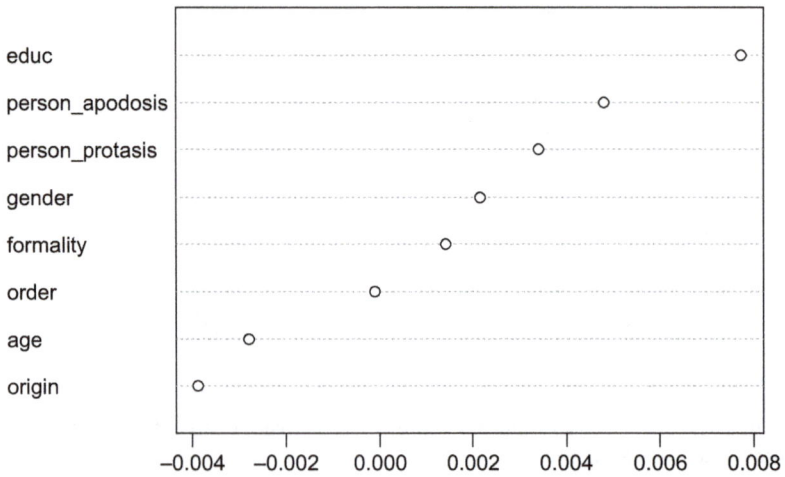

Figure 8: Plot ranking linguistic and extra-linguistic predictors for the occurrence of DOUBLE-IND counterfactual strategies.[11]

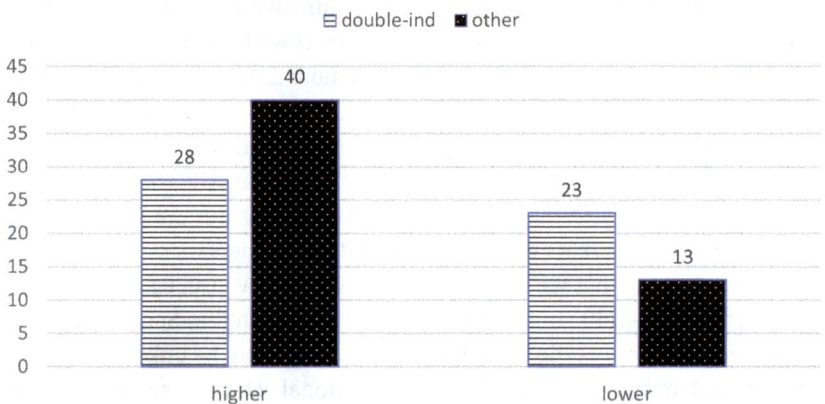

Figure 9: Use of DOUBLE-IND strategy by higher educated and lower educated speakers (in this chart, the absolute numbers are provided).[12]

only weakly connected with a lower degree of educational achievement. In other words, speakers appear to use the symmetric construction with double indicative widely in discourse, both in formal and informal contexts, though with a greater frequency in diastratically lower productions.

---

[11] The model validity is excellent (Goodness of fit): C= 0.8047273.
[12] According to the Fisher exact test, the result is significant at p < .05*, with p=< 0.0389, N=104.

To sum up, the observed correlations are revealing of a gradual expansion of counterfactual ImpfPast indicative in Italian, especially in symmetric constructions, starting from the lower varieties. How can we interpret these data in the light of a larger typological picture? Is the use of symmetric counterfactual constructions a recurrent tendency across languages, as argued by Haiman and Kuteva (2002), which may explain why the use of DOUBLE-IND in Italian appears to be widespread and not closely associated to a specific diastratic or diaphasic variety? And how frequent is the use of an indicative past imperfective form, typically employed for past habitual events and narrations, for counterfactual conditionals? In the next section, we will consider the attested cross-linguistic variation in the expression of counterfactual conditionals, looking for a larger picture, in the light of which the intra-linguistic variation described for Italian could be further explained.

3 Beyond Italian: Cross-linguistic variation in the expression of counterfactual conditionals

3.1 From sociolinguistics to typology: Methodological issues

As already argued in §1, we aim to integrate the analysis of the intra-linguistic variation attested in spoken Italian within a larger picture, to explain the rise and spread of nonstandard conditional constructions in the light of the attested cross-linguistic variation, verifying to what extent the patterns described for Italian in §2 follow or deviate from some general tendencies. In particular, we will focus on two aspects: the use of a symmetrical strategy for counterfactual conditionals and the use of a past imperfective form with counterfactual functions. To achieve this goal, we will compare the results obtained in the sociolinguistic analysis with both the variation attested in a variety 223-language sample and the existing typological literature on counterfactuals.

For each counterfactual construction, we focused on the verbal forms attested (or described) in counterfactual protasis and apodosis, their TAM properties, and on the asymmetry *vs.* symmetry of the construction. In addition, we monitored the presence of an independent dedicated counterfactual marker. For every language we further coded data regarding the strategies attested for hypothetical conditionals (cf. §1.1 for a definition).

We collected data from a variety sample composed of 223 languages (Mattiola 2020, freely available at http://amsacta.unibo.it/6504/). A variety sample is a language sample that aims at maximizing linguistic variety leaving aside (at least partially) the perfect statistical balancing. This kind of sample perfectly fits with our final goal of verifying the existence of cross-linguistic patterns and tendencies. The criteria adopted by Mattiola (2020) to build this sample are the Diversity Value technique (Rijkhoff et al. 1993; Rijkhoff and Bakker 1998) and Ethnologue 2018 language classification (Lewis et al. 2018), as described in Table A.1 published as Appendix 1 in Miestamo et al. (2016) (for further information on this variety sample, see Mattiola 2020).

Our final sample is composed of 203 languages (see Appendix 1) because for some languages we could not have access to some grammatical descriptions. Among these 203 languages, we were able to identify information on counterfactual conditionals for 98 languages.

Before discussing the results of our analysis, it is necessary to highlight some crucial methodological issues that may have affected the study, which act as a big *caveat* in the interpretation of what we found. First of all, our sociolinguistic analysis focuses on spoken language data, without considering data from written language. A crucial issue with typological data from descriptive grammars is that in many cases we have no information about the specific variety that the grammar is describing: is it spoken language? Are we dealing with translations of written data? Field linguists indeed often recur to translations of sacred text (written), elicitation and translations (e.g., translations of sentences created ad hoc), monologues (songs, myths and traditional stories; or personal stories) which cannot account for the intra-linguistic variation of a language.

Furthermore, the sociolinguistic analysis of Italian is based on spontaneous speech, in both formal and informal contexts, but the data we usually find within descriptive grammars are hardly of this type. Most typological data discussed in descriptive grammars do likely not come from spontaneous interactions, but rather from more "controlled" situations, such as the ones involving the use of elicitation tecniques. This can be so for a number of possible reasons, e.g., the interviewer is not part of the informants' community, or there may be an asymmetrical relationship between them, just to name two examples. As a consequence, our typological findings are likely biased towards less spontaneous and informal data.

For an integrated approach as the one we are adopting in this study, the lack of information regarding the specific language variety being described, and, more in general, the sociolinguistically relevant properties of the recorded speakers and contexts of interaction, constitutes a crucial problem.

In comparing Italian data with the attested typological variation, we realized that in most cases we could not know what type of data we were dealing with. Yet, comparability is a crucial issue in typological research: it is indeed extremely important to compare data that can be thought as expressions of the (near-)same varieties, or at least varieties that can be compared among them. Unfortunately, though, data from descriptive grammars usually do not provide information regarding the diastratic and/or diaphasic characterization of the data being described. We believe indeed that it would be important to re-discuss the overall methodology that stands behind fieldwork in order to make the data as informative as possible both for typologically-oriented and sociolinguistically-oriented comparative investigations, fostering the use of spontaneous interactions where possible.

3.2 Typological variation: Focus on symmetry and past tense

Data from the typological sample first of all confirm that the use of a symmetrical counterfactual construction is a widespread phenomenon, allowing us to analyze the DOUBLE-IND Italian strategy as a manifestation of a recurrent construction type. Out of the 98 languages in the sample that show some overtly TAM coding to mark counterfactual, 22 languages indeed show a symmetrical strategy, employing the same verb form for protasis and apodosis. For instance, in Mehek (Sepik), counterfactual conditionals are marked with the conditional morpheme -*na* in both protasis and apodosis,[13] while in Warupu (Skou), they are marked with the irrealis marker *n*-, as shown in the following examples.

(11) Mehek (Sepik; Hatfield 2016: 373)
loko   wate-na   on   ya-na-yun
rain   rain.fall-COND 1SG come-COND-1SG
'If it had rained, I would have come.'

(12) Warupu (Skou; Corris 2005: 340)
Kanro   n-e-n-ikoko,   bârém   beya   n-o-te-ni   vai.
shoes   IRR-1SG.F-1SG.F-wear   thorn   NEG   IRR-3SG.F-shoot-1SG.F   POL
'If I had worn shoes, the thorn would not have spiked me.'

The presence of symmetrical strategies is even more significant if we compare counterfactual to hypothetical conditionals, as shown in Figure 10. While asymmetrical constructions are the most common strategy attested in our sample, symmetrical constructions are more frequent for counterfactual conditionals than for possibility conditionals, to the point of representing almost a quarter of the languages.

---

[13] Interestingly, if the result is a negative outcome, the verb in the apodosis doesn't have the conditional marker but only the negative makers -*nak* (Hatfield 2016: 372).

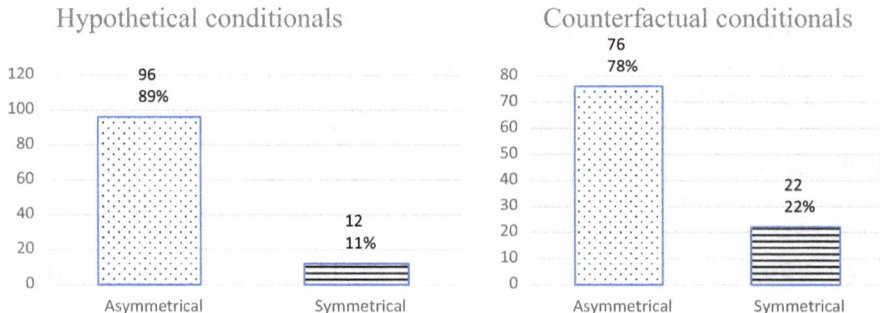

Figure 10: Symmetrical and asymmetrical constructions in counterfactual and hypothetical conditionals: data from the variety language sample.[14]

If we focus on the verbal forms employed in symmetrical constructions, interesting data emerge also from the range of markers used in both protasis and apodosis, as shown in Figure 11.

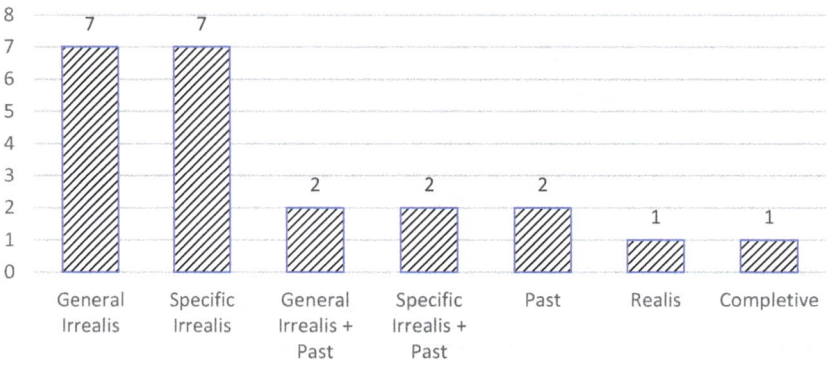

Figure 11: TAM markers in symmetrical counterfactual constructions.

Most symmetrical counterfactual constructions are marked by general irrealis markers, employed to denote a wide range of unrealized situations, or specific irrealis markers, typically mood markers employed for a restricted range of unrealized or potential situations:[15] in other words, in line with the results of Olguín Martínez

---

14 According to the Fisher exact test, the result is significant at p<.05*, with p=< 0.0381, N=205.
15 For a detailed discussion on the notion of irrealis and general irrealis marker, see Mauri and Sansò (2012). We classified as specific irrealis markers all those mood markers employed for a restricted range of unrealized or potential situations, including e.g., conditional markers, subjunctive mood markers, potential markers, hypothetical markers. There is great variation with respect to

and Lester's (2021) study, if the same verb form is used for protasis and apodosis, it is likely to be a form encoding some general or specific irrealis function (this is the case for 18 out of 22 languages showing symmetrical counterfactual strategies, cf. Figure 11). This could be due to an iconic mechanism, motivated by the double contrary-to-fact status of the two linked states of affairs. Whereas it is true that also for counterfactual conditionals the linked states of affairs stand in a consequential relation, which is proper of all conditional relations and motivates the use of asymmetric constructions, it is also true that in counterfactuals the consequential relation is less salient, in that it does not affect the truth values of the states of affairs, which are equally claimed to be contrary to fact.

In six languages, we observe the use of a symmetrical construction employing some past tense marker, either alone, as in example (13) from Tboli (Austronesian), or together with a specific or general irrealis marker, as in example (14) from Wardaman (Australian). In Tboli both protasis and apodosis are marked with *deng* which encodes a completed action:

(13) Tboli (Austronesian; Porter 1977: 153)
 Ke **deng** *ton-em* # **deng** *benli-hem* # *ne.*
 if PAST saw-you it PAST buy-you it now
 'If you had seen it, you would have bought it.' (The fact is he hadn't seen it so he didn't buy it).

(14) Wardaman (Australian; Merlan 1994: 188)
 *bujun yi-ngan-wo-**ndi** ma-jad yi-ngong-wo-**ndi***
 if IRR-3SG/1SG-give-PAST MA-big.ABS IRR-2SG/1SG-give-PAST
 ngawun, ma-jad-wagbawun
 no MA-big-lacking.ABS
 'If he had given me a lot, I would have given you [some], [but] no, [he did not] give a lot.'

The role of past tense in the coding of counterfactual conditionals appears to be far from marginal, especially if we consider also asymmetrical constructions: out of the 98 languages in the sample that show some overtly TAM coding to mark counterfactual, 28 languages use past tense to mark at least one between the protasis and the apodosis. For instance, in Jamsay Dogon (Dogon), counterfactuals are char-

---

the types of markers and the terminology through which they are referred to in descriptive grammars. This classification does not imply any theoretical claim, but is adopted here for descriptive purposes.

acterized by the use of the past particle jì:ⁿ in both protasis and apodosis,[16] while in Kayardild (Australian) the past suffix -*jarra* only marks the verb in the protasis, as shown in the following examples:

(15) Jamsay Dogon (Dogon; Heath 2008: 585)
 nì-dî:ⁿ yĕs-sà-bà   jì:ⁿ   dèy, bé   wɔ̌:-m̀   jì:ⁿ
 here   come-RESLT-3PL.SBJ **PAST** if 3PL.OBJ kill.IMPF-1SG.SBJ **PAST**
 'If they had come here, I'd have killed them.'

(16) Kayardild (Australian; Evans 1995: 260–261)
 ngada   kurri-***jarra***   bukaji-na   dii-n-kina,   ngada   raa-ju
 1SG.NOM see-**PAST**   seahawk-M.ABL   sit-N-M.ABL   1SG.NOM   spear-POT
 'If I had seen a sea-hawk landing, I'd have speared it.'

Interestingly, in most cases, past tense is used in both protasis and apodosis (17 languages out of 28 languages employing past markers in counterfactual constructions). This does not necessarily imply that the construction is symmetrical: in some cases, even though the past marking is present in both verbs, protasis and apodosis can show other differences in the TAM marking. For instance, in Palauan (Austronesian), protasis and apodosis are both marked with the past tense, but the protasis also takes the hypothetical verb form (Josephs 1975: 447). This is the kind of situation that we also find in the SUB-COND strategy described in §2.2 for Italian, where the protasis is marked with a past subjunctive form and the apodosis with a past conditional form (i.e., forms that we would have classified here as specific irrealis).

The relevance of past tense for the coding of counterfactual conditionals is confirmed by the literature. This phenomenon has indeed been analyzed in different languages, such as in English by Langacker (1978), Proto-Uto-Aztecan (Steele 1975), Korean and Japanese (Han 1996; Cho 1997). Other studies have adopted a cross-linguistic perspective, noting that the presence of past tense markers for counterfactual situations is widespread in the world's languages (James 1982, Fleischman 1989). The correlation between past tense and counterfactuality was mostly explained by means of the so-called *past-as-unreal hypothesis* (cf. Dahl 1997). This hypothesis has different formulations, but the basic common premises are the following: past situations are perceived as distant from the realm of immediate realis (i.e., here-and-now) to the point of potentially being associated with unactualized situations (e.g., future events), and thus with irrealis. Therefore, it is argued that, due to some conceptual similarity, past tense markers can extend their functional

---

[16] Occasionally jì:ⁿ can be omitted in the protasis (Heath 2008: 585).

domain to irrealis functions, like counterfactuality (cf. Steele 1975; Langacker 1978; James 1982; among others).

Dahl (1997: 100) points out a major problem with this theory, that is, the fact that the "marking of irreality/hypotheticality is rarely done by means of a past tense alone but normally by the combination of a past tense with something else". This "something else" is typically a marker with some modal meaning or a fully-fledged irrealis marker, as we saw for Wardaman in (14), which uses an irrealis prefix *yi-* and a past suffix *-ndi* to mark both verbs in protasis and apodosis.

In the light of the cross-linguistic variation attested in our language sample, we may thus analyze the two most frequent counterfactual strategies attested in Italian (SUB-COND and DOUBLE-IND) as manifestations of construction types that are recurrent across languages: the SUB-COND construction is an asymmetrical strategy composed of two different specific irrealis verb forms (subjunctive and conditional) inflected for the past tense; the DOUBLE-IND construction is a symmetrical strategy involving the use of a past indicative form, i.e., a verbal form that does *not* encode an irrealis function (cf. example (11) from Tboli). We may further add that also the OTHER constructions types, namely asymmetrical strategies involving the use of the past imperfective indicative form in just one of the linked clauses (cf. §2.2), follow a pattern that is attested in our languages sample, as exemplified by Kayardild (example (16)).

As argued in §2, the PastImpf indicative verbal form employed in nonstandard Italian strategies (that is, DOUBLE-IND and OTHER strategies), is characterized by an imperfective aspect which makes it the preferred strategy to refer to past habitual situations and narrations in the past. Yet, the data we collected in our typological sample do not provide clear patterns regarding aspectual features of the attested forms. Interestingly, as we saw in examples (4) and (5), PastImpf indicative is attested in Italian for a larger range of functions than the sole reference to past imperfective events, including unrealized situations such as fictitious or imaginary situations. May this function widening towards the irrealis domain play a role in the increasing use of PastImpf indicative in asymmetrical and symmetrical counterfactual strategies? The cross-linguistic patterns observed in our sample seem to suggest that the frequency of the DOUBLE-IND construction could be connected at least partially to the acquisition of a more general irrealis function by the PastImpf indicative form.

3.3 Past habituals as counterfactuals: A recurrent pattern

On the basis of a sample of a few dozen languages and focusing only on the marking of the counterfactual apodosis, Lazard (1998, 2006: 62) argues that the combination of some irrealis morpheme and a past tense morpheme is likely the more frequent strategy in the languages of the world. However, he notes that the 'irrealis' morpheme "may assume different shades of meaning" (Lazard 2006: 62). So, for instance, in some languages, the irrealis morpheme is a future marker, like in Ditidaht (17), while in other languages we can find a desiderative, debitive, or potential marker, like in the case of Yimas (18).

(17) Ditidaht (Wakashan; James 1982: 382 citing Klokeid 1976: 31)
('oyi) kab'at'p it qwiy s,
(if) know **PAST** specifier I
hitaqaya 'i:k ibt s 'a:bay 'oyi
come **future PAST** I yesterday time-marker
'If I had known (it), then I would have come yesterday'

(18) Yimas (Ramu-Lower Sepik; Foley 1991: 265)
ampi**-ya-**ntuk**-mp-n   ant-ka-wa-**ntut
POT-come-**RM.PAST**-VII.SG-OBL   **POT**-1SG.A-go-**RM.PAST**
'If those two had come, I would have gone.'

Another frequent situation noted by Lazard is the usage of past subjunctive or optative forms, which convey non-actualized events. This is, for instance, what we find in the counterfactual construction that is ascribed to the standard variety of Italian which, as noted in §2, uses a past subjunctive form in the protasis and a past conditional in the apodosis:

(19) Italian (Indo-European)
ovviamente se poi avesse partorito
obviously if then AUX:SUBJ.PAST:3SG give.birth:PAST.PTCP
'obviously if then she had'
ci saremmo dovuti fermare in ambulanza
REFL.1PL AUX:COND:1PL must:PAST.PTCP:M.PL stop:INF in ambulance
'we should have stopped in an ambulance' [ParlaTO, PTA18]

Finally, Lazard also notes that, in some cases, counterfactuality can be marked by a combination of past marking with habitual marking. Habitual, however, does not refer to irrealis or unactualized situations, it rather conveys an aspectual value typically associated to actualized events: according to Comrie (1976: 30), habitual marking indeed denotes "any situation that can be protracted sufficiently in time, or that can be iterated a sufficient number of times over a long enough period". The correlation between habituals and counterfactual conditionals is addressed by Iatridou (2000, 2010), according to whom imperfective marking, or more precisely, habitual marking, is a crucial grammatical ingredient of counterfactual conditionals.

Italian is thus not isolate, in recurring to a past habitual form to express counterfactuality, but this strategy appears to be attested in several languages, independently of genealogical or areal proximity. For example, in Turkish, the apodosis of counterfactual conditionals is marked by combination of the aorist morpheme -(ı)r and the past tense morpheme -dı, as shown in the following example:

(20) Turkish (Turkic; Caro 2012: 20)
Bir kedi-m ol-sa o-nu okşa-r, sev-er, o-ndan can
one cat-1SG be-COND it-ACC pet-AOR love-AOR it-ABL soul
al-ır-dı-m
take-AOR-PAST-1SG
'If I had had a cat, I would have petted it, loved it, and taken its life.'

The Turkish aorist denotes continuing activity and can be used to mark habitual actions (but interestingly, aorist forms never express progressive aspect, Göksel and Kerslake 2005: 290; Lewis 1985: 117), for instance:

(21) Turkish (Turkic; Göksel and Kerslake 2005: 290)
O zamanlarda Mehmet çok sigara iç-er-di
that at.times Mehmet very cigarette smoke-AOR-PAST.COP
'At that time Mehmet smoked/used to smoke a lot/Mehmet was a heavy smoker.'

The use of past habitual to mark counterfactual conditionals seems also quite frequent in Indo-Iranian languages (Lazard 1975, 1998). For instance, Pashto (Indo-European) has a "past narrative" formed by the particle bə and a finite verb form in the past, which usually expresses habitual events in the past but can also be used in the apodosis of counterfactual conditionals (Grjunberg 1987: 158–159; Vydrin 2011: 73), as shown in the following examples.

(22) Pashto (Indo-European; adapted from Vydrin 2011: 73)
ka obo waṛay wāy no
if water take.PTCP.PAST.M be.OPT then
mor ta bə me dzawāb war-kāwə
mother POST PRTCL 1SG.ENCL.OBL answer PREF-do.PAST.3SG.M
'If the water had taken me, what would I have said to my mother.'

In Yaghnobi (Indo-European), counterfactuality is conveyed by the imperfect (also labelled as "past continuous"), which is formed by the verbal stem with special person/number affixes and the prefix *a-*, and is mainly used to convey past habitual (Xromov 1972: 32; Vydrin 2011: 72):

(23) Yaghnobi (Indo-European; Vydrin 2011: 72 citing Xromov 1972: 32)
 a. *ax sahár ajáxišt*
  he early.morning wake.up.IMPF.3SG
  'He used to wake up early in the morning.'
 b. *agár divári anížimišt aláks, yarm.avírimišt*
  if outside go.out.IMPF.1SG walk.IMPF get.warm.IMPF.1SG
  'If I had gone out for a walk, I would have gotten warm.'

Beyond Indo-Iranian languages, the correlation between counterfactual and habituality in the past is also attested in languages scattered in different areas of the world. Example (24) shows the case of Lavukaleve, an isolate language spoken in the Solomon Islands:

(24) Lavukaleve (Isolate; Terrill 2003: 436)
 aka kini tataveua-re-a la o-e-sia-le
 then ACT be.missing-NF-SG.F SG.F.ART 3SG.F.OBJ-SBD-do-POT
 o-vea ma-me.
 3SG.F.OBJ-know 3PL.SBJ-HAB
 'If [anything] was missing, they would have known it (but it never was).'

Counterfactual conditionals in Lavukaleve are formed by marking the protasis with the potential marker *-le* while the apodosis appears to be marked by the habitual marker *-me*. The absence of a past tense marker is due to the fact that Lavukaleve has explicit ways to mark present and future tense but has no past tense marker (Terrill 2003: 324, 328).

Finally, another interesting case is the one found in Goemai (Afro-Asiatic). In Goemai counterfactual conditionals, the protasis is marked with the conditional marker *lá* while the apodosis is marked with the irrealis marker *t'óng* ('would'). Moreover, both protasis and apodosis are also marked with the morpheme *d'ín* which "probably originated in the close past tense particle *d'ín*" (Hellwig 2011: 463), as shown in (25).[17]

---

[17] The conditional marker *lá* and the irrealis marker *t'òng* are used also to mark other types of conditionals (Hellwig 2011: 457).

(25) Goemai (Afro-Asiatic; Hellwig 2011: 463)
Óerém   mén   **d'ín**   lá   là   hèn=**d'ìn**   **t'óng**
beans   1PL.POSS   **PAST.CL**   **COND** produce(SG)   1SG.S=**PAST.CL** **IRR**
póe   yòe (...)
give   2SGF.O
'If our beans had produced (fruit) (but they didn't), I would have given (the fruit) (to) you.'

Interestingly, both *lá* and *t'óng* can also function as habitual markers, often used together in the same sentence, as shown in the following example:[18]

(26) Goemai (Afro-Asiatic; Hellwig 2011: 243)
[hèn]*_A_*=dók   **lá**   t'ém   [póe   gòe]*_o_*   **t'óng**   gòepé (...)
1SG.S=RM.PAST   **HAB**   tell   give   2SG.M.O   **HAB**   THAT/WHEN
'in the past, I used to tell you that (...)'

To sum up, we can say that despite not being irrealis marker in a narrow sense, habitual markers seem to play an interesting role in the coding of counterfactuality, regardless of specific linguistic families or areas. More generally, the connection between habitual and the irrealis domain has been discussed by various scholars in typology (see for instance Lazard 1975; Chung and Timberlake 1985; Givón 1994; Elliott 2000), in the light of the fact that many languages of the world use the same construction to express both actualized habitual and unactualized events. This connection has been mainly explained postulating a conceptual connection between habituality and irrealis due to the fact that habitual does not relate to a specific action, but rather to a tendency to act. For instance, Givón (1994: 322) argues that habitual is a "hybrid modality" since it shares some features of realis (higher assertive certainty) and some of irrealis (lack of specific temporal reference, lack of specific evidence, non-referring NPs under its scope).

Based on a typological survey, Cristofaro (2004) further notes that "the association between habituality and irrealis takes place for past rather than present habituality" (Cristofaro 2004: 261). In other words, if habituality in the present is expressed through the same construction used also to express any type of unactualized situation, then it is also used to express habituality in the past, however the reverse does not hold (Cristofaro 2004: 262–263). To explain this tendency, Cristofaro argues that once again there is a conceptual correlation between irrealis and

---

[18] Hellwig (2011: 324) comments on this functional extension by proposing the following diachronic development CONDITIONAL > HABITUAL.

habituality in the past (as opposed to habituality in the present). Indeed, as already noted, both habitual events and past events individually have been connected conceptually to unactualized events (irrealis). Therefore, not only habituality in the past relates to situations that do not pertain to any specific actualized instance of the relevant event (like habitual in general), but it also does not hold in the present anymore and is thus perceived as far from the realm of immediate realis (like past in general).

As already noted, in Italian, indicative imperfective past is employed to denote habitual states or events in the past, but it has also developed sort-of irrealis functions related to the domain of imagination or possibility, where the subjunctive or conditional would be required in the standard variety, thus confirming Cristofaro's (2004) account. From this point of view, the widespread use of PastImpf indicative in Italian counterfactual constructions (as in (4), repeated here for convenience as (27)) is to be interpreted as the spread of a strategy employed for both past habituality and unactualized events.

(27) Italian (Indo-European)
      Ah   la   rossi   ci   **faceva il culo**   soltanto se lo
      ah   DEF   Rossi   1PL.DAT   scold:IND.IMPF.PAST:3SG   only   if it
      pensavamo
      think:IND.IMPF.PAST:3SG
      'ah, the Rossi would have scolded us if we had even thought' [KIP, TOA3001]

In the light of the typological variation discussed in this section, Italian is thus not to be seen as an exception to Olguín Martínez and Lester's (2021) predictions: the observed preference for the double use of PastImpf indicative, leading to a symmetric counterfactual strategy, indeed confirms the cross-linguistic tendency towards counterfactual constructions in which both protasis and apodosis are marked as unactualized.

4 Concluding remarks

In this contribution, our main aim was to provide a corpus-based and sociolinguistically-oriented description of counterfactual conditional constructions in spoken Italian, comparing our findings to the more general cross-linguistic variation.

First, through a corpus-based analysis, we identified DOUBLE-IMPF and SUB-COND as the most frequent strategies in Italian to convey counterfactual conditionals, as expected, but alongside these, we were also able to identify some other strategies that are not well depicted in the literature, such as PastImpf Indicative + Past Conditional or Past Subjunctive + PastImpf Indicative. The distribution of the two main strategies is furthermore not balanced in the two corpora examined: while in the KIP corpus, SUB-COND was the most frequent strategy (even though with close percentages), DOUBLE-IMPF was by the far the most frequent in the ParlaTO corpus. The picture is even more unbalanced if we compare the distribution of SUB-COND to the distribution of IND-IMPF strategies, that is, strategies employing PastImpf indicative either in the protasis or in protasis, or in both. On the one hand, KIP shows almost the same percentage of SUB-COND and IND-IMPF strategies (47% *vs.* 53%), on the other hand ParlaTO shows a clear preference for IND-IMPF (84% *vs.* 16%). The reasons behind this imbalance can be traced back to sociolinguistic variables relating to the diaphasic and diastratic axes. SUB-COND strategies are clearly preferred by speakers with higher education and also in formal interactions, while conversely IND-IMPF strategies (especially the symmetric ones) are more often found in informal situations and used by less educated speakers, but also not fully dis-preferred in high communicative situations and by highly educated speakers, too. We can thus presume that counterfactual ImpfPast indicative is expanding its domain of application from nonstandard varieties of Italian.

Second, we tested our language-specific findings from a larger cross-linguistic perspective. From a methodological point of view, integrating data from sociolinguistic and from cross-linguistic investigations is far from being an easy task. The two kinds of data are indeed quite different from each other and can hardly be compared, at least until grammars will thoroughly provide sociolinguistic information about the variety described within. However, the information grammars offer can be useful as well, even though to a lesser extent, as a general litmus test for language-specific linguistic change. Our cross-linguistic investigation of counterfactual conditional constructions confirmed the tendency of Italian strategies for a preference for displaying symmetrical constructions and the frequent presence of past verbal forms.

Finally, we provided some typological considerations on why past imperfective forms are attested to express irrealis functions, such as counterfactual conditional. The fact that past imperfective forms are very often used to convey past habituality indeed leads them to lose their reference to individual and specific situations. Due to this weakening of their referential force, past habituals become conceptually similar to unactualized events, frequently extending their functional domain to irrealis functions. Under this respect, we propose to analyze the spread of a past imperfective form to counterfactual functions in Italian as a manifestation of this more general tendency.

Abbreviations

1,2,3	1st, 2nd, 3rd person
A	subject of transitive verb
ABL	ablative
ABS	absolutive
ACC	accusative
ACT	action (particle)
AOR	aorist
ART	definite article
AUX	auxiliary
CL	close (Past)
COND	conditional
COP	copula
DAT	dative
DEF	definite
ENCL	enclitic
F	feminine
HAB	habitual
IMP	imperative
IMPF	imperfective
IND	indicative
INDEF	indefinite
INF	infinitive
IRR	irrealis
LOC	locative
M	masculine
MA	adjective class
N	nominalization
NEG	negative
NF	non-Finite (verb suffix)
NOM	nominative
O	object pronoun
OBJ	object
OBL	oblique
OPT	optative
PAST	past
PL	plural
POL	polite
POSS	possessive
POST	postposition
POT	potential
PREF	prefix
PRES	present
PRTCL	particle
PTCP	participle

REFL	reflexive
RM	remote (Past)
RESLT	resultative
S	subject (intransitive and transitive) pronoun
SBJ	subject
SBD	subordinate (verb prefix)
SG	singular
SUBJ	subjunctive
VII	class VII

Appendix 1: 203-language sample (based on Mattiola 2020)

Language	Macro-area	Family	Sub-classification
Tamasheq	Africa	Afro-Asiatic	Berber
Buwal	Africa	Afro-Asiatic	Chadic
Goemai	Africa	Afro-Asiatic	Chadic
Hamer-Banna	Africa	Afro-Asiatic	Omotic
Kabuverdianu	Africa	Creole	Portuguese
Khwedam	Africa	Khoe-Kwadi (Khoisan)	Khoe
Bullom So	Africa	Niger-Congo	Atlantic-Congo
Noone	Africa	Niger-Congo	Atlantic-Congo
Chuwabu	Africa	Niger-Congo	Atlantic-Congo
Eton	Africa	Niger-Congo	Atlantic-Congo
Ngemba	Africa	Niger-Congo	Atlantic-Congo
Mungbam	Africa	Niger-Congo	Atlantic-Congo
Obolo	Africa	Niger-Congo	Atlantic-Congo
Yoruba	Africa	Niger-Congo	Atlantic-Congo
Mbembe Tigon	Africa	Niger-Congo	Atlantic-Congo
Cicipu	Africa	Niger-Congo	Atlantic-Congo
Gbari	Africa	Niger-Congo	Atlantic-Congo
Lijili	Africa	Niger-Congo	Atlantic-Congo
Jamsay Dogon	Africa	Niger-Congo	Atlantic-Congo
Godié	Africa	Niger-Congo	Atlantic-Congo
Ikposo	Africa	Niger-Congo	Atlantic-Congo
Mundang	Africa	Niger-Congo	Atlantic-Congo
Bouna Kulango	Africa	Niger-Congo	Atlantic-Congo
Lumun	Africa	Niger-Congo	Kordofanian
Maan	Africa	Niger-Congo	Mande

(continued)

Language	Macro-area	Family	Sub-classification
Ik	Africa	Nilo-Saharan	Kuliak
Zaghawa	Africa	Nilo-Saharan	Saharan
Gumuz	Africa	Nilo-Saharan	Satellite-Core
Lango	Africa	Nilo-Saharan	Satellite-Core
Ma'di	Africa	Nilo-Saharan	Satellite-Core
Koyra Chiini Songhay	Africa	Nilo-Saharan	Songhay
N|u	Africa	Tuu	!Ui
Gooniyandi	Australia & New Guinea	Australian	Bunaban
Wardaman	Australia & New Guinea	Australian	Gunwingguan
Bardi	Australia & New Guinea	Australian	Nyulnyulan
Warungu	Australia & New Guinea	Australian	Pama-Nyungan
Kayardild	Australia & New Guinea	Australian	Tangic
Worrorra	Australia & New Guinea	Australian	Worrorran
Garrwa	Australia & New Guinea	Australian	Yanyi
Imonda	Australia & New Guinea	Border	Waris
Lavukaleve	Australia & New Guinea	Central Solomons	//
Moskona	Australia & New Guinea	East Bird's Head-Sentani	East Bird's Head
Mali	Australia & New Guinea	East New Britain	Baining
Kuot	Australia & New Guinea	Isolate	//
Kwomtari	Australia & New Guinea	Kwomtari	Nuclear Kwomtari
Warembori	Australia & New Guinea	Lower Mamberamo	//
Yaul	Australia & New Guinea	Mongol-Langam	//
Nimboran	Australia & New Guinea	Nimboran	//
Rotokas	Australia & New Guinea	North Bougainville	Rotokas
Motu, Hiri	Australia & New Guinea	Pidgin	Motu
Yimas	Australia & New Guinea	Ramu-Lower Sepik	Lower Sepik
Mehek	Australia & New Guinea	Sepik	Tama
Warupu	Australia & New Guinea	Skou	Skou-Serra-Piore
Siwai	Australia & New Guinea	South Bouginville	Buin
Wára	Australia & New Guinea	South-Central Papuan	Morehead-Upper Maro
Yapunda	Australia & New Guinea	Torricelli	Wapei-Palei
Asmat, Central	Australia & New Guinea	Trans-New Guinea	Amsat-Kamoro
Menya	Australia & New Guinea	Trans-New Guinea	Angan
Duna	Australia & New Guinea	Trans-New Guinea	Duna-Bogaya
Kwewa, East	Australia & New Guinea	Trans-New Guinea	Engan
Yagaria	Australia & New Guinea	Trans-New Guinea	Kainantu-Goroka
Mauwake	Australia & New Guinea	Trans-New Guinea	Madang
Marind	Australia & New Guinea	Trans-New Guinea	Marind

(continued)

Language	Macro-area	Family	Sub-classification
Mian	Australia & New Guinea	Trans-New Guinea	Ok-Awyu
Oksapmin	Australia & New Guinea	Trans-New Guinea	Oksapmin
Daga	Australia & New Guinea	Trans-New Guinea	Southeast Papuan
Makasae	Australia & New Guinea	Trans-New Guinea	West
Tidore	Australia & New Guinea	West Papuan	North Halmahera
Aka-Jeru	Eurasia	Andamanese	Great Andamanese
Chukchi	Eurasia	Chukotko-Kamchatkan	Northern
Armenian	Eurasia	Indo-European	Armenian
Lithuanian	Eurasia	Indo-European	Balto-Slavic
Breton	Eurasia	Indo-European	Celtic
Frisian, Northern	Eurasia	Indo-European	Germanic
Greek	Eurasia	Indo-European	Greek
Palula	Eurasia	Indo-European	Indo-Iranian
Catalan	Eurasia	Indo-European	Italic
Basque	Eurasia	Isolate	//
Burushaski	Eurasia	Isolate	//
Laz	Eurasia	Kartvelian	Zan
Korean	Eurasia	Koreanic	//
Bonan	Eurasia	Mongolic	Eastern
Hinukh	Eurasia	North Caucasian	East Caucasian
Udihe	Eurasia	Tungusic	Southern
Uyghur	Eurasia	Turkic	Eastern
Nenets	Eurasia	Uralic	Samoyed
Ket	Eurasia	Yeniseian	//
Southern Yukaghir	Eurasia	Yukaghir	//
Arapaho	North America	Algic	Algonquian
Pawnee	North America	Caddoan	Caddoan
Ineseño	North America	Chumash	Chumashan
Havasupai-Walapai-Yavapai	North America	Cochimí-Yuman	Yuman
Yupik, Central	North America	Eskimo-Aleut	Eskimo
Chilcotin	North America	Eyak-Athabaskan	Athabaskan
Haida, Northern/Southern	North America	Haida	//
Huave, San Dioniso del Mar	North America	Huavean	//
Karok	North America	Isolate	//
Klamath-Modoc	North America	Isolate	//

(continued)

Language	Macro-area	Family	Sub-classification
Kutenai	North America	Isolate	//
Molale	North America	Isolate	//
Tonkawa	North America	Isolate	//
Washo	North America	Isolate	//
Yuchi	North America	Isolate	//
Zuni	North America	Isolate	//
Kiowa	North America	Kiowa-Tanoan	//
Maidu, Northwest	North America	Maiduan	//
Itza'	North America	Mayan	Yucatecan-Core Mayan
Ohlone, Southern	North America	Miwok-Costanoan	Costanoan
Popoluca, Highland	North America	Mixe-Zoquean	Zoquean
Muskogee	North America	Muskogean	Muskogean
Zapotec, Coatlán / San Baltazar Loxicha	North America	Otomanguean	Eastern Otomanguean
Pomo, Southern	North America	Pomoan	Western
Yakama	North America	Sahaptian	Sahaptin
Halkomelem	North America	Salish	Central Salish
Hidatsan	North America	Siouan-Catawban	Siouan
Purepecha, Western Highland	North America	Tarascan	//
Chontal, Lowland Oaxaca	North America	Tequistlatecan	//
Tepehua, Huehuetla	North America	Totonacan	Tepehua
Nisga'a	North America	Tsimshian	Nass-Gitksan
Ute-Southern Paiute	North America	Uto-Aztecan	Northern Uto-Aztecan
Nuu-chah-nulth	North America	Wakashan	Southern Wakashan
Wintu	North America	Wintuan	//
Witoto, Murui	North America	Witotoan	Proto-Huitoto-Ocaina
Yuki	North America	Yukian	Core Yukian
Jamamadí	South America	Arauan	Jamamadi
Awa-Cuaquier	South America	Barbacoan	Northern
Trió	South America	Cariban	Tiriyó
Pakaásnovos	South America	Chapacuran	Wari
Kuna, Border	South America	Chibchan	Chibchan B
Uru	South America	Chipaya-Uru	//

(continued)

Language	Macro-area	Family	Sub-classification
Emberá, Northern	South America	Chocoan	Emberá
Cholón	South America	Cholonan	//
Tehuelche	South America	Chon	//
Guahibo	South America	Guajiboan	Guajibo
Pilagá	South America	Guaykuruan	Southern
Kwaza	South America	Isolate	//
Movima	South America	Isolate	//
Trumai	South America	Isolate	//
Urarina	South America	Isolate	//
Apinayé	South America	Jean	Northern
Wampís	South America	Jivaroan	Jívaro
Karajá	South America	Karajá	//
Katukína (/ Kanamarí)	South America	Katukinan	//
Qawasqar	South America	Kaweskaran	//
Tariana	South America	Maipurean	Northern
Mapudungun	South America	Mapudungu	//
Sanapaná	South America	Mascoyan	//
Maxakalí	South America	Maxakalian	//
Mískito	North America	Misumalpan	//
Tsimané	South America	Mosetenan	//
Mamaindé	South America	Nambikwara	Nambikwara Complex
Páez	South America	Paezan	Paezan
Kakataibo-Kashibo	South America	Panoan	Mainline
Hupdë	South America	Puinavean	Hupda
Quechua, Yauyos	South America	Quechuan	Central Quechua
Maco	South America	Sálivan	Piaroa-Maco
Cavineña	South America	Tacanan	//
Tanimuca-Retuarã	South America	Tucanoan	Western Tucanoan
Ninam	South America	Yanomaman	//
Semelai	Southeast Asia & Oceania	Austro-Asiatic	Mon-Khmer
Stieng, Bulo	Southeast Asia & Oceania	Austro-Asiatic	Mon-Khmer
Pnar	Southeast Asia & Oceania	Austro-Asiatic	Mon-Khmer
Kharia	Southeast Asia & Oceania	Austro-Asiatic	Munda
Atayal	Southeast Asia & Oceania	Austronesian	Atayalic
Bunun	Southeast Asia & Oceania	Austronesian	Bunun
Siraya	Southeast Asia & Oceania	Austronesian	East Formosan
Bali	Southeast Asia & Oceania	Austronesian	Malayo-Polynesian

(continued)

Language	Macro-area	Family	Sub-classification
Ibatan	Southeast Asia & Oceania	Austronesian	Malayo-Polynesian
Tboli	Southeast Asia & Oceania	Austronesian	Malayo-Polynesian
Tukang Besi North	Southeast Asia & Oceania	Austronesian	Malayo-Polynesian
To'abaita	Southeast Asia & Oceania	Austronesian	Malayo-Polynesian
Pampangan	Southeast Asia & Oceania	Austronesian	Malayo-Polynesian
Chamorro	Southeast Asia & Oceania	Austronesian	Malayo-Polynesian
Bajau, West Coast	Southeast Asia & Oceania	Austronesian	Malayo-Polynesian
Cebuano	Southeast Asia & Oceania	Austronesian	Malayo-Polynesian
Javanese	Southeast Asia & Oceania	Austronesian	Malayo-Polynesian
Bakati'	Southeast Asia & Oceania	Austronesian	Malayo-Polynesian
Madura	Southeast Asia & Oceania	Austronesian	Malayo-Polynesian
Malay, Jambi	Southeast Asia & Oceania	Austronesian	Malayo-Polynesian
Tondano	Southeast Asia & Oceania	Austronesian	Malayo-Polynesian
Moken	Southeast Asia & Oceania	Austronesian	Malayo-Polynesian
Ida'an	Southeast Asia & Oceania	Austronesian	Malayo-Polynesian
Iraya	Southeast Asia & Oceania	Austronesian	Malayo-Polynesian
Ilocano	Southeast Asia & Oceania	Austronesian	Malayo-Polynesian
Nias	Southeast Asia & Oceania	Austronesian	Malayo-Polynesian
Palauan	Southeast Asia & Oceania	Austronesian	Malayo-Polynesian
Makasar	Southeast Asia & Oceania	Austronesian	Malayo-Polynesian
Subanen, Northern	Southeast Asia & Oceania	Austronesian	Malayo-Polynesian
Paiwan	Southeast Asia & Oceania	Austronesian	Paiwan
Payuma	Southeast Asia & Oceania	Austronesian	Payuma
Rukai	Southeast Asia & Oceania	Austronesian	Rukai
Saaroa	Southeast Asia & Oceania	Austronesian	Tsouic
Thao	Southeast Asia & Oceania	Austronesian	Western Plains
Miao, Western Xiangxi	Southeast Asia & Oceania	Hmong-Mien	Hmongic
Mai Brat	Southeast Asia & Oceania	Maybrat	//
Dera	Southeast Asia & Oceania	Senagi	//
Mandarin Chinese	Southeast Asia & Oceania	Sino-Tibetan	Chinese
Naga, Ao	Southeast Asia & Oceania	Sino-Tibetan	Tibeto-Burman
Karbi	Southeast Asia & Oceania	Sino-Tibetan	Tibeto-Burman
Katso	Southeast Asia & Oceania	Sino-Tibetan	Tibeto-Burman
Gahri	Southeast Asia & Oceania	Sino-Tibetan	Tibeto-Burman
Yakkha	Southeast Asia & Oceania	Sino-Tibetan	Tibeto-Burman
Lao	Southeast Asia & Oceania	Tai-Kadai	Kam-Tai

References

Berretta, Monica. 1993. Morfologia. In Alberto A. Sobrero (ed.), *Introduzione all'italiano contemporaneo. Vol. I*, 193–245. Roma/Bari: Laterza.
Berruto, Gaetano. 1983. L'italiano popolare e la semplificazione linguistica. *Vox Romanica* 42. 38–79.
Berruto, Gaetano. 2012. *Sociolinguistica dell'italiano contemporaneo*. Roma: Carocci.
Berruto, Gaetano. 2014. Esiste ancora l'italiano popolare? Una rivisitazione. In Paul Danler & Christine Konecny (eds.), *Dall'architettura della lingua italiana all'architettura linguistica dell'Italia. Saggi in omaggio a Heidi Siller-Runggaldier*, 277–290. Frankfurt am Main: Peter Lang.
Bertinetto, Pier Marco. 1986. *Tempo, aspetto e azione nel verbo italiano. Il sistema dell'indicativo*. Firenze: Accademia della Crusca.
Caro, Ryan. 2012. Semantics of the Turkish non-past. Unpublished manuscript, Yale University. Retrieved from: https://ling.yale.edu/sites/default/files/files/alumni%20senior%20essays/CaroSeniorEssay.pdf
Cerruti, Massimo. 2018. Il parlato regionale oggi: un italiano composito? *LId'O Lingua italiana d'oggi* 15. 15–31.
Cho, Eun. 1997. Counterfactuals in Korean and Japanese: Interaction between verbal morphology and interpretation. Unpublished manuscript, Cornell University, Ithaca, NY.
Chung, Sandra & Alan Timberlake. 1985. Tense, aspect, and mood. In Timothy Shopen (ed.), *Language Typology and Syntactic Description, Volume 3: Grammatical categories and the lexicon*, 202–258. Cambridge: Cambridge University Press.
Comrie, Bernard. 1976. *Aspect*. Cambridge: Cambridge University Press.
Comrie, Bernard. 1986. Conditionals: A typology. In Elisabeth Closs Traugott (ed.), *On Conditionals*, 77–99. Cambridge: Cambridge Univerity Press.
Corris, Miriam. 2005. *A grammar of Barupu, a language of Papua New Guinea*. Sydney: University of Sydney dissertation.
Crewe, William J. 1984. *Singapore English and Standard English: Exercises in awareness*. Singapore: Eastern Universities Press.
Cristofaro, Sonia. 2004. Past habituals and irrealis. In Yuri A. Lander, Vladimir A. Plungian &. Anna Yu Urmanchieva (eds.), *Irrealis and Irreality*, 256–272. Moscow: Gnosis.
Dahl, Östen. 1997. The relation between past time reference and counterfactuality: A new look. In Angeliki Athanasiadou & René Dirven (eds.), *On Conditionals Again*, 97–114. Amsterdam/Philadelphia: John Benjamins.
Elliott, Jennifer R. 2000. Realis and irrealis: Forms and concepts of the grammaticalization of reality. *Linguistic Typology* 4(1). 55–90.
Evans, Nicholas. 1995. *A grammar of Kayardild*. Berlin/New York: Mouton de Gruyter.
Fleischman, Suzanne. 1989. Temporal distance: A basic linguistic metaphor. *Studies in Language* 13(1). 1–50.
Foley, William. 1991. *The Yimas language of Papua New Guinea*. Stanford, CA: Stanford University Press.
Givón, Talmy. 1994. Irrealis and the subjunctive. *Studies in Language* 18(2). 265–337.
Göksel, Aslı & Celia Kerslake. 2005. *Turkish: A comprehensive grammar*. London: Routledge.
Grjunberg, Aleksandr L. 1987. *Ocherk grammatiki afganskogo jazyka (pashto) [Grammar of the Afghan language (Pashto)]*. Leningrad: Nauka.

Haiman, John & Tania Kuteva. 2002. The symmetry of counterfactuals. In Joan L. Bybee & Michael Noonan (eds.), *Complex sentences in grammar and discourse: Essays in honor of Sandra A. Thompson*, 101–124. Amsterdam/Philadelphia: John Benjamins.

Han, Chung-hye. 1996. Comparing English and Korean counterfactuals: The role of verbal morphology and lexical aspect in counterfactual interpretation. In Anthony D. Green & Virginia Montapanyane (eds.), *Proceedings of the Eastern States Conference on Linguistics '96*, 124–138. Ithaca, NY: Cornell University.

Hatfield, Adam. 2016. *A grammar of Mehek*. Buffalo, NY: State University of New York at Buffalo dissertation.

Heath, Jeffrey. 2008. *A grammar of Jamsay*. Berlin/New York: Mouton de Gruyter.

Hellwig, Birgit. 2011. *A Grammar of Goemai*. Berlin/New York: Mouton de Gruyter.

Iatridou, Sabine. 2000. The grammatical ingredients of counterfactuality. *Linguistic Inquiry* 31(2). 231–270.

Iatridou, Sabine. 2010. Some thoughts about the imperfect in counterfactuals. Unpublished manuscript, MIT.

James, Deborah. 1982. Past tense and the hypothetical: A cross-linguistic study. *Studies in Language* 6(3). 375–403.

Josephs, Lewis S. 1975. *Palauan reference grammar*. Honolulu, HI: University of Hawaii Press.

Klokeid, Terry J. 1976. *Topics in Lardil grammar*. Cambridge, MA: MIT dissertation.

Langacker, Ronald W. 1978. The form and meaning of the English auxiliary. *Language* 54(4). 853–882

Lazard, Gilbert. 1975. La catégorie de l'éventuel. In René Amacker (ed.), *Mélanges linguistiques offerts à Émile Benveniste*, 347–358. Paris: Peeters.

Lazard, Gilbert. 1998. L'expression de l'irréel: essai de typologie. In Leonid Kulikov & Heinz Vater (eds.), *Typology of verbal categories: Papers presented to Vladimir Nedjalkov on the occasion of his 70th birthday*, 237–247. Tübingen: Niemeyer.

Lazard, Gilbert. 2006. More on counterfactuality, and on categories in general. *Linguistic Typology* 10(1). 61–66.

Levshina, Natalia. 2015. *How to do linguistics with R: Data exploration and statistical analysis*. Amsterdam/Philadelphia: John Benjamins.

Lewis, Geoffrey L. 1985. *Turkish grammar*. New York, NY: Oxford University Press.

Lewis, M. Paul, Gary F. Simons & Charles D. Fennig (eds.). 2018. *Ethnologue: Languages of the world*. 21st edn. Dallas, TX: SIL International. http://www.ethnologue.com/

Mattiola, Simone. 2020. *Two language samples for maximizing linguistic variety*. Bologna: AMS Acta.

Mauri, Caterina & Andrea Sansò. 2012. What do languages encode when they encode reality status? *Language Sciences* 34(2). 99–106.

Mauri, Caterina & Andrea Sansò. 2016. The linguistic marking of (ir)realis and subjunctive. In Jan Nuyts & Johan van der Auwera (eds.), *The Oxford Handbook of mood and modality*, 166–195. Oxford: Oxford University Press.

Mauri, Caterina, Silvia Ballarè, Eugenio Goria, Massimo Cerruti & Francesco Suriano. 2019. KIParla corpus: a new resource for spoken Italian. In Raffaella Bernardi, Roberto Navigli & Giovanni Semeraro (eds.), *Proceedings of the 6th Italian Conference on Computational Linguistics CLiC-it*. https://ceur-ws.org/Vol-2481/paper45.pdf

Mazzoleni, Marco. 2013. Le concordanze dei periodi ipotetici tra italiano antico, dialetti italoromanzi ed italiano contemporaneo, *inTRAlinea* [=Special Issue *Palabras con aroma a mujer. Scritti in onore di Alessandra Melloni*. Edited by Maria Isabel Fernández García & Mariachiara Russo].

Merlan, Francesca C. 1994. *A grammar of Wardaman: A language of the Northern Territory of Australia*. Berlin/New York: Mouton de Gruyter.

Miestamo, Matti, Dik Bakker & Antti Arppe. 2016. Sampling for variety. *Linguistic Typology* 20(2). 233–296.
Olguín Martínez, Jesús & Nicholas Lester 2021. A quantitative analysis of counterfactual conditionals in cross-linguistic perspective. *Italian Journal of Linguistics* 33(2). 147–182.
Porter, Doris. 1977. *A Tboli grammar*. Manila: Linguistic Society of the Philippines.
Rijkhoff, Jan, Dik Bakker, Kees Hengeveld & Peter Kahrel. 1993. A method of language sampling. *Studies in Language* 17(1). 169–203.
Rijkhoff, Jan & Dik Bakker. 1998. Language sampling. *Linguistic Typology* 2(3). 263–314.
Schachter, Jacqueline C. 1971. *Presupposition and counterfactual conditional sentences*. Los Angeles, CA: University of California Los Angeles dissertation.
Steele, Susan. 1975. Past and irrealis: Just what does it all mean? *International Journal of American Linguistics* 41(3). 200–217.
Sweetser, Eve E. 1990. *From etymology to pragmatics*. Cambridge: Cambridge University Press.
Tagliamonte, Sali A. & Harald Baayen. 2012. Models, forests, and trees of York English: Was/were variation as a case study for statistical practice. *Language Variation and Change* 24(2). 135–178.
Taylor, John R. 1997. Conditionals and polarity. In Angeliki Athanasiadou & René Dirven (eds.), *On conditionals again*, 289–306, Amsterdam/Philadelphia: John Benjamins.
Terrill, Angela. 2003. *A grammar of Lavukaleve*. Berlin/New York: Mouton de Gruyter.
Thompson, Sandra A., Robert E. Longacre & Shin Ja J. Hwang. 2007. Adverbial clauses. In Timothy Shopen (ed.), *Language typology and syntactic description. Vol.2: Complex constructions*, 237–300. 2nd edn. Cambridge: Cambridge University Press.
Vydrin, Arseniy. 2011. Counterfactual mood in Iranian. In Agnes Korn, Geoffrey Haig, Simin Karimi & Pollet Samvelian (eds.), *Topics in iranian linguistics*, 71–88. Wiesbaden: Reichert.
Wiberg, Eva. 2010. Imperfetto. In Raffaele Simone, Gaetano Berruto & Paolo D'Achille (eds.), *Enciclopedia dell'Italiano*. Roma: Istituto della Enciclopedia Italiana Treccani. http://www.treccani.it/enciclopedia/imperfetto_(Enciclopedia-dell%27Italiano)/
Xromov, Albert L. 1972: *Jagnobskij jazyk*. Moscow: Nauka.
Zaefferer, Dietmar. 1991. Conditionals and unconditionals: Cross-linguistic and logical aspects. In Dietmar Zaefferer (ed.), *Semantic Universals and Universal Semantics*, 210–236. Berlin/New York: Mouton de Gruyter.
Ziegeler, Debra. 1994. Conditionals and counterfactuality in Singaporean English. *Journal of Intercultural Studies* 15(1). 29–49.

Bert Cornillie and Malte Rosemeyer
7 Syntactic elaboration in the domain of periphrasticity: Evidence from Spanish

Abstract: In this paper we offer a multidimensional account of the evolution of periphrastic expressions that (i) addresses the sociolinguistic variation in terms of texts being situated along the continuum between communicative immediacy and communicative distance; (ii) presents clause linking strategies as a workable tool for cross-linguistic typology; and (iii) adopts a diachronic approach to auxiliaries on the basis of statistical correlations between different types of auxiliaries and linkage scores so as to determine the nature of syntactic elaboration. Our data show that periphrastic expressions cannot be associated with communicative distance only, yet it is in texts with higher linkage scores, associated with communicative distance where frequent auxiliaries and periphrastic expressions expand most clearly. With the rise of humanism after 1400, we find a significant increase in the usage frequencies of this group of periphrastic expressions, which was bound to syntactic elaboration processes in the communicative distance. Yet, our analysis also suggests that, although emblematic for the humanist era, Latinisms are rather marginal in the evolution of the overall linguistic system. Hence, our linkage-based account is also a call for proportionality in the analyst's attention to specific linguistic phenomena that are less entrenched in the linguistic system.

1 Introduction

In this paper we address the possible intersection between historical sociolinguistic variation and typology by accounting for the evolution of different types of auxiliaries in a historical Spanish corpus as instances of *syntactic elaboration*, defined as the creation and actualization of new and more specific syntactic expressions replacing others or covering meanings that were left implicit. We understand the sociolinguistic dimension of this enterprise as the continuum between *communicative immediacy* and *communicative distance* and, more specifically, as the elaboration of languages towards higher levels of scripturality, as opposed to higher levels

---

Bert Cornillie, KU Leuven, e-mail: bert.cornillie@kuleuven.be
Malte Rosemeyer, Freie Universität Berlin, e-mail: malte.rosemeyer@fu-berlin.de

https://doi.org/10.1515/9783110781168-007

of orality. Scholars are well aware of the challenge inherent to accounting for sociolinguistic variation in the past, in that no interviews or experiments are possible (cf. Labov's bad data problem). Yet, written documents may witness different Discourse Traditions and are often produced with an eye to specific audiences, e.g., different types of letters (cf. the attention paid to the dynamics of Audience Design in the framework of Historical Sociolinguistics; Bell 1984).

Sociolinguistic variation in a typological perspective needs to be accounted for on the basis of comparable criteria. In the field of Romance linguistics, discourse traditionality (cf. Octavio de Toledo y Huerta 2018) offers an analytic tool to compare usage in one language to usage in other languages. However, the heavy focus on European literacy is a challenge for joining forces with present-day typological research, although awareness of the continuum of discourse traditions from communicative immediacy to communicative distance, both in oral and written texts, is a first important step that allows us to go beyond the established European languages.

More than twenty years ago typologists and Romance linguists, the latter 'group' being the one to which we belong, engaged in an intense collaboration in the discipline of language typology, integrating insights from the conceptual continuum proposed by Peter Koch and Wulf Oesterreicher. At the end of the 1990s Martin Haspelmath, Ekkehard König, Wulf Oesterreicher and Wolfgang Raible co-edited the seminal second volume of *Language Typology and Language Universals. An International Handbook* (with translations of the title in German and French, published in 2001). In this paper we attempt, on the one hand, to rescue part of this legacy, and, on the other hand, we want to enrich it methodologically, by exploring new statistical methods for the study of discourse traditions. We believe that anchoring linguistic subsystems in specific communicative and sociolinguistic contexts, with special attention to the textual traditions (and the prestige attached to them), allows for an empirically refined and methodologically sound description. In this paper, we will test whether (subgroups of) auxiliaries are part of elaboration processes that typically lead to the expansion of linguistic expressions belonging to the Communicative Distance ("learned") (Kabatek 2005a; Koch and Oesterreicher 1990; López Serena 2021; Octavio de Toledo y Huerta 2018).

Using data from the CODEA corpus of historical Spanish texts, we propose to model the difference between orality and scripturality ("escrituralidad") in terms of the usage frequency of clause linkage strategies such as conjunctions or non-finite clauses, which mark the type of semantic relationship between the matrix and the subordinate clause. Our results indicate that the emergence and expansion of use of a specific group of infinitival periphrastic expressions, namely, periphrases that were already used in Classical Latin, and were continued into Old (and sometimes Classical) Spanish, was bound to higher levels of scripturality. By contrast, this correlation is much weaker for periphrastic expressions that were Spanish innovations, entering the language either as the result of language change on the level of informal interaction or as calques from Latin. This result supplements existing analyses of the creation of verbal periphrases on the basis of the principle of extravagance (Haspelmath 1999) in informal interaction.

2 Periphrasticity and elaboration

2.1 The emergence of periphrastic expressions

In languages such as Spanish, the prototypical verb phrase consists of a simple verb form that agrees with its subject. Hence, auxiliaries and periphrastic expressions are hypothesized to be instances that display a certain degree of grammatical and conceptual complexity. Auxiliaries may be used to express various qualificational categories such as Tense, Aspect and Modality (Heine 1993; Kuteva 2004; Anderson 2006). In functional terms, these categories add a special perspective to the state of affairs, with Modality having the widest scope over the sentence. Needless to say, within the realm of Modality differences between semantic subtypes can be observed (see Section 3.2).

As Haspelmath (2000: 656–659) points out, periphrases do not typically arise as "gap fillers", i.e., they are not developed to express meanings that were not previously codified in a language. Rather, we can use Haspelmath's (1999) principle of *extravagance* ("Talk in such a way as to be noticed") to account for the creation of periphrases. The use of periphrastic expressions in a situation where syntactically simpler expressions for the same meanings exist may serve an important social function. Consequently, auxiliaries are a universal means of creating *ad-hoc* grammatical meanings. There is, indeed, a general need for making explicit a specific perspective to the state-of-affairs. The universal dimension also explains why analytic expressions in general, and auxiliaries and periphrases in particular, are not only common in highly prestigious written texts but are also frequent in pidgins and creoles. Michaelis and Haspelmath (2020: 1118) explain accelerated functionalization in pidgins and creoles with the *Extra-Transparency Hypothesis*:

> In social situations with many (or even mostly) adult second-language speakers, people need to make an extra effort to make themselves understood. This naturally leads to the overuse of content items for grammatical meanings, which may become fixed when more and more speakers adopt the innovative uses.

In comparison to monolingual situations, there is an extra need for transparency in many contact situations. In contexts of pidgin and creole formation, speakers cannot expect their interlocutors to have mastered the grammar of the lexifier language. A more promising strategy is to employ lexical material for the expression of grammatical meanings and rely on inferencing processes in comprehension.

As a result, it appears that two very different motivations (extravagance and need for clarity) can lead to the creation of periphrases. It is our contention that such innovative processes can be described as instances of elaboration in a broad sense: the creation of new linguistic routines that serve to express meanings not yet codified in a language system, whether it be a dialect, pidgin, register or discourse tradition. Moreover, it can be expected that some auxiliaries are clearly on the side of 'intensive elaboration' and communicative distance, whereas other auxiliaries rather belong to communicative immediacy. The first type of auxiliaries can then be considered instances of syntactic elaboration in the domain of scripturality. We will show that the different origins of the auxiliaries in Spanish are related to different linking strategies.

2.2 Periphrasticity and communicative distance

Diachronically, syntactic elaboration can be defined as the creation and actualization of new and more specific syntactic expressions replacing others or covering meanings that were left implicit. These elaboration processes are generally associated with languages reaching advanced degrees of formality and scripturality, through the broadening of the linguistic repertoire in discourse traditions belonging to the pole of communicative distance. In the words of Koch, Oesterreicher and López Serena (2007: 188):

> Intensive elaboration comprises, for instance, the settlement of textual coherence in a purely linguistic context, strong syntactic integration, oriented toward the sentence as canonical form of expression, the intensification of hypotaxis, great lexical variation and precision, the preference for the symbolic field versus deictic means, etc. (our translation)

The same line of reasoning is found in Raible (2001), who emphasizes the relationship between juridical texts and linking techniques as an example of elaboration and scripturality:

> In the case of lots of European languages, the first purely nominal technique are prepositional groups like ENGLISH *on account of, on behalf of, with respect to, in spite of*; SPANISH *con finalidad de, (con) respecto a, al respecto de, a causa de, debido a, gracias a, merced a, por causa de*; FRENCH *à cause de, par suite de, pour cause de, en vertu de*; ITALIAN *a causa di, grazie a, a forza di, in virtù di*; GERMAN *infolge von, aufgrund von, in Bezug auf*, etc.

In most cases, such prepositional groups occur for the first time in juridical texts. This is due to the fact that jurists like precision (the underlying idea is ruling out ambiguities) and that prepositional groups offer the most precise possibility of expressing certain relations. As a result, they are relatively rare in other textual genres. Above all, they tend not to occur in the genres of spoken language, thus showing once more the relation holding between the linking techniques and the Ausbau of a language system by scripturality. (Raible 2001: 596)

In this paper, we will show that we can have elaboration both in the communicative proximity (e.g., pidgins and creoles) and the communicative distance (original concept of *Sprachausbau*). Spanish periphrastic expressions are a good example in that their usage has been described as typical for either informal or formal registers. Some periphrastic expressions are the result of a grammaticalization process that started in the realm of Communicative Immediacy: e.g., deontic modals *haber de* and *tener de* 'have to', the former analytical future that emerged from the infinitive + *habere* construction (*illum cantare habeo* > *cantar lo é* >> *lo cantaré* 'I will sing it') or the periphrastic future (*voy a ir*) in informal spoken speech (cf. Fleischman 1982). Also, an opposition can be observed between *deber* + infinitive and *deber* + *de* + infinitive, where the more complex and elaborate *deber* + *de* + infinitive was promoted by the Real Academia Española, leading to an increase of its use in formal registers (cf. Blas Arroyo and Vellón Lahoz 2014; Rosemeyer 2017). More generally, there was also a continuous renewal of deontic auxiliaries in Old Spanish texts (*uviar* + (*a*) + infinitive (cf. Garachana 2017a), as well as lexical substitution processes with *haber* 'to have' by *tener* 'to have': *haber de, haber que, tener de, tener que* etc.). As a result of these considerations, we assume that syntactic elaboration on the sentence level can also be attested in the elaboration or development of the verbal group through auxiliation. So, what are the implications of this formal and conceptual diversity for an 'elaboration' account of the historical development of verbal periphrases? First of all, we cannot posit that, due to their inherent complexity, all periphrases belong to the communicative distance. Hence, we hypothesize that the emergence of periphrases can be located both in the communicative immediacy and the communicative distance. However, the original distribution of auxiliaries along the continuum from immediacy to distance may also vary according to particular communicative needs. The specific location of such emergence might depend on the type of meaning expressed: modal (especially deontic) meanings are more typical of the linguistic practices of the communicative distance, temporal meanings are more typical of the deixis present in the communicative immediacy.

3 Data

3.1 Corpus and data extraction

We extracted all verb clusters combining a finite verb inflected for present tense and an infinitive from the CODEA corpus (Corpus de Documentos Anteriores a 1800, Githe 2018). The CODEA is a "primary" corpus of Spanish historical documents (Miguel Franco and Sánchez-Prieto Borja 2016), containing about 2500 documents (about 1,4 million words) in Peninsular Spanish dated between the 11th and 19th centuries. While these documents represent different registers, from chancellery to private letters, the majority of these documents represent rather formal registers. In general these documents are relatively short, with some texts comprising fewer than 25 words. The CODEA is exceptionally well-edited, and contains both the facsimile and rigorous paleographic and critical transcriptions. Given that only original manuscripts were included, a great number of the texts are dated to the exact year. In sum, the high degree of philological exactness and its focus on more formal registers make the CODEA a more than adequate corpus for the analysis of the relationship between periphrasticity, linking strategies and syntactic elaboration.

For this study, we restricted the queries to the timeframe from the 13th to the 19th century due to the scarcity of earlier data. Likewise, we restricted the corpus to texts that contained at least 25 words and eliminated all undated texts, resulting in a final corpus of n = 2179 texts. The extraction procedure was realized using regular expressions; both regular and irregular verb forms were extracted. This extraction procedure yielded n = 2167 verb clusters, excluding the voice periphrases, which include finite verbs and participles. Inspection of the data revealed that a majority of these verb forms expressed modal meanings, with only n = 66 verb clusters expressing temporal-aspectual meanings. This effect is likely due to the fact that the CODEA mostly contains texts from more formal registers, in which modal meanings and the associated speech acts (requesting, ordering etc.) are more frequent than narrations. In order to increase the consistency of the data, we eliminated verb clusters with temporal-aspectual meanings, leaving us with a total dataset of n = 2101 verb clusters. Of the n = 2179 texts in our corpus, such verb clusters were found in n = 980 texts. In other words, modal verb clusters are used in about 45 percent of the texts of our corpus. We have not examined any correlation between the established textual labels of CODEA+ and the frequency of verbal periphrases, since we wanted to adopt the more systematic, perhaps universal, criterion of linking strategies (cf. Mazzola, De Pascale and Rosemeyer 2023).

3.2 Types of periphrasticity

Before describing the types of verb clusters documented in our data, a brief remark on the notion of periphrasticity employed in this paper is in order. We have consciously refrained from using the term "verbal periphrasis" until now in order to avoid a premature categorization of our data in these terms. There is an ongoing discussion in Spanish linguistics regarding the question of what counts as a verbal periphrasis, with some authors employing a more or less rigid system of categorization to distinguish "true" verbal periphrases such as the progressive *estar* 'to be' + gerund (1a) from transitive-like verb clusters such as *querer* 'to want to' + infinitive (2b) (Fernández de Castro 1999; RAE/ASALE 2009).

(1) a. *Estoy   cant-ando.*
       be.PRS.1SG sing-PROG
       'I am singing.'
    b. *Quier-o   cant-ar.*
       want-PRS.1SG sing-INF
       'I want to sing.'

Forms such as (1a) are said to have a non-compositional meaning that cannot be predicted from the semantics of the individual verbs, while the same is not true for verbs such as *querer* in (1b). The difference in grammaticalization between (1a) and (1b) is also evinced by syntactic parameters related to coalescence. For instance, pronominalization of the non-finite verb form is possible for (1b), but not for (1a) (cf. *Lo quiero* vs. ?*Lo estoy*, where *lo* refers to the respective actions). Likewise, word order seems more flexible for (1b) than for (1a) (cf. *CanTAR quiero* vs. ?*CanTANdo estoy*).

However, such descriptions of verbal periphrases lead to unsurmountable definitional problems, such as the status of grammaticalized temporal-aspectual periphrases (e.g., *haber* + participle, which is frequently described as a verb tense), the status of layered auxiliary uses with more frequent non-auxiliary counterparts (Cornillie 2007), or the fact that even highly grammaticalized verbal periphrases continue to impose distributional restrictions on the subject (Garachana Camarero 2017b; Rosemeyer and Garachana Camarero to appear). As was outlined in Section 2 of this chapter we consider that periphrasticity can be a strategy for syntactic elaboration, meaning that authors recruit verb clusters as more elaborate/extravagant forms of expression. This assumption does not necessarily imply a high degree of grammaticalization of these verb clusters. We consequently adopt a more encompassing definition of periphrasticity, including all cases in which a finite verb form is combined with a non-finite verb form, irrespective of their degree of grammaticalization.

In order to avoid confusion with the traditional, more restricted, term "verbal periphrasis", we will use the more neutral term "periphrastic expression" (abbreviated PeX), limiting ourselves to the ones in which an auxiliary combines with an infinitive. This definition is very much in line with the existing typological literature, which has pointed out that auxiliation is a gradient notion. To cite Anderson (2006: 8):

> [...] as a form–function continuum, auxiliary verb constructions are necessarily vaguely definable, dynamic, ever-emergent and changing. These may constitute a closed class from a strict synchronic perspective but not when viewed diachronically in any sense [...]

The n = 2101 PeX in our corpus fall into n = 76 syntactic types. A complete list of these types can be found in the Appendix. Table 1 gives the most frequent modal periphrastic expressions in our data. These six PeX make up almost 75 percent of all modal PeX.

Table 1: Six most frequent modal periphrastic expressions (PeX) in CODEA.

Periphrastic expression	Typical meaning	Frequency
haber + de + infinitive	must do something	686
poder + infinitive	can do something	336
deber + infinitive	must do something	252
ser + a + infinitive	have to do something	169
querer + infinitive	want to do something	75
convenir + a + infinitive	it is appropriate to do something	47

Crucially, the PeX in our data differ with respect to their historical origins, and we will show in this chapter that this fact is strongly correlated with the extent to which they are recruited for syntactic elaboration processes. We categorized the PeX in our data in terms of a three-way distinction regarding their historical origins, which is summarized in Table 2.

Table 2: Categorization of historical origin of PeX in our data.

Group	Description	Frequent PeX	Usage frequency
I	PeX that were already used in Classical Latin, and were continued into Old (and sometimes Classical) Spanish	*poder* + infinitive	n = 762
II	PeX that were already used in Classical Latin, but lost in Proto-Spanish. These PeX were reintroduced into Spanish as Latin calques during Humanism.	*ser + a* + infinitive	n = 213
III	PeX that did not exist / were infrequent in Classical Latin, and which experienced a grammaticalization process from Vulgar Latin in Old and/or Classical Spanish	*haber + de* + infinitive	n = 1126

In terms of the parameter of communicative distance, the typology described in Table 2 makes the prediction that type I and II PeX are most likely to be recruited as devices for syntactic elaboration due to their Latin origin. In contrast, type III PeX would seem to be less ideal candidates for syntactic elaboration processes, because they come from grammaticalization processes in informal interaction, bound to the communicate immediacy. Note also that type II PeX are distinctly less frequent in our data than type I and III PeX.

3.3 Operationalizing conceptual distance and immediacy in terms of junction

The concepts of conceptual distance and conceptual immediacy, already described in Section 2, suggest that texts can be classified in terms of both their communication environments and the preferred linguistic strategies (Kabatek 2005b; Koch and Oesterreicher 1990; López Serena 2021). In terms of communication environments, conceptual immediacy is characterized by a high degree of intimacy, involvement, emotionality, cooperation, dialogicity and spontaneity, whereas the opposite holds for conceptual distance. In terms of linguistic strategies, conceptual immediacy is characterized by a low degree of planning, a high degree of provisionality, and a preference for syntactic aggregation, whereas conceptual distance typically involves a high degree of planning and a low degree of provisionality, as well as a preference for syntactic integration.

In this chapter we will examine the development and presence of PeX against the background of syntactic aggregation and integration. Previous studies have shown that one of the key aspects of the aggregation – integration dimension is clause linking strategies (cf. Raible 1992, 2001 and Kabatek, Obrist and Vincis 2010: 252). Consider, as a first example, the letter accompanying an abandoned child left at the door of a monastery in (2). This short letter of eleven words contains three sentences linked through aggregation with the linking device *y* 'and', which is also called a 'junctor' by Raible (1992).

(2) *Cristiano esta*
   'He is Christian'
   y tiene por nombre antonio
   'and is named Antonio'
   y es hijo de la tierra
   'and is a son of this place'   (CODEA-1520, Madrid, 1593)

Now, consider the sentence in (3), from a letter by a certain Juan Chacón, in which he informs an ecclesiastical authority of an incident at the monastery of Santa Cruz at Valladolid. The sentence can also be divided into three separate clauses. These clauses are linked through integration using the temporal junctor with a past participle *después de acabados* 'lit. after finished' and the absolute construction *no aviendo quedado* 'lit. not having remained'. These junctors serve to make explicit the complex semantic relationships between the sentences (here, anteriority and simultaneity).

(3) **Después de acabados** *los oficios*
'after the services had ended'
se mudó este bulto o persona cerca del coro y comulgatorio,
'this bulk or person moved close to the choir and altar rail'
no aviendo quedado *en la iglesia sino el maestro de capilla de la iglesia mayor, y María de Santana, Catalina Martín, Gerónima de Texada y otras cuatro o cinco muxeres...*
'while only the chapel master of the church, María de Santana, Catalina Martín, Gerónima de Texada and four or five other women had remained in the church' (CODEA-1269, Valladolid, 1634)

The two examples in (2) and (3) illustrate how clause linkage strategies can be taken as proxies for the degree of communicative immediacy or distance of texts. This idea has already been exploited in a number of studies. Raible (1992, 2001) established a typology of clause linkage strategies (in his terms, "junction" by means of "junctors") that served to measure stages between aggregation and integration.[1] This typology is reproduced in Table 3, using examples from our data. Note that in order to facilitate the computational implementation of the typology, we changed the original scale (ranging between 1 and 7) to a scale between 0 and 6. Likewise, we did not find any clear examples of the nominalization strategy in our data, which is why no examples for this level are given. Simple juxtaposition refers to a lack of junctors.

---

[1] Raible's original theory is more complex, as a second, semantic dimension measuring the relational complexity of sentences is also considered. In this paper, we will refrain from establishing a more complete model of clause linkage strategies that includes this second, also important, dimension, and concentrate on syntactic aspects of clause linkage.

Table 3: Typology of clause linkage strategies in Raible (1992; 2001); translation based on the adaption in Kabatek, Obrist and Vincis (2010: 252).

Integration weight	Type	Examples
0	Simple juxtaposition	*Vine, vi, vencí* 'I came, I saw, I won'
1	Junction by (phrasal) adverbs	*por cuanto/ende/esta razón/ond(e)* 'given that'
2	Coordinating conjunctions	*y/e* 'and', *pero/mas* 'but'
3	Subordinating conjunctions	*porque* 'because' *después que* 'after'
4	Non-finite verbs (gerunds, participles or infinitives)	*Leída la carta,...* 'the letter read' *Aviendo estado* 'having been'
5	Prepositional groups with non-finite verbs	*En llegando* 'upon arriving'
6	Nominalization	

As was already recognized in a study by Kabatek, Obrist and Vincis (2010), the model by Raible can be easily applied to a corpus in order to quantify the degree to which texts implement syntactic aggregation or integration strategies. Their analysis of a corpus of Spanish historical texts (dated between 1200 and 1499) following Raible's typology showed a general increase in the use of more integrative clause linkage strategies. However, their results also showed considerable intertextual variation (Kabatek, Obrist and Vincis 2010: 257). Given that their corpus only contained seven texts, of which only three were composed later than the 13th century, their results have to be described as preliminary.

Kabatek, Obrist and Vincis (2010) described the frequency of each of the stages of aggregation/integration. In our case, however, we are interested in measuring the degree to which the historical increase in the usage frequency of verbal periphrases can be described as a syntactic elaboration process. Consequently, we made use of Raible's typology as represented on an ordinal scale (the higher the number, the more integration). This allowed us to create aggregate scores measuring the usage of more integrated clause linkage strategies for each text in our corpus. First, we simply extracted each full stop (.) from each text in the corpus and classified the following first words in terms of Raible's typology. This procedure resulted in the detection of $n = 1029$ clause linkage markers, which are distributed as summarized in Table 4.

Table 4: Absolute usage frequency of types of clause linkage markers in CODEA (selection of texts).

Type	1	2	3	4	5
Frequency	79	359	187	306	5

Second, in keeping with previous approaches to register analysis in texts (Biber and Finegan 2004; Rosemeyer 2019), each text was assigned a "clause linkage score" that consisted of the added scores for each clause linkage marker found in the text, normalized by 1000 words. This variable measured the extent to which a given text in the corpus makes use of more integrated clause linkage strategies.

Figure 1 visualizes both the historical development of the usage frequency of modal PeX (left plot) and aggregate clause linkage scores (right plot) in our data. The data were logarithmized in order to facilitate visual inspection of the effect. Regarding the development of PeX, we document a consistent increase in usage frequency from 1200 to about 1600, after which usage frequencies of PeX seem to have reached a plateau. The usage frequency of PeX and date of composition of the text were found to be moderately positively correlated, with $r(2177) = .22$, $p<.001$***. This result confirms recent historical studies on Spanish PeX (cf., e.g., the papers united in Garachana Camarero 2017a; Garachana Camarero 2020).

With respect to the development of aggregate clause linkage scores, we first find a marked decrease between 1200 and 1400, which is followed by a monotonic increase between 1400 and 1800. The overall picture is that of an increase in aggre-

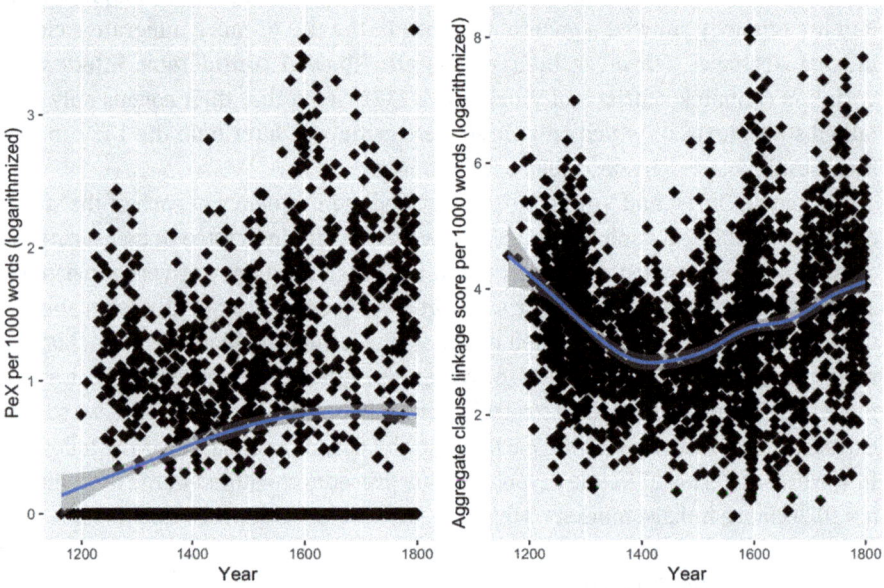

Figure 1: Historical development of the logarithmized usage frequency of modal PeX (left plot) and aggregate clause linkage scores (right plot) in CODEA (selection of texts). Each point represents a text. The blue smoother lines were calculated using generative additive modeling (GAM). Shades around the smoother lines represent confidence intervals.

gate clause linkage scores, as aggregate clause linkage scores and date of composition of the text were found to be weakly positively correlated, with $r(2177) = .08$, $p<.001$***. Note that our results of a decrease of aggregate clause linkage scores until 1400 contradict the findings from Kabatek, Obrist and Vincis (2010). One possible explanation for this difference could be the fact that Kabatek, Obrist and Vincis (2010) use prose texts, whereas our corpus is mostly composed of short documents. On the other hand, the increase in aggregate clause linkage scores after 1400 can likely be explained in terms of syntactic elaboration processes associated with the rise of humanism and the adoption of more elaborate linguistic models (see Section 2).

4 Periphrasticity and syntactic elaboration

Having presented the data and measurements used in the study, we are now in a position to analyze the extent to which the historical increase in usage frequency of PeX can be explained in terms of syntactic elaboration processes. We will analyze our data both from a synchronic (Section 4.1) and a diachronic perspective (Section 4.2), and demonstrate that, in order to justify this twofold perspective, it is crucial to consider the historical origins of the different PeX (cf. Section 3.2).

4.1 Synchronic analysis

In line with the historical scenario developed in Section 2, we assume that the historical increase in the usage frequency of PeX is at least partially due to syntactic elaboration processes in the communicative distance. This hypothesis can be tested by measuring the correlation between the normalized usage frequencies of the PeX and aggregate clause linkage scores in our corpus. If our hypothesis is correct, we would expect a positive correlation between these measurements, i.e., a higher usage frequency of PeX in texts associated with conceptual distance through aggregation.

Figure 2 visualizes the relationship between these two measurements for each text in our corpus. In line with our hypothesis, the usage frequencies of PeX and aggregate clause linkage scores were found to be weakly positively correlated, with $r(2177) = .07, p<.001$***.

We also predicted that the correlation between usage frequency of modal PeX and aggregate clause linkage scores is moderated by the origin of PeX. We predicted that PeX that were either continued from Latin (type I) or later Latin calques (type

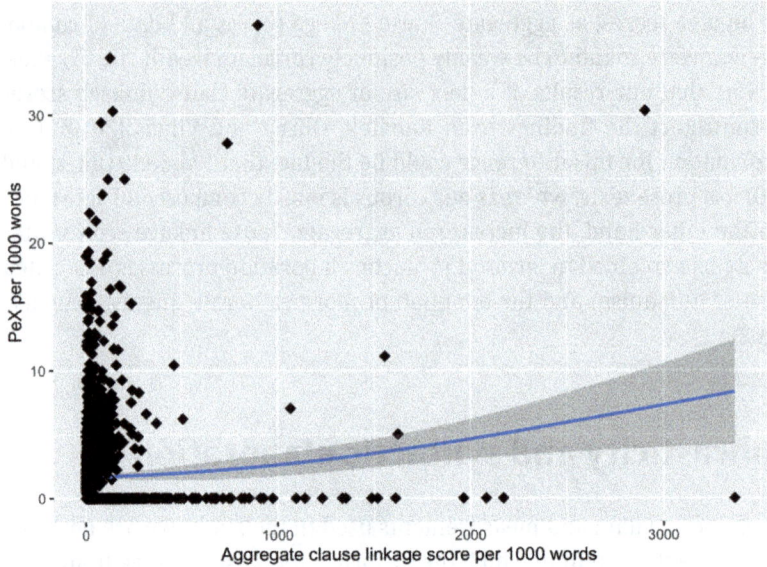

Figure 2: Correlation between usage frequency of modal PeX and aggregate clause linkage scores in CODEA (selection of texts). Each point represents a text. The blue smoother line was calculated using generative additive modeling (GAM). The shades around the smoother line represent the confidence intervals.

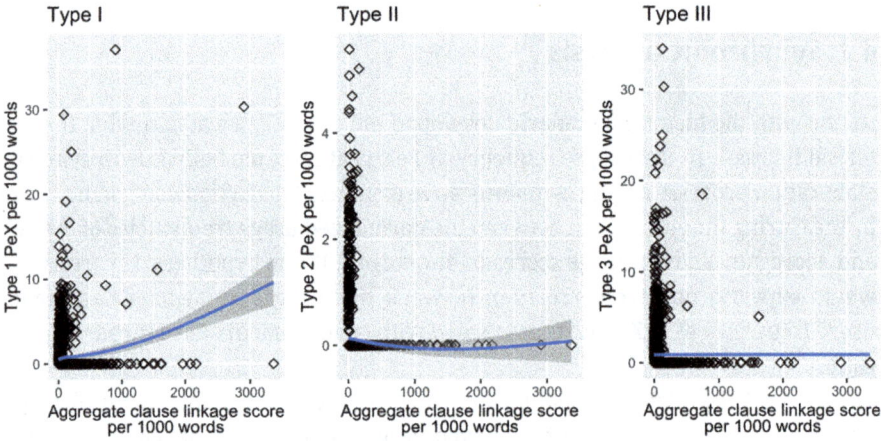

Figure 3: Correlation between usage frequency of modal PeX and aggregate clause linkage scores in CODEA (selection of texts), by type of PeX. Each point represents a text. The blue smoother lines were calculated using generative additive modeling (GAM). The shades around the smoother lines represent the confidence intervals.

II) are more likely to have been recruited for syntactic elaboration processes than PeX resulting from grammaticalization processes in the conceptual immediacy (type III). Figure 3 visualizes the relationship between usage frequencies of modal PeX and aggregate clause linkage scores for each text in our corpus, taking into account the different PeX types. It demonstrates that the global positive correlation between these measurements, reported in Figure 2 above, is indeed almost entirely restricted to type I PeX, i.e. PeX such as *poder* 'can' + infinitive, which were continued from Latin. Restriction to type I PeX consequently leads to a much better correlation measure, in that the usage frequencies of PeX and aggregate clause linkage scores were found to be more strongly positively correlated, with $r(2177) = .16$, $p<.001$***, for type I PeX than in the analysis for all PeX types.

4.2 Diachronic analysis

The synchronic analysis reported in Section 4.1 has confirmed our expectation of a positive correlation between the usage frequency of PeX and aggregate clause linkage, which we take to indicate that PeX were recruited as linguistic elements in processes of syntactic elaboration. In addition, our analysis seems to indicate that this generalization only applies to type I PeX, which were continued into Spanish from Latin.

However, such a synchronic analysis of the data fails to take into account the fact that syntactic elaboration is a historical process that should be modeled using diachronic data. For instance, the fact that we did not find a positive correlation between the usage frequency of type II PeX and the degree of communicative distance of the texts might be due to unaccounted diachronic variation. Consequently, in this section we analyze the degree to which the relationship between the usage frequencies of PeX and the degree of communicative distance is moderated by time.

Figure 4 visualizes the complex interaction between (a) usage frequency of PeX, (b) aggregate clause linkage score, (c) PeX type, and (d) date of composition of the text. It replaces the finding of a historical increase in the usage frequencies of PeX in our corpus (cf. also Figure 1). It is now clear that this trend is clearly moderated by PeX type. Until about 1450 we witness a relative predominance of type I PeX, while both type II and type III PeX have a lower usage frequency. This situation is expected given that type I PeX were simply inherited from Latin. For Old Spanish (ca. 1200–1400), we document a decrease in the usage frequencies of type I PeX, while there is a mild increase in the usage frequencies of type III PeX. This trend might be explained by the fact that in this period, syntactic elaboration processes went hand in hand with an avoidance of Latin, the previously dominant language in textual production (Fernández-Ordóñez 2004). Crucially for our analysis, with the beginning of humanism after 1400, this tendency is inverted. In particular, we find a strong increase in the usage frequencies of both type I and type III PeX after about 1400.

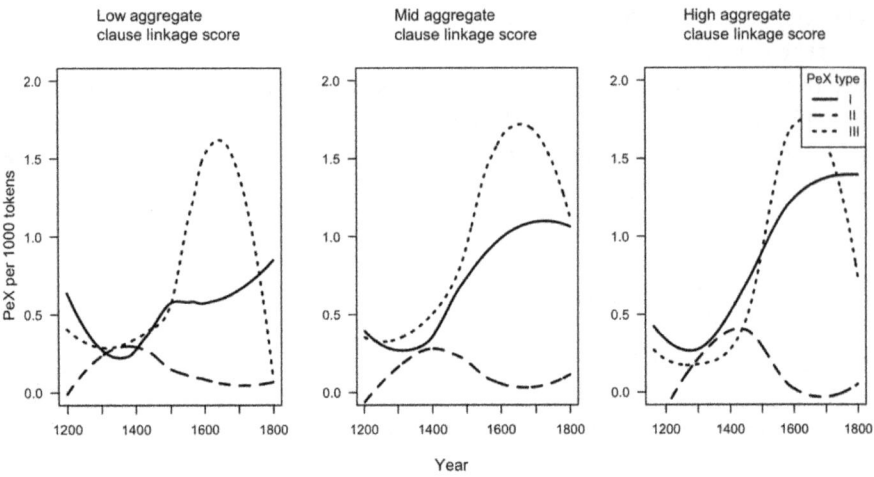

Figure 4: Usage frequency of PeX by aggregate clause linkage score (factor variable with three levels representing tertiles), PeX type, and Date of composition of the text. Curves represent results from polynomial regression models conducted using the function 'loess'.

Again, the usage frequencies are moderated by an additional factor, namely aggregate clause linkage scores. Crucially, we find a stronger, earlier, and more consistent increase in the usage frequencies of type I PeX in texts with higher aggregate clause linkage scores (here, scores classified as "mid" and "high"). In contrast, the increase in the usage frequencies of type III PeX is not affected by differences in aggregate clause linkage scores. For type II PeX, we find a weak effect, in that the increase in their usage frequencies until 1400 seems slightly stronger in texts with the highest aggregate clause linkage scores.

4.3 Discussion of results

We interpret the findings from our synchronic and diachronic corpus analyses as evidence for the prediction that the historical increase in the usage frequencies of PeX can be partially attributed to syntactic elaboration processes. Our analysis has evinced a positive correlation between the usage frequency of PeX in the texts in the CODEA and the degree to which these texts exhibit more integrated clause linkage strategies. A more fine-grained analysis has shown that this correlation is mostly restricted to type I PeX, which originated in Latin and continued into Spanish, whereas usage frequencies of type III PeX, which resulted from autochthonous grammaticalization processes, are not correlated with the aggregated clause linkage scores of the texts.

The diachronic analysis has confirmed our claim that the historical spread of the usage of PeX is partially due to syntactic elaboration strategies. In particular, we found a stronger, earlier, and more consistent increase in the usage frequencies of type I PeX in texts with higher aggregate clause linkage scores. Moreover, our analysis demonstrates that these changes took place in the time between 1400 and 1600, which from a socio-historical perspective can be described as the time at which humanist scholars implemented syntactic elaboration processes. In contrast, the increase in the usage frequencies of type III PeX was not affected by the degree to which texts exhibit more integrated clause linkage strategies. As a result, we argue that these grammaticalization processes were independent from the syntactic elaboration processes documented for type I PeX.

5 Conclusions

In this chapter we have offered an account of the evolution of periphrastic expressions that touches upon different dimensions: it adopts a view of sociolinguistic variation in terms of texts being situated along the continuum between communicative immediacy and communicative distance; it presents a study of clause linking strategies as a workable tool for cross-linguistic typology; and it operationalized a diachronic approach to auxiliaries on the basis of statistical correlations between different types of auxiliaries and linkage scores so as to determine the nature of syntactic elaboration.

The analysis has yielded mixed results. On the one hand, our data have shown that periphrastic expressions cannot be associated with communicative distance only. On the other hand, it is in texts with higher linkage scores where frequent auxiliaries and periphrastic expressions expand most clearly. Moreover, the evolution of periphrastic expressions witnesses an S-curve, showing a consistent increase in usage frequency from 1200 to 1600, stabilizing afterwards. Notably, we document a sharp increase of linking strategies in the period between 1400 and 1600, in which text production was strongly influenced by humanism.

The differentiation of three types of auxiliaries on the basis of their origins has shed new light on the rather similar role of auxiliaries that already existed in Latin versus that of autochthonous auxiliaries stemming from the century-long evolution from Vulgar Latin over Romance to modern Spanish. In particular, the analysis suggests a decrease in the usage frequency of periphrastic expressions of Latin origin that continued into Old Spanish (1200–1400), reflecting the fact that during this time period, authors such as Alfonse X sought to establish Castilian as the dominant language in written text production. With the rise of humanism after 1400, however, we find a significant increase in the usage frequencies of this group of periphrastic expressions, which was bound to syntactic elaboration processes in the communicative distance. Although we also find a strong increase in the usage frequencies of autochthonous periphrastic expressions after 1400, our analysis did not find a significant correlation between this change and the difference between communicative immediacy and communicative distance. Consequently, there is no evidence for the assumption that the rise of non-Latinate periphrastic expressions was a part of syntactic elaboration processes.

Likewise, only weak evidence was found for the assumption that periphrastic expressions that were copied from Latin into Spanish (so-called Latin calques) played an important role in syntactic elaboration processes. While the diachronic analysis showed that the increase in the usage frequencies of this group of PeX was somewhat stronger in texts with the highest aggregate clause linkage scores, this effect was much weaker than for auxiliaries that already existed in Latin. Likewise, the use of these constructions was not found to be more frequent in texts scoring high on the dimension of communicative distance. Moreover, with only 213 tokens, Latin calques constituted by far the least frequent group of PeX. Compared to the other groups of PeX, calquing from Latin seems to have been a rather unproductive strategy and the impact of this strategy on the overall development of PeX was negligible. This is a case in point, because the bulk of the literature on elaboration has focused on special Latinate constructions (cf., for instance, the papers in Castillo Lluch and López Izquierdo 2010; Cornillie and Drinka 2019). Our analysis suggests that although emblematic for the humanist era, these Latinisms are rather marginal in the evolution of the overall linguistic system. Hence, our linkage-based account may also be seen as a call for proportionality in the analyst's attention to specific linguistic phenomena that are less entrenched in the linguistic system.

Appendix

Table 5: Periphrastic expressions with modal meanings in CODEA, sorted by frequency.

Periphrastic expression	Typical meaning	Frequency	Type
haber + de + infinitive	must do something	686	III
poder + infinitive	can do something	336	I
deber + infinitive	must do something	252	I
ser + a + infinitive	have to do something	169	II
querer + infinitive	want to do something	75	I
convenir + a + infinitive	it is appropriate to do something	47	I
mandar + infinitive	order something to happen	45	III
tener + de + infinitive	have to do something	30	III
obligarse + de + infinitive	obligate someone/oneself to do something	26	III
haber + a + infinitive	must do something	24	III
obligarse + infinitive	obligate someone/oneself to do something	24	III
convenir + infinitive	it is appropriate to do something	23	I
deber + de + infinitive	must do something	23	III
ser + de + infinitive	have to do something	23	II
esperar + infinitive	hope to receive something	19	III
pertenecer + infinitive	must do something	18	III
parecer + infinitive	something it is likely to be the case	16	III
soler + infinitive	habitually do something	15	I
atorgar/otorgar + infinitive	declare that something is the case	12	III
prometer + de + infinitive	promise to do something	12	III
obligarse + a + infinitive	obligate someone/oneself to do something	11	III
ser + participio + de + infinitive	have to do something	11	II
otorgar + infinitive	obligate oneself to do something	9	III
saber + infinitive	know to do something	9	I
ser preciso + infinitive	it is necessary to do something	9	III
tener + que + infinitive	have to do something	9	III
acordarse + infinitive	remember to do something	8	III
atorgar/otorgar + de + infinitive	obligate oneself to do something	8	III
pertenecer + de + infinitive	must do something	8	III
entender + infinitive	can do something	7	III
pretender + infinitive	want to do something	7	III
atorgarse + infinitive	obligate oneself to do something	6	III
prometer + infinitive	promise to do something	6	III
deber + a + infinitive	must do something	5	I
ser + participio + a + infinitive	have to do something	5	II
atreverse + a + infinitive	dare do something	4	III
estar + de + infinitive	should do something	4	III
estar + participio + a + infinitive	must to something	4	III
ofrecer + infinitive	offer to do something	4	III
entender + de + infinitive	can do something	3	III

Table 5 (continued)

Periphrastic expression	Typical meaning	Frequency	Type
ofrecerse + a + infinitive	offer to do something	3	III
pensar + infinitive	think about doing something	3	III
tratar + de + infinitive	try to do something	3	III
aguardarse + infinitive	to wait (for)	2	III
caber + a + infinitive	it is appropriate to do something	2	III
haber + infinitive	must to something	2	III
necesitar + de + infinitive	it is necessary to do something	2	III
ofrecerse + infinitive	offer to do something	2	III
pensar + de + infinitive	think about doing something	2	III
plegar + a + infinitive	be happy about something	2	II
plegar + infinitive	be happy about something	2	II
servirse + infinitive	use something	2	III
temer + infinitive	fear to do something	2	III
tocar + a + infinitive	have to do something	2	III
aguardarse + a + infinitive	to wait (for)	1	III
animarse + a + infinitive	to decide to	1	III
deliberar + infinitive	obligate oneself to do something	1	III
fincar + de + infinitive	must to something	1	III
haber + que + infinitive	must to something	1	III
holgar + de + infinitive	be happy about something	1	III
holgarse + de + infinitive	be happy about something	1	III
mover + a + infinitive	obligate oneself to do something	1	III
necesitar + infinitive	it is necessary to do something	1	III
obligar + a + infinitive	obligate someone/oneself to do something	1	III
obligar + infinitive	obligate someone/oneself to do something	1	III
osar + infinitive	dare to do something	1	III
permitir + infinitive	permit to do something	1	III
plegar + de + infinitive	be happy about something	1	II
pretender + de + infinitive	aspire to do something	1	III
procurar + infinitive	try to do something	1	III
reflexive + quedar + de + infinitive	have to do something	1	III
tocar + de + infinitive	have to do something	1	III
tocar + infinitive	have to do something	1	III
usar + de + infinitive	habitually do something	1	III
usar + infinitive	habitually do something	1	III

References

Anderson, Gregory D. S. 2006. *Auxiliary Verb Constructions*. Oxford: Oxford University Press.

Bell, Allan. 1984. Language style as audience design. *Language in Society* 13(2). 145–204.

Biber, Douglas & Edward Finegan. 2004. Historical drift in three English genres. In Geoffrey Sampson & Diana McCarthy (eds.), *Corpus Linguistics: Readings in a Widening Discipline*, 67–77. London: Continuum.

Blas Arroyo, José Luis & Javier Vellón Lahoz. 2014. La supervivencia de *deber de* + infinitivo en el español moderno (ss. XVIII-XX). *Revista de Filología Española* 94(1). 9–38.

Castillo Lluch, Mónica & Marta López Izquierdo (eds). 2010. *Modelos latinos en la Castilla Medieval*. Frankfurt/Madrid: Vervuert.

Cornillie, Bert. 2007. *Evidentiality and Epistemic Modality in Spanish (Semi-)Auxiliaries: A Cognitive-Functional Approach*. Berlin/New York: Mouton de Gruyter.

Cornillie, Bert & Bridget Drinka (eds.). 2019. *Latin Influence on the Syntax of the Languages of Europe*. [=Special Issue of *Belgian Journal of Linguistics* 33].

Fernández de Castro, Félix. 1999. *Las perífrasis verbales en el español actual*. Madrid: Gredos.

Fernández-Ordóñez, Inés. 2004. Alfonso X en la historia del español. In Rafael Cano Aguilar (ed.), *Historia de la lengua española*, 381–422. Barcelona: Ariel.

Fleischman, Suzanne. 1982. *The Future in Thought and Language: Diachronic Evidence from Romance*. Cambridge: Cambridge University Press.

Garachana Camarero, Mar (ed.). 2017a. *La gramática en la diacronía. La evolución de las perífrasis modales en español*. Frankfurt/Madrid: Vervuert.

Garachana Camarero, Mar. 2017b. Los límites de una categoría híbrida. Las perífrasis verbales. In Mar Garachana Camarero (ed.), *La gramática en la diacronía. La evolución de las perífrasis modales en español*, 35–80. Frankfurt/Madrid: Vervuert.

Garachana Camarero, Mar (ed.). 2020. *La evolución de las perífrasis verbales en español. Una aproximación desde la gramática de construcciones diacrónica*. Berlin: Peter Lang.

Githe, CODEA + 2015 (=Corpus de Documentos Españoles Anteriores a 1800). 2018. Available online at http://demos.bitext.com/codea/. [last access 23 July 2018].

Haspelmath, Martin. 1999. Why is grammaticalization irreversible? *Linguistics* 37(6). 1043–1068.

Haspelmath, Martin. 2000. Periphrasis. In Geert Booij, Christian Lehmann & Joachim Mugdan (eds.), *Morphologie: Ein internationales Handbuch zur Flexion und Wortbildung*. Vol. 1, 654–664. Berlin/New York: Mouton de Gruyter.

Heine, Bernd. 2003. *Auxiliaries: Cognitive Forces and Grammaticalization*. Oxford: Oxford University Press.

Kabatek, Johannes. 2005a. *Die Bolognesische Renaissance und der Ausbau romanischer Sprachen. Juristische Diskurstraditionen und Sprachentwicklung in Südfrankreich und Spanien im 12. und 13. Jahrhundert*. Tübingen: Niemeyer.

Kabatek, Johannes. 2005b. Tradiciones discursivas y cambio lingüístico. *Lexis* 29(2). 151–177.

Kabatek, Johannes, Philipp Obrist & Valentina Vincis. 2010. Clause-linkage techniques as a symptom of discourse traditions: methodological issues and evidence from Romance languages. In Heidrun Dorgeloh & Anja Wanner (eds.), *Syntactic Variation and Genre*, 247–275. Berlin/New York: Mouton de Gruyter.

Koch, Peter & Wulf Oesterreicher. 1990. *Gesprochene Sprache in der Romania: Französisch, Italienisch, Spanisch*. Tübingen: Niemeyer.

Koch, Peter, Wulf Oesterreicher & Araceli López Serena. 2007. *Lengua hablada en la Romania: español, francés, italiano*. Madrid: Gredos.

Kuteva, Tania. 2004. *Auxiliation. An Enquiry into the Nature of Grammaticalization*. Oxford: Oxford University Press.

López Serena, Araceli. 2021. Algunas cuestiones pendientes en el modelo distancia vs. inmediatez. Los parámetros situacionales que determinan las formas de la variación concepcional. In Teresa Gruber, Klaus Grübl & Thomas Scharinger (eds.), *Was bleibt von kommunikativer Nähe und Distanz? Mediale und konzeptionelle Aspekte von Diskurstraditionen und sprachlichem Wandel*, 171–204. Tübingen: Narr.

Michaelis, Susanne & Martin Haspelmath. 2020. Grammaticalization in creole languages: Accelerated functionalization and semantic imitation. In Walter Bisang & Andrej Malchukov (eds.), *Grammaticalization Scenarios: Cross-Linguistic Variation and Universal Tendencies*. Volume 2: *Grammaticalization Scenarios from Africa, the Americas, and the Pacific*, 1109–1128. Berlin/New York: De Gruyter Mouton.

Miguel Franco, Ruth & Pedro Sánchez-Prieto Borja. 2016. CODEA: A "Primary" Corpus of Spanish Historical Documents, *Variants* 12–13. 211–230.

Octavio de Toledo y Huerta, Álvaro. 2018. ¿Tradiciones discursivas o tradicionalidad? ¿Gramaticalización o sintactización? Difusión y declive de las construcciones modales con infinitivo antepuesto. In Alconchel José Luis Girón, Francisco Javier Herrero Ruiz de Loizaga, Daniel M. Sáez Rivera (eds.), *Procesos de textualización y gramaticalización en la historia del español*, 79–134. Frankfurt/Madrid: Vervuert.

RAE/ASALE. 2009. *Nueva gramática de la lengua española*. Madrid: Espasa.

Raible, Wolfgang. 1992. *Junktion: eine Dimension der Sprache und ihre Realisierungsformen zwischen Aggregation und Integration*. Heidelberg: Universitätsverlag Winter.

Raible, Wolfgang. 2001. Linking clauses. In Martin Haspelmath, Ekkehard König, Wulf Oesterreicher & Wolfgang Raible (eds.), *Language Typology and Language Universals/ Sprachtypologie und sprachliche Universalien/ La typologie des langues et les universaux linguistiques – An International Handbook/ Ein internationales Handbuch/ Manuel international*, Vol. 1, 590–617. Berlin/New York: De Gruyter.

Rosemeyer, Malte. 2017. La historia de las perífrasis *deber / deber de* + INF: variación, norma y géneros textuales. In Mar Garachana Camarero (ed.), *La gramática en la diacronía. La evolución de las perífrasis modales en español*, 147–195. Frankfurt/Madrid: Vervuert.

Rosemeyer, Malte. 2019. Actual and apparent change in Brazilian Portuguese wh-interrogatives. *Language Variation and Change* 31(2). 165–191.

Rosemeyer, Malte & Mar Garachana Camarero. To appear. Semantic bleaching as an indicator of degrees of periphrasticity: an experimental approach. In Katrin Pfadenhauer & Evelyn Wiesinger (eds.), *Motion Verbs in Language Change: Grammar, Lexicon, Discourse*. Berlin/New York: Mouton de Gruyter.

Index

actuation vs. diffusion 115
agglutination 56, 62, 64–66, 72, 78
aspect 31, 39, 98, 103, 160, 179
- imperfective 19, 155, 157–161, 173–180, 184–185
- habitual 19, 102, 155–156, 159, 161, 173, 179–184, 215–216
- progressive 99–100, 105, 181, 203
- perfective 98, 100, 160
auxiliary 99–100, 160, 197–204, 213–214

bilingual see bilingualism
bilingualism 16, 56–57, 60, 62–63, 76–78, 87–91, 95, 108, 122, 132–133

cliticization 16, 34–36, 39–41, 71
- copula cliticization 56, 70
- object clitic 34–35
- clitic fusion 35, 38–40
- clitic string 38
code-switching 60, 66–67, 133
communicative distance 19, 197–198, 200–202, 205, 209, 211, 213–214
communicative immediacy 20, 197–198, 200–201, 206, 213–214
comparative concept 3–5
complexification see complexity
(linguistic) complexity 6, 10, 16, 30–32, 39–40, 42, 44, 48–49, 130, 133
conditional constructions see conditionals
conditionals 122–123, 126–128, 134, 138, 141– 145, 147–149 155–158, 163, 169, 173–178, 180–185
- asymmetric constructions 158, 166, 171, 175–179
- symmetric constructions 19, 156–159, 171–179, 184–185
- conditional markers 127–128, 135, 143, 176
- counterfactual 19, 123–126, 135, 155
- hypothetical 123–124, 126, 135, 156–159, 173–179
coordinating conjunctions 207
corpus 10, 155, 162–163, 198, 202, 207
- treebank 10, 79

diachrony 2, 12–14, 20, 30, 40, 54, 56, 64, 66, 69, 72, 130, 183, 198, 200, 204, 209, 211–214
discourse marker see pragmatic marker

enclisis see cliticization
enhancement see hardening

formal see formality
formality 3, 96, 134, 162–164, 169–172, 200

grammaticalization 12–13, 122, 128, 133, 147, 201, 203–205, 211, 213

hardening 41–43
heritage language 90, 109–111, 116

implicational hierarchies 7, 13
implicational scales 7
in-group language 90, 95, 109, 116
informal see formality
intertwined languages 88–89, 104, 106, 110, 112
irregular morphology 30, 97
irrealis 155, 157–160, 175–180, 182–185
isomorphy 31

L2-speakers 122, 129–130, 136–137, 147
language contact 29–30, 49, 54, 56–58, 61, 64, 67–68, 77–79, 86–90, 92, 107, 109, 111–112, 132, 137, 141–143, 146, 149, 199
language mixing 89, 112, 133
layering 14
relative clause 58, 63, 70, 74–75, 79, 102
lexical borrowing 61, 103, 110
linguistic minority 85
linguistic type 5–6, 19, 30
literature tradition 122, 131–132, 137–138, 140–141, 145, 147–148
identity 67, 77, 86, 88–91, 96, 106–113, 116

matrix language 62, 88
migration 30, 92–93, 107–108
mixed language 55–57, 62–64, 78, 86–92, 104–109

mixed marriage 17, 88, 90–91, 105, 107, 111–113
multilingual *see* multilingualism
multilingualism 11, 105, 122, 133, 136–137, 139–140, 143, 145–146

non-standard 17, 157–159, 173

orality *see* spoken language
OV language 72–75
overspecification 31

pattern replication 64, 73
periphrastic expressions *see* periphrasticity
periphrasticity 19, 98, 198–201, 203–204, 209, 213–214
phylogenetic 129, 134, 136, 138–143, 145, 148–149
population size 122, 129–130, 133–134, 139–140, 147–149
pragmatic marker 67, 74
pronoun 61, 101
– object pronoun 16
– demonstrative pronoun 102–103
– personal pronoun 73

questionnaire 8–9, 93

(language) sample 9, 17–19, 122–123, 125, 133–138, 147, 157, 173–175, 187
scripturality *see* written language
self-repair 165
simplification 30, 40, 45
social network 18, 30, 42, 46, 48, 130

social structures 20, 129
socio-demographic factors 8, 15, 30
– age 43, 104, 163–164, 170, 172
– education 136, 138, 140–142, 144–147, 162, 185
– gender 172
sociolinguistic typology 30, 49
split language 62–63
spoken language 10, 105, 130–132, 157, 174, 198, 201
stereotype 42–44
structural elaboration 31, 40, 42
subjunctive 157, 159–161, 166, 169–171, 178–180, 185
subordination 102, 131–132
– subordinator 69–70, 124, 126, 128, 132, 147, 217
sub-standard 14, 158, 169
syntactic elaboration 198, 201, 203, 205, 207, 209–214

thetical (element) 66–67
token-based typology 10
transparency 30–31, 39, 199
typological shift 54, 55–56, 61–62, 64–67, 69–70, 72, 78

variety 5, 12, 49
vocabulary 90, 97, 130
voicing 38, 41
vowel harmony 69–70

written language 105, 132, 149, 197–198, 200–201

www.ingramcontent.com/pod-product-compliance
Lightning Source LLC
Chambersburg PA
CBHW050524170426
43201CB00013B/2074